TOM BISSELL
MAGIC HOURS

Tom Bissell was born in Escanaba, Michigan, in 1974. He is the recipient of the Rome Prize and a Guggenheim Fellowship and the author of nine books, including *The Father of All Things*, *Extra Lives*, and *Apostle*. Two of his short stories, "Expensive Trips Nowhere" and "Aral," were adapted into feature films by directors Julia Loktev and Werner Herzog, and his book *The Disaster Artist*, co-written with Greg Sestero, was made into a feature film by James Franco and Seth Rogen. He has also done scriptwriting for several popular video-game franchises, including *Gears of War*, *Battlefield*, and *Uncharted*. He currently lives in Los Angeles with his partner, Trisha Miller, and their daughter, Mina.

BOOKS BY TOM BISSELL

Chasing the Sea (2003)

Speak, Commentary (2003) (with Jeff Alexander)

God Lives in St. Petersburg and Other Stories (2005)

The Father of All Things (2007)

Extra Lives (2010)

The Art and Design of Gears of War (2011)

Magic Hours (2012)

The Disaster Artist (2013) (with Greg Sestero)

Apostle (2016)

MAGIC HOURS

Magic Hours

Essays on Creators and Creation

TOM BISSELL

Vintage Books
A Division of Penguin Random House LLC
New York

FIRST VINTAGE BOOKS EDITION, FEBRUARY 2018

The Cataloging-in-Publication data is on file at the Library of Congress.

Vintage Books Trade Paperback ISBN: 978-0-525-43394-1
eBook ISBN: 978-0-525-43395-8

www.vintagebooks.com

Printed in the United States of America
10 9 8 7 6 5 4 3 2 1

For Trisha Miller and Mina Miller Bissell,
with whom every hour is magic

I think you are in love with more than
a story this is the story of stories and what
you have done with it.

—JAMES TATE,
"Brother of the Unknown Ancient Man"

CONTENTS

AUTHOR'S NOTE

I have never studied journalism. Until my early twenties, in fact, I almost never *read* nonfiction. When I first started writing for magazines, I imagined that I would use nonfiction writing as a way to fund my fiction writing. This did not go exactly as planned. Insofar as I am known as anything today, it is as a nonfiction writer. Earlier in my career, I was neurotic enough to let this bother me. When I started out as a writer, I regarded fiction—novels, especially—as the supreme achievement of the human imagination. While I still hold fiction in very high regard, and continue to write it, I no longer believe in genre chauvinism. Life is difficult enough.

When I am asked by students and younger writers for advice on how to get started as a nonfiction writer, I tell them to start small and look around. You need to find a story you are uniquely well situated to tell, a story that literally cannot be told without you. In my case, my first stories concerned my experience of republishing the work of Paula Fox and a film shoot in my hometown of Escanaba, Michigan. No one was particularly crying out for these stories, I knew, but both, I felt certain, had larger implications if properly explored. Shortly after "Escanaba's Magic Hour" was published, a magazine editor asked me if I wanted to go to the Canadian Arctic and write about NASA's Mars training camp. Yes. Yes I did.

Shortly before the trip, though, I had second thoughts and called the editor. "You're aware," I said, "that I'm not actually a journalist? That I have no idea how to interview someone?" The editor was undeterred. "Look," he said, "just go up there and write about what you see."

Most of what I have learned about writing nonfiction has

come, practically speaking, on the job. However, I am quite certain that my years of writing fiction provided me with the necessary tools of storytelling, observation, and empathy—all that stuff that is as hard to teach as it is hard to learn without doing it badly for a long and necessary time. When I began to think about assembling a collection of my nonfiction, I noticed how often I wrote about people engaged in some aspect of creation. To create anything—whether a short story or a magazine profile or a film or a sitcom—is to believe, if only momentarily, you are capable of magic. These essays are about that magic—which is sometimes perilous, sometimes infectious, sometimes fragile, sometimes failed, sometimes infuriating, sometimes triumphant, and sometimes tragic. I went up there. I wrote. I tried to see.

—TCB
Portland, OR
October 19, 2011

MAGIC HOURS

UNFLOWERED ALOES

*We do not possess a thousandth part of the writings of the Ancients:
it is Fortune's favour which grants them a short life or a long one.*
—Michel de Montaigne, "On Glory"

Destiny—the quaint notion that things happen as a matter of necessity—no longer retains much intellectual currency. But a curious vestige of faith endures in many otherwise skeptical intellectuals, and nothing indicates it more than how they view literature. For intellectuals, destiny as it applies to life is a ludicrous thought, but destiny as it applies to works of fiction and poetry goes largely unquestioned. Call it literary destiny: the faith that great literature will survive and achieve recognition commensurate to its value. We read of Kafka's deathbed plea to his friend and literary executor Max Brod to consign his fiction to the hearth, and grin with the realization that Kafka's survival was ordained. (Never mind the fact that Kafka's girlfriend, Dora Dymant, loved him enough to take his identical plea to her seriously, and put to the torch a large portion of material.) In a similar vein, we read the contemporaneous reviews that pilloried Melville ("trash belonging to the worst school of

Bedlam literature") and Whitman ("his failure to understand the business of a poet is clearly astounding") as dusty scuttlebutt. Yes, we console ourselves, great work may be greeted with scorn and may even disappear altogether for some stretch of time, but the slow process of literary recognition assures that the sweetest cream eventually rises to the top.

The simple problem is that this happy story is, in art as in life, not true. What determines a work's longevity is in many cases an accumulation of unliterary accidents in the lives of individuals years and sometimes even decades after the writer has gone unto the white creator. "The race is not to the swift," the author of Ecclesiastes tell us, "nor the battle to the strong...but time and chance happen to them all." Nowhere is this truer than literary survival. Some work, through no fault of its own, has simply not made it. If Max Brod had been as obedient as Dora Dymant, the twentieth century would have lost its most emblematic writer. In the face of this alarming possibility, Kafka's greatness seems pale reassurance indeed.

W. W. Norton & Company stands among the last of the independent American publishing houses, and I came to work there more or less by accident. After a Peace Corps hitch and a magazine internship, I was hired by Norton as an editorial assistant, one of modern civilization's least remunerative, most thankless, yet intensely interesting jobs. With my new worm's-eye view of the publishing process, I became aware of the many invisible determinants in a book's journey to hardback. Editorial meetings, for instance. Where I work, editors and salespeople gather every week to determine which books they will buy. A week or two before the meeting, an editor circulates a manuscript or proposal he or she is interested in; at the meeting, the editor makes a case for the book, and discussion ensues. At this point the vagaries of taste and personality cast an inordinately long shadow. (Most editors can tell chilling stories of a cutting, off-the-cuff comment from a colleague that irretrievably turns an entire room against the project at hand.) Immense too is the influence wielded by a house's sales director, who is forced to make immediate, hard-hearted judgments on what books will sell and how much. Indeed, I suspect that many writers would hang themselves in despair if handed the transcript of an editorial meeting commenced within even a literary house.

It still never occurred to me to question the mechanisms of literary survival. Certainly I believed, then as now, that the publishing industry as a whole does literature few favors. ("Publication is the Auction of the Mind of Man," Emily Dickinson wrote, and I doubt there is an editor alive who would disagree, or an agent who would want to.) But I had faith in the books themselves. Every great work, I felt sure, eventually rises above base commerce and sheer indifference. How can one embark upon any serious study of literature without believing this? Accident may misrule the corridors of history and science, but the course of literature is charted by more attentive forces. (Even if, as the generalissimos of political correctness insist, these forces are racist and sexist.)

I had spent five months at Norton when I was invited to join its paperback committee. The ominous addendum was that I have "ideas." As it happened, I did have an idea. When I first arrived in New York, I wandered the aisles of the Strand, the famous clearinghouse for used books, hunting for Paula Fox's *Desperate Characters*. I'd first gotten wind of the book in Jonathan Franzen's *Harper's* essay "Perchance to Dream," which I'd read and admired as an undergraduate. At the time, Franzen's reference to Fox's "classic short novel" struck me with dismay. Could there be a classic of which I'd never even heard? I lit out to buy a copy, but found it out of print. Two years after reading Franzen's essay, not even the Strand could help. Now, with the opportunity afforded by Norton, I wrote Franzen for Paula Fox's address, and she, in turn, sent me a copy of *Desperate Characters*. I read of Otto and Sophie Bentwood, forty-something Brooklynites whose lives of quiet, bitter unrest erupt over a long weekend after Sophie is bitten by a stray cat. From such quotidian material, Fox wrests a dread-soaked exploration of American life. A week later, I sat at a large polished wooden table and sheepishly explained to my colleagues why I thought restoring to print a thirty-year-old novel about a cat bite was a good idea. To my surprise, my colleagues agreed.

Months later, armed with a new introduction from Franzen and fresh encomia from David Foster Wallace, Jonathan Lethem, Rosellen Brown, Shirley Hazzard, and Andrea Barrett, *Desperate Characters* was republished. It received a harvest of publicity virtually unheard of for a paperback reprint. Upon the strength of this showing, Norton signed up more of Fox's out-of-print novels, including what I believe to be her best work, *The Widow's Children*.

One might assume all this would make a young editor very happy. The longer I thought about it, however, the more troubled I became. I could not stop reflecting upon how arbitrary—how *unliterary*—the whole business was. *Desperate Characters*'s republication, despite the book's greatness, seemed merely the yield of an inert aggregate of chance. I felt something akin to what I imagine haunts the recipient of a Hail Mary touchdown pass. Not only was the ball not meant for him, it was not meant for *anyone*. The joy of victory is cut with a terrifying void. Outcome is particulate; modulating the tiniest variable can spell ruin. In football, we accept this. But for writers, editors, and readers who view literature itself with quasi-religious reverence, this is intolerable.

Of course, that *any* good book sees publication is a miracle on par with the loaves and fishes. New books are, by their nature, subject to the cruelest happenstance. A novelist can be hit by a bus, manuscript under arm, on her way to the mailbox. But *rediscovering* a work creates an altogether different quandary. Smuggling forgotten titles back into print is more difficult than ever. When such an opportunity presents itself, the majordomos of modern publishing will reliably issue a stark mandate on one of several themes: It is money poorly spent. It is effort wrongly exerted. It is throwing away a spot on the list better reserved for short story collections detailing the adventures of young women and their diaphragms.

Publishing is a business with little consolation but the books themselves. Republishing *Desperate Characters* made me wonder if this was a most fleeting solace. Is greatness, in the end, no purer guarantee for survival than awfulness is for swift dispatch?

Art, Wallace Stevens wrote, "lives uncertainly and not for long." Nothing illustrates how uncertainly better than what remains of ancient literature. The first performance of Aristophanes's *The Clouds* was held at a festival in 423 BCE. Judged today by many critics to be Aristophanes's greatest satire—it is almost certainly his funniest—it disappointed its author's hopes by placing third in the festival's competition. It was defeated by Kratinos's *The Wineflask* and Ameipsias's *Konnos*. It must have particularly galled Aristophanes to place second to Ameipsias. Among other things, *The Clouds* attacks the sophistic movement then sweeping Greece, satirizing its leader, Socrates, with such glee that Plato believed it helped create the atmosphere that led to Socrates's death. "Konnos" was the name of Socrates's music teacher, and thus it is likely that Ameipsias's play mounted a similar assault. We must rely on such phrases as "likely" because Ameipsias's play, like a number of Aristophanes's, no longer survives. Whether these works were abandoned by copyists, incinerated in a doomed library, or carried off by plundering Ostrogoths, we can never know. All we can know is that individual excellence is a virtually useless consideration when pondering their disappearance.

For obvious reasons, religious literature has been better safeguarded against the obliterating levers of time. But one event in particular demonstrates the precarious stewardship to which all ancient literature is subject. In 1945 an Egyptian peasant named Muhammad Ali al-Samman discovered in caves near the town of Nag Hammadi one of the most significant caches of religious manuscripts in history. They would come to be known as the Gnostic Gospels. Contrary to the workings of popular imagination, the Gnostics were heterodox groups of Christians of highly varying beliefs. Prior to Muhammad Ali's discovery, all scholars had to piece together Gnosticism was the denunciation of church fathers like Irenaeus and Tertullian and the odd recovered fragment from works like the *Gospel of Thomas*. Texts in hand, and completely ignorant of what they contained, Muhammad Ali took them home and dumped them in a pile near the oven. Over the next few days, his mother burned an unknown number of manuscripts for the noble cause of preparing dinner for her family.

As Nazism demonstrates, censorship and genocide are part of the same continuum of eradication. As monstrous as intentional book-burning is, something more troubling flickers along the margins of the Muhammad Ali episode. For work that has survived nearly two thousand years to find itself sacrificed to the domestic pyre clearly reveals that literature is less vulnerable to concentrated efforts to destroy it than blind, innocent accident.

Herman Melville, Walt Whitman, and Emily Dickinson form American literature's most influential troika. Their appearances are unprecedented; their innovations immeasurable. Mark Twain,

Henry James, and Nathaniel Hawthorne, great nineteenth-century writers of equal if less profound influence, would have left unfazed one early judge of American literature. In 1840, Alexander de Tocqueville could write, to general agreement, that "Americans have not yet, properly speaking, got any literature." By that, he meant no American writer had yet kicked over the traces of European influence. James and Hawthorne never really would. As for Twain, Tocqueville's comment, "Only the journalists strike me as truly American," seems instantly, if unhappily, applicable.

Melville and Whitman share both a birth year (1819) and a death year (1891). Dickinson, a decade younger than either, died in 1886. But for post-mortem developments that had, at best, oblique connections to their work, it is possible that Melville would be familiar only to a small group of antebellum scholars, Whitman remembered only as the author of the Lincoln eulogy "Oh Captain! My Captain!," and Emily Dickinson enduring only in the whispers of Dickinson descendants as the unmarried shut-in who wrote abstruse verse.

Of the three, Whitman's survival is least perilous. Before embarking on his career as a poet, Whitman failed at everything he attempted. He was a newspaper editor (publicly fired, on one occasion, for laziness), a hack journalist, and the author of a forgettable temperance novel. He became a poet, at least initially, to amuse himself. Trained as a printer, he set *Leaves of Grass*'s first edition on his own. (The printer's term for experimental writing then was "grass," a larky job to be done during downtime.) In Whitman's day, poets were freighted with tripartite names like Oliver Wendell Holmes and Henry Wadsworth Longfellow. Whitman was America's first literary bohemian, and for that crime endured many stripes by its reigning establishment gentlemen—all but Ralph Waldo Emerson, to whom Whitman sent a first edition of *Leaves of Grass*. Emerson's 1855 response is probably the most celebrated blurb in literary history. One of its less famous sections reads: "I rubbed my eyes a little to see if this sunbeam were no illusion; but the solid sense of the book is a sober certainty. It has the best merits." Whitman, to Emerson's undying annoyance, promptly printed Emerson's words in gold print on the cover of the second edition, which still sold no better than the first.

But he soldiered on, writing new poems and endlessly tinkering with *Leaves of Grass*. Little by little, thanks to relentless self-promotion and a somewhat shameless exploitation of his Civil War experiences, he became the Maya Angelou of his day, filling commissions for commemorative poems and sought after by magazine editors for his views. He often concluded his packed lectures with a reading of the hoary chestnut "Oh Captain! My Captain!," now regarded by Whitman scholars as his silliest. Although it was the favorite of the poet's unliterary brother George, Whitman himself once complained, "I'm almost sorry I ever wrote it." It would be this slight Civil War curio, in the uncertain years following Whitman's death, that kept him fixed in prominent anthologies of post-war American literature.

Whitman was subject to nearly universal critical condemnation during his lifetime, his poems regarded as egomaniacal and obscene. Thomas Wentworth Higginson, the premier tastemaker of his time and by all counts a dashing, valiant man who led one of the first black regiments into battle during the Civil War, attacked Whitman repeatedly. He claimed that *Leaves of Grass* made him "seasick," and several scathing pieces in prominent magazines assured that Whitman would never be highly regarded in East Coast publishing cozies. Of his foes, Whitman once said they "wanted for nothing better or more than simply, without remorse, to crush me, to brush me, without compunction or mercy, out of sight."

One of the only critical boosts Whitman received in his

lifetime came from abroad. When the esteemed English critic William Michael Rossetti received, as a gift, a remaindered copy of *Leaves of Grass*, bought from a London book-peddler in 1856, he wrote Whitman a letter of praise. When the 1867 edition appeared, Rossetti wrote publicly that *Leaves* was "the largest poetic work of our period." This chance accolade ensured that, for many years, Whitman's reputation in Europe would be much higher than in the States. It would allow Ezra Pound, in 1909, the paternalistic complaint that American criticism had not yet come to appreciate Whitman's artistry.

Whitman's first American champion was William O'Connor, who became a devoted disciple after Whitman was fired by the Department of Interior for being a "dirty poet." (O'Connor would later ascend to the bone-headed constellation of literary conspiracy theorists by trying to prove that Bacon wrote Shakespeare's plays.) In the aftermath of Whitman's sacking, O'Connor churned out, with Whitman's help, *The Good Gray Poet* in 1866—a pure chunk of hagiography. The book did much to enlarge Whitman's fame (if not reputation; it was largely savaged), leading the good gray poet himself to reflect, "I wonder what *Leaves of Grass* would have been if I . . . had never met William O'Connor?"

Whitman's true champion, though, the man without whom one can say there might be no Walt Whitman, was the bisexual socialist Horace Traubel. When the two met after a Philadelphia lecture in 1886, Whitman had probably never been more famous. Four years earlier, the most recent edition of *Leaves of Grass* had been banned in Boston, and though its first two printings sold out instantly, support from fringe elements like the New England Free Love League did little to change Whitman's critical reputation. Before long, Traubel would be serving as Whitman's amanuensis. Traubel's greatest accomplishment was *Walt Whitman in Camden*, a day-to-day compendium of his thirty-minute conversations with the aging poet. His other contribution to Whitman's survival was his founding, in 1890, of *The Conservator*, which served as the *Pravda* of Whitman worship until Traubel's death in 1919. Rebuking anyone who dared impugn Whitman's name, it attempted single-handedly to beat back the onslaught from the literary establishment's broadswords.

But even all this was not enough. One of Whitman's last poems, "To the Sun-Set Breeze," was rejected by *Harper's*, and appeared in a less prestigious magazine in 1890. The *New York Times* said in its final review of *Leaves of Grass* that Whitman could not be called "a great poet unless we deny poetry to be an art." The same day, the paper printed his obituary. A decade after his death, Walt Whitman's works were out of print, his worst poem the one trace he left. Only Traubel's agitation, and a few scolding voices from abroad, gradually forced American criticism to look again at Whitman. If Traubel's great faith had faltered, Longfellow (or Holmes, or any number of others) might today be regarded as the preeminent American poet of his time.

No writer's critical woes are more famous than Herman Melville's. "Melville took an awful licking," Charles Olson wrote. "He was bound to. He was an original, aboriginal. It happens that way to the dreaming man it takes to discover America." Any novelist smarting from a vicious review is inevitably reminded of the disdain to which *Moby-Dick* first appeared. The story is used to illustrate the Potemkin village in which criticism is permanently decamped. Full knowledge of the story reveals just the opposite. The critics succeeded beyond their pettiest dreams of killing *Moby-Dick*.

Melville seems to have anticipated the troubles he would face. When he finished writing *Moby-Dick*, he wrote to Hawthorne, "I have written a wicked book, and feel as spotless as the lamb," suggesting he was aware of the inherently conservative notions of novelistic form his book then defied. "When big hearts strike together," he went on to Hawthorne, "the concussion is a little stunning."

He had some reason to feel buoyant. His first books, *Typee* and *Omoo*, were critical and popular successes. *Typee*, in particular, thanks to its frank descriptions of native sexual practices, made Melville, for a time, a most unlikely literary heartthrob. His early success was harpooned by the failure of *Mardi* in 1849. When he offered *Mardi* to a friend, he wrote in an accompanying letter: "[It] may possibly—by some miracle, that is—flower like aloe, a hundred years hence—or not flower at all, which is more likely by far, for some aloes never flower." In dire need of money, Melville cranked out the novels *Redburn*, about his cabin-boy experiences, and *White-Jacket*, a reformist fiction concerning, of all things, naval flogging. His reputation as a reliable sea-story spinner restored, he turned his freed-up intellect toward writing *Moby-Dick*.

Moby-Dick is the first true American novel, an affront to every retiring habit of mind that prevailed in the nineteenth century. As Melville's first biographer, Lewis Mumford, noted: "[*Moby-Dick*] is not Victorian; it is not Elizabethan; it is, rather, prophetic of another quality of life." Despite the unwieldiness of the novel (it first appeared in three volumes), Melville's publisher was hopeful about the book's success. *Moby-Dick* had appeared a few months earlier in England, and Melville and his publisher waited with glistening expectation for the one review that truly mattered, that of the London *Athenaeum*, a journal read avidly in Boston and New York publishing cliques. It is either immensely heartening or unbearably distressing to know that publishers in Melville's day were also helpless before the judgment of a single, inexplicably important critical organ. Today, of course, that monolithic power belongs to the *New York Times Book Review*. When *Athenaeum*'s review appeared, it proved fatal to *Moby-Dick*'s success. "Our author," it read, "must be henceforth numbered in the company of the incorrigibles who . . . summon us to endure monstrosities, carelessness, and other such harassing manifestations of bad taste as daring or disordered ingenuity can devise." Blood was in the surf, and American critics fell over one another to carve off a piece of *Moby-Dick*'s beached carcass. While very few of the reviews were as scathing as *Athenaeum*'s, some even grudgingly acknowledging Melville's odd brilliance, the book was a disaster. It went out of print, thirty-six years later, with a total of 3,180 copies sold.

Melville's critical standing was not helped by the publication of *Pierre* the following year. The reviews it received were so damning Melville gave into a depression from which he never fully recovered. When he died of heartbreak in 1891, the ever-obliging *New York Times* got his name wrong in its obituary, though Melville's death did stir a brief flurry of reappraisals that kept *Moby-Dick* barely afloat in the American literary underground.

As with Whitman, Melville was more prized as an artist in England, thanks largely to the efforts of Henry S. Salt, virtually the only person to write critically about Melville between 1890 and World War I. Salt was a member of a luminous British literary circle that included George Bernard Shaw and J. M. Barrie, and apparently his passion for Melville infected them. Shaw's letters from the period mention *Moby-Dick* in furtive tones normally reserved for samizdat, and Barrie modeled *Peter Pan*'s Captain Hook on Melville's Ahab. In 1907, Oxford University Press issued an edition of *Moby-Dick* in its "World Classics" line. The press's editors had invited Joseph Conrad to write an introduction, but he was not convinced of the book's (then) status as a minor classic. "A rather strained rhapsody with whaling for a subject," Conrad said, "and not a single sincere line in the 3 volumes of it." The edition did not sell well, and soon went out of print.

It is commonly thought that the centenary of Melville's birth in 1919 laid the red carpet for *Moby-Dick*'s new American appreciation. While this is partly true, that rug would have remained obdurately furled without one breathtakingly random incident. The influential critic Carl Van Doren happened upon an ancient copy of *Moby-Dick* in a used bookstore sometime in 1916. He subsequently wrote an essay on *Moby-Dick* that deemed it "one of the greatest sea romances in the whole literature of the world." The essay caught the eye of D. H. Lawrence, then in the midst of writing *Studies in Classic American Literature*, his still-seminal attempt to rip away American literature from the smothering Velcro of European critical prejudice. He too included an essay on Melville's masterpiece in his overview, and it remains one of the most entertaining pieces of criticism ever produced: "Nobody can be more clownish, clumsy, and senticiously in bad taste than Herman Melville, even in a great book like *Moby-Dick*. . . . So unrelieved, the solemn ass even in humor. So hopelessly *au grand serieux*, you feel like saying: Good God, what does it matter? If life is a tragedy, or a farce, or a disaster, or anything else, what do I care? Let life be what it likes. Give me a drink." Lawrence's essay was the first indication that, much like the doubloon Ahab nails to the *Pequod*'s mast, *Moby-Dick* is prismatically appropriated by each generation of readers. When first published it was viewed as an insane grab bag of religious allegory. In Lawrence's time, it was the first novel to show Europe where the hands stood on the clock. Later it would be a source text for the New Critics, then the litter box for post-colonial theorists. In 1927, *Moby-Dick*'s status all but assured, E. M. Forster devoted to it a long, cautious appraisal in *Aspects of the Novel*, and Melville's greatest work, as we today know it, was born seventy-six years after its initial publication.

* * *

Emily Dickinson achieved critical and popular acclaim much earlier than Whitman or Melville, though final validation did not occur until well into the twentieth century. "Just how good is she?" one critic demanded, with growing frustration, long after the appearance of the groundbreaking 1955 edition of Dickinson's poems. Despite the relatively sudden acceptance of her work after her death, Dickinson's survival is the least likely of all, subject to family quarrels and fortuitous breaks.

Dickinson's life is the stuff of biographers' night terrors: so many relationships, and so much shadowy speculation concerning them. Dickinson's brilliant letters, less than a tenth of which survive, are often as nebulous as scripture. Dickinson's brother Austin is probably the most significant figure in her Amherst home life. Most similar of all the Dickinsons to Emily in temperament (though least similar in taste and intellect), Austin's adulterous personal life would form the unlikely impetus that gradually forced Dickinson's poems into public prominence.

Dickinson's invincibly sedentary love of home is, from our modern standpoint, rather pathetic. Her letters from Mount Holyoke (which she left after three terms) ache with sonorous longing for Amherst. When she arrived back home, she wrote: "Never did Amherst look more lovely to me & gratitude rose in my heart to God, for granting me such a safe return." (Mount Holyoke is ten miles from Amherst.) Within a few years of Dickinson's homecoming, Austin would begin a relationship with Susan Gilbert, whom he would eventually marry. Recently, scholarly eyebrows have raised at Susan and Emily's relationship. Susan exchanged with Dickinson many letters, some of which are strikingly erotic. But like much of Dickinson's life, these are speculative matters. For the next several decades, Dickinson did little but write letters and poems, very occasionally traveling, with her younger sister, Lavinia, to Washington and Philadelphia, among other far-flung locales. Vinnie, as Lavinia was known, was utterly unlike her sister. Dickinson called Vinnie her "Soldier & Angel," and Vinnie responded with a devotion that would not abate in the coming unpleasantness.

In 1881, a brilliant young woman named Mabel Todd moved to Amherst with her professor husband. Austin and Susan immediately welcomed the Todds into their Amherst salon, and an open-secret affair between Austin and Todd began. Despite her great intellectual gifts, Todd came to Amherst very much untouched clay. Her literary aspirations to become a novelist made her uniquely susceptible to the legends already shrouding Austin's increasingly sequestered sister. Two months after arriving in Amherst, she wrote: "I must tell you about the *character* of Amherst . . . a lady whom the people call the *Myth*." Within a year, Todd and Dickinson would be exchanging lengthy missives, flowers, and gifts. Sometimes Todd would sing in the Dickinson house for Emily, who listened upstairs, composing poems on the spot. Thus Dickinson and the woman who eventually edited the first volume of her work never met face-to-face. An odder relationship in the history of American letters would be hard to fathom.

After Dickinson died in 1886, Vinnie pressured anyone possessing an ounce of literary acumen to do something about her sister's orphaned poems. Susan initially agreed to edit them, then backed out, claiming the poems would never sell. Vinnie turned to, among others, the same Thomas Wentworth Higginson who had assailed Walt Whitman. As Vinnie was aware, her sister's correspondence with Higginson began in 1862, after the appearance of a Higginson essay in *The Atlantic* called "Letter to a Young Contributor," which assured that editors are "always hungering and thirsting after novelties." Dickinson was thirty-one when she sent along a short letter and four poems, asking Higginson, famously, if her "Verse is alive." Although he offered Dickinson some guarded praise, Higginson said to *The Atlantic*'s editor, "I foresee that 'Young Contributors' [*sic*] will send me worse things than ever now." In the following epistolary exchanges, a strange friendship formed. In time, Higginson came to see Dickinson as a remarkable, if not publishable, talent, and despite occasional reluctance served her as a valuable friend. Although he spoke at Dickinson's funeral, Higginson declined Vinnie's plea to edit her poetry.

In desperation, Vinnie approached Mabel Todd. Todd had many reasons for turning Vinnie down, her own literary ambitions among them. But she was deeply depressed with Amherst and her battles with Susan. Dickinson's troubled, eerie poems seemed, as she later wrote, "to open the door into a wider universe than the little sphere surrounding me." Actually faced with transcribing the poems—sheer illegibility and Dickinson's grammatical peculiarities making it immensely difficult—soon convinced her she could not manage the job alone. She contacted Higginson herself, who told Todd that, while he admired Dickinson's verse, he deplored its undisciplined form. Only after listening to Todd read some poems aloud did Higginson, at long last, assent to involvement. The growing toxicity between Austin, Susan, Vinnie, and Todd complicated the editing process, as did Higginson's stuffy insistence on titling Dickinson's poems. "Because I could not stop for Death" appeared in 1890's *Poems* under the Higginsonian title of "The Chariot."

Their task completed, Higginson sent the poems to Houghton Mifflin, where they were quickly rejected as "queer." Humiliated, Higginson more or less bowed out from the publishing process, and after months of failure and negotiation, the firm Roberts and Brothers agreed to publish Dickinson's poems, requiring that Vinnie pay for the printer's plates. After an ordeal whose vicissitudes could have derailed the project any number of times, the poems were published in 1890. Public reception was immediate. *Poems* would go through eleven printings within the next two years.

What, then, do we have to thank for the survival of American literature's three greatest figures? Remaindered copies bought from book peddlers. A man, sitting at his desk, an oxidized copy of a forgotten novel beside him, cobbling together an essay with no idea of what it would accomplish. The lovely devotion of solitary women and men. Essays published at the right time, in the right journals or books, noticed by the right people. Clearly, these are not the props of fate. They are, rather, the stagecraft of chance.

The comfort we take in these writers' survival is undercut by some quietly nagging questions: How many novels did Carl Van Doren's hand pass over to find *Moby-Dick*? How many poets' work sits moldering in New England attic trunks, no one having lobbied on its behalf? What of a novel like Helen Hunt Jackson's *Ramona*, a beautifully searing reproach to federal treatment of Native Americans? *Ramona* actively changed American history, something neither Melville, Whitman, nor Dickinson's work can claim. *Ramona* was praised when it first appeared, not the least by Jackson's friend Emily Dickinson, who wrote, "Pity me, I have finished Ramona." *Ramona* lives on, of course, much in the way of *Moby-Dick* before 1917—a minor classic attended by the tepid enthusiasm of a few. We may laugh at Thomas Wentworth Higginson's antique taste today, but that taste once belonged to everyone. Is it impossible to imagine what unpredictable events might allow us a shocked recognition of that taste again?

For many months after *Desperate Characters* reappeared, writer friends, agents, and strangers sent to me numerous works of fiction and poetry they maintained never met with proper acclaim. The books came in, one after another, accompanied by nth-generation Xeroxes of effulgent reviews from *Publishers Weekly* and stamped with enthusiastic blurbs from James Baldwin, Stanley Elkin, and

Rita Mae Brown. Brokenhearted postscripts revealed the miserable delicacy of our literary machinery:"Although it sold well, the publisher let it go out of print. . . . ""The *Times* review came out eleven months after its publication. . . . ""There was no paperback sale. . . . " I soon felt as though I were deep in the peaty bowels of some awful literary purgatory, where hundreds of books are lashed with their own obscurity, many no worse than those considered—in an irritating oxymoron—"contemporary classics." I floated one or two of these projects before Norton's board, but failed to convince anyone of the fiduciary soundness of further revivals. It did not auger well that Graywolf Press's ambitious Rediscovery series, which republished, among other books, Larry Woiwode's *Beyond the Bedroom Wall,* one of the greatest American novels I have ever read, had been recently discontinued.

With all this in mind, I don't know if I could have read a less comforting book than Joseph Blotner's landmark biography *Faulkner*. Even Faulkner was forced to sneak past checkpoints into demilitarized literary immortality. Here again, in this century, were all the hard-luck accouterments of ill-starred nineteenth-century scriveners. With every book but *Sanctuary* out of print, Faulkner was living in Hollywood, drinking too much, reduced to reworking screenplays for films like *The Amazing Dr. Clitterhouse.* (Of course, he also scripted *To Have and Have Not* and *The Big Sleep.*) While many writers and critics revered him, Faulkner's popular status was so obscure that Faulkner was asked by the actor Clark Gable who Faulkner felt were the best living writers. Faulkner replied, "Ernest Hemingway, Willa Cather, Thomas Mann, John Dos Passos, and myself." A surprised Gable asked Faulkner if he wrote fiction. "Yes, Mr. Gable," Faulkner said. "What do you do?"

In 1944, a despondent Faulkner came across a letter that had lain unopened in his desk for months. Faulkner opened his mail only when he recognized the return address, or to scavenge any return postage stamps. The three-month-old letter, torn open on a whim, was from the young critic Malcolm Cowley, who wanted to write an essay on Faulkner that would "redress the balance" between his worth and reputation. Faulkner gave Cowley his delighted blessing, but the essay was rejected several times by editors who maintained that Faulkner was an unsalable commodity. It finally appeared in the *New York Times Book Review*, which for once found itself on the right side of history. Soon after that, Viking Press contracted Cowley to edit a collection of Faulkner's work for the Viking Portable Library, a book that remains in print to this day. Thanks to Cowley's essay and the windfall of reappraisals that followed, Faulkner no longer had to "eke out a hack's motion picture wages" to support his financially hopeless fiction. Five years later, he would win the Nobel Prize.

I don't doubt that many writers eventually receive their due returns, but the fact remains that *many* is not *all*. For those of us who love literature, only the all-encompassing justifies complacency. Our situation today is not altogether grim. In recent years, several writers have been revived thanks mainly to the efforts of individuals, my Norton colleague Robert Weil's heroic republication of Henry Roth and Tim Page's equally heroic salvage of Dawn Powell among them. Occasionally, I pull from my shelf my favorite contemporary novels—Robert Antoni's *Divina Trace*, Philip Caputo's *Horn of Africa*, Mark Jacobs's *Stone Cowboy*, and Gayl Jones's *The Healing*, to name a vastly underappreciated few— and wonder what will become of them. These questions were much less troubling when I was merely a reader who believed that the captains of the industry that now employs me were, at heart, attentive and just. Critics deserve their portion of blame—too many incapable of all but obvious commonplaces. Those few critics of higher caliber are often given to asking, "Will we be reading this fifty years from now?" The implication of this last-resort rhetoric is clear: I am a noncombatant observer upon literature's battlefield. The implication is also false. Whatever a book's merits, it can do little to fulfill such prophecy by itself.

What faith, then, can the poet or novelist place in his or her work's survival? Is literary destiny simply yet another god that failed? Although I know what I now believe, I hope I am wrong. Nevertheless, I cannot help but imagine that literature is an airplane, and we are passengers on it. One might assume that behind the flimsy accordion door sit pilots of skill and accomplishment. But the cockpit is empty. It has always been empty. The controls are abandoned. They have always been abandoned. One needs only to touch them to know how mutable our course.

—2000

ESCANABA'S MAGIC HOUR

Movies, Robot Deer, and the American Small Town

MAGIC HOUR: *The brief periods of dawn and dusk that allow enough time for shooting, but also create some striking effects on film.*
—*The Complete Film Dictionary*

EXT. ESCANABA AREA HIGH SCHOOL ATHLETIC FIELD—TWILIGHT

In the hard cold of a waning afternoon in early March, I stand on the hash-marked permafrost of my hometown football field in Escanaba, Michigan, and wait for a motion picture to be filmed. So far, I have seen almost nothing of what moviemaking is rumored to consist. I *have* seen a brief game of touch football break out among the crew. I *have* seen the film's star, writer, and director, Jeff Daniels, field the same question from four different journalists. I *have* been introduced to one of those journalists by Daniels, an irreducibly dreamlike introduction, since that journalist happened to be my childhood best friend, Mike. I *have* seen many, many lights—enormous, mutant lights whose wattage is equal to a perpetual camera flash—moved all over the place and overheard complicated justifications for doing so. And I *have* listened to three Escanabans, standing together near the field's entrance gate, tell me what they think of the production: "It's interesting," "It's interesting," and "Pretty interesting."

The one scene on tonight's call sheet is a nightmare sequence in which Daniels's character realizes he is standing in his underwear before a stadium of Escanabans. The film's producers were hoping for a turn-out of 4,000 local extras. What looks to be 600 have been herded into the center section of the bleachers, leaving huge swaths of seating utterly empty. The trouble no doubt began with the request for extras the Movie People placed in Escanaba's daily newspaper. There were three provisos.

Proviso One: *No one would be allowed to bring alcoholic beverages.* Why this is a problem: Escanaba is the sort of place where family friends earn nicknames like A Liter Later. Booze is, quite simply, a cultural staple.

Proviso Two: *No one would be allowed to wear "any clothing from professional sports teams,"* since to do so would force the producers to pony up permissions fees. Why this is a problem: Escanaba is the sort of place where people (*people*, meaning more than one) paint their homes the colors of their favorite football team. More often than not, this means the green-and-gold of the Green Bay Packers. It is immensely difficult for many grown-up Escanabans to leave their homes without some NFL logo displayed somewhere on their bodies. Many people's "good" coats happen to be expensive leather jackets, the breasts of which are emblazoned with a gigantic Packers G. This is not to suggest that these people don't own other, non-NFL-related clothing, only that to forbid it, for whatever reason, is to disapprove of it, and since rural Midwesterners are highly self-conscious, a good way to ensure that large numbers of them will not show up for your movie shoot is to tell them what they can and cannot wear.

Proviso Three: *No one would be allowed to leave his or her seat, not even for bathroom breaks.* Why this is a problem: From what I was able to gather earlier in the day, this simply baffled everyone. A woman I ran into at the mall all but scoffed at the idea of sitting still for four hours "without a bathroom." The Movie People's fatal error here was their failure to explain *why* no one could leave his or her seat. At stake, of course, is the film's continuity. If people are getting up to relieve themselves, a scene that takes hours to shoot yet occupies thirty seconds of film time will be riddled with hundreds of inconsistencies. So what was a sensible request on the part of the Movie People came off to Escanabans as a veiled if really weird threat.

Mike and I are not the only members of the press here to cover the film, which is nothing less than the biggest story in Escanaba's history. The film's producer, Tom Spiroff, a Michigan-born, Los Angeles–residing man in his early forties, approaches our journalistic flotilla. He is wearing a small fortune's worth of North Face arcticwear and, in a gesture of superhuman kindness, greets every one of us by name. This includes the pretty redhead from the local television station, a tall fellow from the *Flint Journal*, and a reporter from a national wire service who interviewed Mike three days ago. Mike, a graduate of a top-flight midwestern law school, has reason to believe that he will find himself cast in the man's coming dispatch as Escanaba's rube reporter, which he does not relish at all.

The remaining two journalists, both locals, ignore the filming entirely and discuss last night's barnburner between the Carney-Nadeau Wolves and the Rapid River Rockets:

"Good game there, eh?"

"Oh, yeah. That was really something."

Their accents are rich with the atonal music of the Upper Midwest, so this exchange is more accurately rendered as:

"Good game dare, eh?"

"Oah, yah. Dot was reely sumptin."

To appreciate just how newsworthy, by Escanaba standards, this film is, one needs only to peruse a recently published millennial Escanaba retrospective, which includes in its "Faces of the 20th Century" a local chemist who invented something called "bloodberry gum" and a man who "helped bring natural gas service to the area." What's more, the Movie People are here not to use this lonely ore town in Michigan's Upper Peninsula as an anonymous backdrop; they are here to carry Escanaba to the silvery brink of eponymous fame. Daniels's film is titled *Escanaba in da Moonlight*, a bit of marketing audacity equal to setting a sitcom in Qom. They've been here, filming, for a little over a week, and within a month they will be gone. "Like gypsies," promised Daniels, a little cruelly, to the local newspaper, in one of the several thousand articles it has so far published on the film. (Most of these articles were written by Mike, who has privately—and, I fear, quite seriously—vowed to shoot himself in the face if asked to write another.) But Daniels is mistaken. I know Escanaba's delicate musculature too well. The Movie People might leave, but they will never be gone. This movie will be, forever, a part of it.

An incidental curiosity of living in New York City, as I do, is how often one finds oneself on the entertainment industry's participatory edge. One learns quickly to correct one's path as to leave undisturbed the crew doing exterior shots for *Law & Order* as they wait for the perfect wash of Sunday-morning light to fall across Beekman Street. Cities, like movies, are extradimensional, most easily defined by what they are not: neither suburb nor town, neither novel nor play. The immense grandeur of cities is often the hatch through which people escape places like Escanaba. Although the city escape is spatial and difficult to repeal, the movie escape is much simpler—a temporal hegira of ninety minutes in familiar darkness. This is what makes the Movie People's presence in Escanaba so incongruous. Rather than supply

Escanaba with their industry's latest distraction, the Movie People will make Escanaba itself distraction's newest template. In return, Escanaba will play the part of that myth-fogged place so popular with Hollywood's illusionists: the American small town.

Escanaba is an Ojibway word meaning either "red buck" or "flat rock." (Local gallows humor holds that the Ojibway were exterminated before this could be cleared up.) It is not a wholesome town, no clean-living idyll where Clark Kent comes of age. The summers are lovely but brief, the winters long and Siberian. Its industries are extractive and blue-collar. Its tourists, who usually come from nearby, even tinier towns, refer to Escanaba as "the city." The good-looking, athletic boys I went to high school with did not go on to Yale or Wall Street. Many are still here, managing restaurants or selling cars. The people are not especially nice, which is not to say Escanaba does not have many fine people. "Nice" is a surface with little relation to inner decency. It takes some doing in our Pentium-processed time to be Caucasian and poor, but there is a lot of solemn Caucasian poverty in Escanaba. This is best illustrated by the local newspaper's personal ad section, in which a disproportionate number of ads begin: "DWF, 21, single mother ..."

The question remains whether "small town" signifies anything today beyond its modest adjective-noun mandate. The Census Bureau refuses to define what a "small town" is. A city, according to its definition, is any settlement of more than 25,000 people. Anything below that is, in an enigmatic tautology, a "place." A sad fate for a way of life upon which whole architectures of faith were once built, and one wonders if the Movie People are here as apostates or revivalists or for one last sweep through the small town's abandoned pews.

Whether one is from Nashville or the Upper West Side, one's hometown *means* something that often outstrips our ability to explain what. Small hometowns, in considerable ways, tend to mean even more. A young woman with a mohawk becomes immeasurably more intriguing when she claims Portage, Wisconsin, as her birthplace rather than Westport, Connecticut, and one can safely assume that the young urban striver who hails from Winner, South Dakota, regards himself differently from his fellow straphangers from Westchester. I, too, have always privately cherished telling people I'm from rural Michigan, especially in a city in which very few can say the same. Imagine my alarm, then, to learn that a film will soon offer an entire nation its own vicarious Escanaba. And so I have returned to the place in which I was born and raised and love very much to determine how much of it the Movie People will take and how much they will leave behind. Will Peoria play in Peoria?

I abandon my colleagues and sidle toward the half dozen Movie People gathered at mid-field, all of them huddled around Daniels's stand-in, an Escanaban named Rob Hosking. A Steadicam operator walks a tight circle around Rob, beginning his sweep focused on Rob's face and ending it with a clinching shot of the stadium's bleachers. Gary Goldman, Daniels's assistant director, watches the shot's rehearsal within a hand-held monitor. Gary is a good-natured, ruthlessly efficient commercial director from New York. He wears sunglasses regardless of available daylight and a tight white ball cap one suspects is in place to keep his skull from detonating. "Let's do it again," Gary tells the Steadicam operator, and speaks, commando-style, into the miked collar of a sporty Day-Glo orange jacket. "Right side. Camera right side. Copy."

As the sun sets behind the thick pine stand that perimeters the football field, the lack of extras begins to become a problem. To appreciate how crucial extras are to tonight's filming, one must know several things about Michigan's Upper Peninsula. First, citizens of the Upper Peninsula are known as "Yoopers," an inelegant transliteration of "U.P.," as this underpopulated and fearsomely bleak stretch of land is known. The U.P. is separated from the rest of Michigan culturally and geographically, connected only by the Mackinac Bridge, an architectural marvel built as recently as 1957. The U.P. might be the most rural part of the country, as well as its least familiar. Some maps neglect to include the border separating the U.P. from Wisconsin, an accidental annexation that, if made official, would please the vast majority of Yoopers, who feel a stronger cultural identification with Wisconsin anyway. Finally—and in light of tonight's scene, not to mention the whole film, this is a key point—for Yoopers, deer hunting has near religious significance. The first day of deer season is actually a school holiday—Deer Day, it is called—and the entire place is a hotbed of gun crazies and gun-craziness. Despite this, there were, in 1997, in the Upper Peninsula, a land mass larger than Massachusetts and Connecticut combined, and which contains a population of 300,000 Schlitz-drinking, deer-slaying yahoos, a grand total of eight murders.

In *Escanaba in da Moonlight*, Daniels plays Reuben Soady, a luckless forty-year-old who stands in danger of becoming the oldest Soady in history to have never bagged a buck. The film—which is, incidentally, a comedy—details Reuben's efforts to kill a deer. Some will perhaps be unsurprised that the film is being independently produced. Even Daniels, in my interview with him, was quick to point out that he "doesn't hunt," and that the film is really a love story. Let me say that, as an erstwhile Yooper, I am not especially fazed by the script's deer-murdering aspects, even though I do not hunt either. Hunting occupies an elemental chamber within the consciousness of rural Americans, for whom the semantic schism between *pig* and *pork* and *deer* and *venison* is

harder to justify. More to the point, deer are the stupidest ter-
restrial mammals the planet has so far known. They are essentially locusts with hoofs. When not eating or breeding, they like to
launch themselves into traffic. If hunting in Upper Michigan were
abolished, thousands of deer would starve during its brutal winter,
and its highways would be a living obstacle course.

Reuben's nightmare, then, finds him before his mocking fellow
Escanabans, all of whom chant "Buckless! Buckless!" and wave aloft
signs that say things like "Da Buckless Yooper." If the scene comes
off, *Escanaba in da Moonlight* could mark the first instance in cinematic history of a central character being derided for his inability
to slaughter a highly beloved constituent of the animal kingdom.

I mention the crowd problem to a unit publicist, who explains
that tonight's filming is in direct competition with the Escanaba
Area High School athletic department's Fan Club Fund Raiser
across town. "It's a really big deal here," she tells me. I nod, even
though it is the first time I have ever heard of this Fan Club Fund
Raiser. The Movie People hoped to counteract the Fan Club
Fund Raiser by staging one of their own. By paying two dollars,
each extra can sit on his or her oversized Midwestern kiester and
know that not only will they appear in the film, but their money
will go to benefit the high school's athletic department.

This explains the mysterious presence of the high school athletic director himself, who ambles along the set's edge with a displaced air. He is a gigantic, yeti-like man well known for bullying
the athletes he dislikes and granting unseemly quarter to those he
does not. He is obviously feeling put out, and I feel a small pang of
sympathy until I recall the inspirational leaflets he used to stuff in
his players' lockers during football practice, each filled with nug-
gets of inadvertently chilling advice: "In matters of principle, stand
like a rock; in matters of taste, swim with the current." I remember the final game of the catastrophic season I spent as a hapless

nose guard for Escanaba's Catholic junior high squad, the Holy Name Crusaders, a massacre commenced upon this very field. After being bulldozed by the opposing fullback, I walked to the sideline, removed my helmet, and fainted. It was my third concussion of the year. When the emergency-room doctor informed me I would never play football again, I nearly wept with relief.

The walk-throughs are done. The sun has set and the blue-black Midwestern sky is shotgunned with nebulae. Some gaffers are placing oval filters over the gigantic 600-watt HMI lights. As the crowd is hit with their celestial illumination, Jeff Daniels emerges from the stadium's adjacent locker room and walks across the field. Upon sight of him, the crowd lets out a small gasp that flatlines into courteous applause. Daniels is bearded, flanneled, clad in long underwear, and convincingly rural, which is by way of saying he looks terrible. This is the first film he has directed, and each twenty-hour workday has etched some new crag into the topography of his face. Since the film's finances were raised privately, whether he will ever do this again depends largely on its success.

Daniels confers with Tom and Gary, his breath unfurling in long white banners. Tom and Gary stand there, listening, their own breath chugging out of their noses in little locomotive puffs. Daniels looks tired in that scary, familiar way one's father looked tired, pouring himself a drink at the dry bar, after letting some-one go that day at work. I have always found Daniels's stardom slightly puzzling. Not in the way one finds the stardom of, say, Tom Hanks, in such clear defiance of celebrity's iron laws, but puzzling in a pleasing, even inspiring way. Daniels looks like any number of big clumsy Midwesterners I grew up around, and I am not at all shocked to learn he was born in Michigan. I wonder if Daniels's appeal has something to do with the fact that many men, if asked to cast their lives without undo conceit, might settle on Jeff Daniels to play themselves.

Tom, Gary, and Daniels break apart, and suddenly Daniels jogs out to the strip of track at the base of the bleachers and raises his hands to the crowd. A small, startled cheer. Daniels mock-reproves them and raises his hands again. Six-hundred suddenly animated voices shout back some innominate huzzah. Daniels segues into a prancing burlesque, whipping off his flannel and throwing it over his shoulders like a feather boa. "Hey, we like it!" one undeniably intoxicated voice shouts back at Daniels, who, as he turns away from the crowd, is smiling not the rictus of celebrity but an actual human smile.

"Well," Daniels mutters as he walks past me. "We got a few people. It *is* three degrees out here. They're not stupid."

As some final preparations are undertaken, I wander up into the stands, looking for someone I know. The crowd is not my demographic, most of its members very old or very young. I do see in the stands a number of well-dressed middle-aged women who "support" the town in its every endeavor, whether it happens to be turning out for the filming of a movie or the construction of internment camps. My PRESS button earns me several "Hello!"s from crowd members, each followed by a hurt silence when they realize I do not plan on interviewing them. A duo of ear-muffed junior high girls assails me, both asking if I write for the local newspaper. I tell them why I'm here. "*Herpes Magazine?*" one gasps, and rushes over to a gaggle of friends. "*Herpes Magazine*" sees a quick, contagionlike spread throughout this small portion of crowd. I am on my way back to the field when I see two quiet boys sitting in the front row. Both are decked out in green-brown camouflage, and they observe the Movie People very closely. I sit next to the boys and ask them what they think. "I think it's really cool," the older one, Scott, tells me. He shakes his head. "Nothing really *happens* in this town. Now that there's something pretty big happening, people will think Escanaba's pretty cool."

Scott knows nothing of the difficulty Daniels faces in getting this film distributed. He does not know that, despite the alien style with which the Movie People comport themselves, fully nine tenths of them are from Michigan. All he knows is that a movie camera will soon turn our way, and that, when it does, our small hometown in the middle of nowhere will be the only place in the world that matters. Scott's anticipation is so intense that, for a moment, I believe this too.

EXT. MAIN STREET—NIGHT

After tonight's filming, Mike and I drive down Main Street. It is 10:00 p.m. on a Saturday night and the streets are empty, the stoplights set on hypnotic yellow blink. Escanaba seems vaguely unwell. Nearly everything is closed. When one thinks of small towns, no two words are as suggestive as *Main Street*. They call up tableaux of a tree-lined avenue where the day's business is leisurely but efficiently transacted, a bustling vena cava through which every citizen passes to reach her town's rejuvenating heart. But Escanaba's heart has been stopped dead by the coronary thrombosis of commercial expansion out on Lincoln Road, a McDonald's- and Burger King– *and* Wendy's- *and* Blockbuster- *and* Walmart-beset thruway that streaks past Escanaba's western edge. Largely underdeveloped when I was a child, Lincoln Road has now made Main Street a pale mercantile ancillary. A number of Main Street's storefronts are abandoned, with no one rushing in to fill the void. And I am devastated to see that Sakylly's Candy, a Main Street stalwart, has opened a slick new headquarters right off Lincoln Road.

Not that Lincoln Road is a commercial dynamo. As Mike and I turn onto it, I am struck by a curious lack of entrepreneurial cunning. Every restaurant and strip mall has a sign, and beneath every sign is a glowing white marquee. Instead of festooning

these marquees with some incentive to stop in, Escanaba's bright-
est business-owning lights have, almost to the one, opted for
William Carlos Williams–like austerity. "Buffet," reads Country
Kitchens's marquee. That of Elmer's Country Restaurant is comparatively encyclopedic: "Polish sausage, kraut." The marquee
belonging to Suds N' Sun tanning salon, while informative, seems
to address some grievous past oversight: "New tanning bulbs."
Only Nanoseconds, a quick-stop found off Lincoln Road's main
drag, does much to bring meaningful tidings: "Marlboro Carton
$21.58."

The new radio station, Mix 106 FM, has scored Mike's and
my roaming to Smashing Pumpkins and Wyclef Jean. I have difficulty accepting this. Not too many years before, I nearly lost
my board operator gig at a local radio station by playing Public
Enemy's "Welcome to the Terrordome" at three o'clock in the
morning. We take a spin by the new cineplex, where actual, profitable motion pictures are playing. As teenagers, Mike and I used
to drive two hours to the nearest big city—this was Green Bay,
Wisconsin—hungry for escape. Only there could we see *Reservoir
Dogs* or *Malcolm X*, since all Escanaba's moribund theater had to
offer was *The Exorcist III* or *Rocky V* epochs after their opening
weekend. Mike and I relied on family safaris to Chicago to procure
rap albums, but when we coast past one of Escanaba's new dance
clubs, we feel within the cockpit of my father's Mountaineer the
concussive urban thud of base. Mike and I special-ordered *Life of
Brian* from Southside Video, whose uniquely crappy selection of
slasher flicks we'd exhausted, but one pass by the new Blockbuster
reveals unending walls of videos and DVDs.

After I left Escanaba, I felt some dignity that I had come of
age far beyond the fallout of the cultural atom smasher. The movies I saw or albums I bought or, later, books I read were not much
colored by the inducements of culture brokers. The pickings were

slimmer, sometimes maddeningly so, and not always sophisticated, but I was never less than certain that I had picked them. This is what makes rural, small-town people so opinionated. Strong opinion is the necessary attendant of choice, however limited, while fashion is the bootlick of exacting coercion.

If I were growing up in Escanaba now, Amazon.com would happily suggest which books or compact disks to buy. Over the Internet, I could chat with people as distant as Newark or Portland, erasing the demarcations of isolation, a visible suburbanite to a vast, invisible city. The Movie People have come to capture Escanaba's isolation, which exists, still, in every empty street and darkened storefront, but it is an isolation that is, increasingly, identical to that of a thousand towns just like it. All of them are attuned to the same cultural pulsar, as distant as it is familiar, as relentless as it is indifferent.

INT. ROSY'S DINER—MORNING

While driving to today's shoot, I find that the Movie People have closed off several blocks of Main Street. A small crowd of Escanabans stands at the barricade, shaking their heads in outrage. I would like to point out to these furnaces of rural anger that driving a single block north will grant them passage to wherever it is they wish to go, but I also know this is not the point. Routine in small towns is not ruptured lightly.

I park and walk down Main Street to Rosy's Diner, where I see that the Movie People's infestation has already taken root. I suddenly realize that I have not, as clearly as I can remember, ever before *walked* down Main Street. As a boy I dirt-biked the whole of Main Street almost daily, and as an adult I have driven down it thousands of times, but the slow-moving vista of its storefronts and clean sidewalk slabs is disassociating in a revelatory way. *No one* walks in Escanaba. Ever. No doubt this bears some relation to the astonishing fatness of many of its citizens.

Rosy's Diner is a small, sensationally yellow building found a few doors down from the bank where my father works—the kind of place that serves Coke in glass bottles and where lunch for two rarely vaults into double digits. During the grim summer following my early withdrawal from the Peace Corps, my father and I ate lunch here every day and tried to figure out what I would do with my life. I arrive at Rosy's to find the Movie People adjusting the set's lighting.

"Wait," one gaffer tells another, after placing a light. "This one'll be dangerously close to being in the shot." I ask the gaffers, Isn't *every* light here dangerously close to being in the shot? There are five different batches of lights: three outside, shining into Rosy's, and two even brighter ones inside. Every possible place upon which the camera will not turn is a bulwark of hot white light. One gaffer smiles, walks over to me, and explains that movie-making is 10 percent good lighting, 10 percent production value, and 80 percent standing around and eating Gummi Bears, of which he offers me several.

I am squired to the back door of Rosy's, my escort and I stepping over cables and heavy black boxes stenciled with "Mid America Ciné Support." As we muscle our way through the sound equipment crowding the kitchen, I see that, in the diner proper, Daniels is in the midst of directing a scene. Wearing a thick flannel shirt and fingerless hobo gloves, he kneels next to a table where his three actors are seated and will soon pretend to chat over tepid coffee. Daniels speaks quietly, every word freighted with consequence. The actors listen, eyes narrow and mouths tamped, while a makeup artist dabs their faces with white foam cubes.

Gary Goldman wanders around Daniels and the actors, pointing out every possible disruptive influence within the scene's frame: "There's spilled water on the table. Do we care? There's no steam coming off that coffee. Do we care?" Watching all this adamant preparation, I try to conceive of how a bad film is ever made. Daniels's budget is only a little over $2 million, yet nothing seems to fall outside consideration. Nothing seems hurried or rushed. Rosy's is filled to its gunwales with incredibly conscientious, hard-working Movie People whose focus on getting down the scene well has made the room a cauldron of concentration. Did a mandarin like David Lean prepare this thoroughly, or was his vision so honed he merely willed things into place? What of the journeyman director tapped for the new Martin Lawrence vehicle? Does he sit down with his AD night after night, day after day, and debate how to light Lawrence? Through what alchemy does the leaden spectacle of three actors surrounded by lights and cameras and twenty other people transform into art's precious metal? One can only conclude that no one, least of all the Movie People, is quite sure of how this happens. Their preparation is backlit by this terrified lack of surety, and just as David Lean collapsed in bed at night, certain of total failure, the journeyman director holds a small cameo of expectancy that he will, finally, wrest from his overworked script and unappealing star something with which the declining remains of his conscience can abide.

Behind me, Tom Spiroff stands in the kitchen, talking to a *Detroit Free Press* reporter. He will later be quoted as saying: "I'm completely confident we're making a movie any studio is going to want to distribute.... The novelty is these Yoopers, who are a special breed of people you haven't seen in movies before."

"Last looks, everybody!" Gary hollers. Tom and the reporter break off their conversation. A subterranean silence falls within Rosy's. The second assistant director snaps his slate. Daniels nods in a deep, comprehending way. Gary yells, "Action!," a moment-specific imperative, like "Charge!" or "Full speed ahead!" that no human being could ever tire of being paid to shout.

They shoot the scene—three hunters talking—several times. Movie People really *do* say things like, "That was perfect. Let's do it again." Between takes, an elderly woman standing to my left asks me, "Do I have to yell out 'Flash!' if I'm taking a picture?" She is clearly a native Escanaban, and I wonder how she has bypassed the wranglers whose job it is to keep Escanabans off the set. I whisper that I don't think flash photography is allowed during filming. She then asks, "Is that man in the chook from Escanaba?" Since the man in the "chook" is an actor, I feel confident in telling her no. "Is Jeff here?" she whispers. I fix her with a long, icy stare. When the takes are completed, Daniels walks over and introduces the elderly woman to the *Detroit Free Press* reporter.

She is the owner of a deer camp the Movie People are using for exterior shots. I now feel like a jackass, and compound this by eavesdropping on the woman's subsequent interview. Her use of "Jeff" is not framed in grossly arriviste terms at all. She'd never heard of Daniels before the filming. The delighted *Free Press* reporter asks her if she ever thought her camp would be used in a motion picture. "Not really," she says.

I wander outside to see Tom Spiroff valiantly holding up his conversational end with a stout Escanaban and his young son. The man talks animatedly of just about everything. Tom remains heart-rendingly kind, even after his responses have fallen to a take-me-to-your-leader tonelessness. "Really," he says. "Huh," he says. The man sallies forth into some new topic, and I can sense the psychic battle being waged behind Tom's faceplate: I *will* be nice. I . . . *will* . . . be *nice*. This is another skirmish in the undeclared emotional war between Escanaba and the Movie People. The Movie People, so far, have been regarded in Escanaba as surprisingly courteous. "Good, normal folks," one person told me. But they are not normal folks.

They are making a movie, one of the more abnormal endeavors a group of human beings can undertake. One senses that Tom knows that the smallest lapse with this Escanaban will poison the garden of friendly relations he has assiduously pruned. One senses further that Tom also knows, and detests, how unfair a burden it is to have to disprove the negative of Movie People's reputed baseness to an entire town twenty-four hours a day.

Here two selves stand in naked confrontation, the Small-town Self and the Hollywood Self, each severed from its context, each forced to create a new, precarious reality. For the Escanaban, this reality holds that, while he is impressed with Tom, he is not overwhelmed by him, and by enjoying with him everyday conversation, he will allow this Hollywood movie producer a respite from the fakery he believes makes up Tom's world. For Tom, the reality is defensive and turns back on itself, a metaphysical hairpin that actually *forces* him to portray the normal, friendly person he is. Having to concentrate, in interaction after interaction, on being oneself must be ontological hell, and I catch a sudden glimmer of why so many famous people lose their minds.

I simply cannot bear to watch any more of this, and hurry away.

INTERMISSION

"In some ways," John Clayton writes in *Small Town Bound*, a primer on abandoning the toxic urban lifestyle, "moving to a small town is like moving to a foreign country.... Compared to your old neighbors, these people really are different....A slip-up may be costly. Despite the best of intentions, your statements or actions ... may send the wrong message, and you'll find yourself disliked." Even for a booster like Clayton, the small town is ineffably the Other. Some of Clayton's pointers ("If you truly have a secret that absolutely nobody should know, then tell absolutely nobody") read like transcriptions from a counterintelligence manual; others ("Your brash New York sales technique may offend reticent dairy farmers") come off as deconstructions of *New Yorker* cartoons. But in the face of lifestyle decompression, Clayton is optimism's archangel. Small-town folk may at first be unsophisticated and a little frightening, he assures, but by obeying draconian rural protocol and (the implication is clear) not expecting very much, you will soon become a welcome member of the community.

Clayton's evidence-gathering in the case of *Small Town* v. *City* will be greeted by many without skepticism. Most Americans, after all, do not live in small towns but in suburbs or micropolitan "edge cities," such as those outside of Phoenix, Houston, and Atlanta. Whether hated, loved, mourned, or celebrated, the small town is, to those who do not live in them, an alternate universe whose values fall hideously short or gloriously surpass those of their referents. Many of our stumping politicians speak plangently of their small-town origins, while most mass entertainments prefer a more cynical vision of small-town life. However small towns are portrayed, they are never Now, and they are never You.

For browbeaten city-dwellers whose rural flight needs more codified guidance than the bromides of *Small Town Bound*, there is Norman Crampton's *The 100 Best Small Towns in America*. Crampton ranks small towns according to their "uniqueness" and "quality." His complicated formula involves average income, percentage of nonwhites, crime rate, and local government spending on education, among other brow-wrinkling concerns. Communities like Beaufort, South Carolina, and Provincetown, Massachusetts, with their singular mission of providing summer housing for millionaires and sucking money out of tourists, score highly in Crampton's playoff. (Escanaba, needless to say, does not merit a mention.)

When discussing the thousands of anti-Provincetowns lacking the restorative power of boutique art and agreeable socio-economics, small-town boosterism goes only so far. "The good small towns are booming," John Clayton writes. "The bad ones are dying." Probably, Clayton would toe-tag my home town in an instant. Escanaba offers its citizens almost nothing appreciable beyond a stagnant local economy and community theater. Despite this, a good chunk of each graduating class hangs around. Every year enough old high-school acquaintances migrate back from Milwaukee or Detroit to give vague misgivings to those of us with no such designs. In a small town, success is the simplest arithmetic there is. To achieve it, you leave—then subsequently bore your new big-city friends with accounts of your narrow escape. Indeed, when I was younger, I felt certain that what kept small-town people in their small towns was some tragic deficiency.

My stridency was fortified by American literature's constellation of small-town exiles. Willa Cather, Ernest Hemingway, F. Scott Fitzgerald, Sinclair Lewis, and Sherwood Anderson all wrote their best work after abandoning their small Midwestern hometowns. Only Cather opted for aria. Hemingway, typically, chose silence, not once writing about Oak Park, Illinois. Fitzgerald seemed to hold his Minnesota boyhood in a regard that is half sneering, half heartbroken. In *Main Street* and *Babbit*, Lewis horse-whipped America's small towns so ferociously the latter has become synonymous with everything strangling and conformist about them. Anderson is the most influential small-town anatomist, his *Winesburg, Ohio* famously coining the term "grotesques" for small-town people and inspiring what might best be called the "Up *Yours*, Winesburg" tradition in American literature.

But I am left with the nagging feeling that, long after leaving my small town, I remain a small-town person. While suburbs tend to produce protoplasmic climbers for whom ascension to the city is a divine right, small towns leave a deep parochial stamp.

I have dwelled happily in New York City for several years yet still find edgy discomfort in cell phones and being kissed in greeting by acquaintances. I would like to credit my dislike for swanky Greenwich Village drinking holes to high-minded asceticism, but I know it is animated by the same wretched self-consciousness that kept many Escanabans away from the filming. Small-town people live in dread of any substantiation of how out of it they secretly suspect themselves to be. This is why many small-town men dress so hideously, and why many small-town women do such upsetting things to their hair. One never risks rejection when one has made that rejection inevitable.

EXT. NORTHTOWN—DAY

On my way out the door for the last day of location filming, my father asks where the Movie People are shooting today. I tell him where "we" are shooting and, while driving to the set, marvel at my unthinking use of the first-person plural. My self-election to the parliament of movie-making is not star-fucking solipsism as much as it is an involuntary submission. When your town is incorporated into another reality, your very identity succumbs to the resultant vortex.

Today the Movie People are filming in Northtown, Escanaba's economically depressed district. In perfect storybook synchronicity, the division between Northtown and its flusher counterpart, Southtown, is the long stretch of Main Street. Since Escanaba lacks any minority presence, Northtowners and Southtowners are forced to dislike one another. I am from Southtown. Worse yet, I grew up on its toniest street, Lake Shore Drive, a descendent of an *ancien régime* Escanaba family whose kingly house overlooks the city park and the oceanic glory of Lake Michigan.

Today's scene takes place at Reuben's house, where he attempts détente with his unhappy wife. The Northtown home the Movie People have selected to film is a biggish, olive-colored two-story on the corner of Fourteenth Street and Second Avenue; it is in sore need of a paint job. Despite the fact that it is the coldest day of filming yet, a savage temperature not unlike that of the moon's solar lee side, a fairly large group of Escanabans has materialized to watch the filming and been corralled into a line across the street. Gary Goldman, in his ever-present sunglasses and white ball cap, paces up and down the sidewalk while talking into his cell phone.

Two large production trucks pull up and are gingerly emptied of equipment. One guy, loaded with an armful of walkie-talkies, calls alms: "Get your red-hot walkies!" Movie-making might be the only occupation without potential lethality that encourages such rampant walkie-talkie use. Several of the gaffers and grips are wearing "I love Escanaba" buttons on their jackets. Even though they are busy, this inspires me to strike up some conversation. For just about all of them, *Escanaba in da Moonlight* is their first "feature" experience, though many have done production work in commercials and public service announcements. They are counting on this movie's success no less keenly than Daniels: the best boy, Hans, is working his way through community college in Lansing at a garage-door manufacturer. I am about to ask whether they truly love Escanaba when I see an old high school friend, Doug, talking with Daniels's stand-in.

Doug is both Mike's cousin and the fullback against whom I concussed myself in that junior-high football game. He is also the only person I know who has been shot for non-geopolitical reasons, taking an accidental bullet in the leg while deer hunting a few years ago. Doug's femur was shattered, and he walks with a noticeable limp. Doug, I learn, has signed onto the film as its Gun Safety Consultant. I congratulate him on his gig, and he regales me with amused but not at all mean-spirited stories of the Movie People's innocence in things ungulate.

The Movie People arrived with the thought of using a tranquilized farm deer for the hunting scenes. But a tranquilized farm deer proved difficult to procure. A mechanical deer was thus obtained from the local branch of the Department of Natural Resources, a notion so oxymoronical I swoon at the thought of it. Why, I ask, does the DNR have a mechanical deer? "To catch poachers," Doug replies. Robot deer are patrolling the forests of Upper Michigan, and clearly I am here covering the wrong story.

A couple approaches the set with a mixture of trepidation and privilege. They are, it is quickly determined, the owners of the house that a whole troop of Movie People are recklessly stomping into and out of. I ask the woman, Michelle, if she's worried about her home. She's not, she tells me, jerking a little as the screen door bangs shut for the fiftieth time. "They gave us excellent insurance."

A stressed-looking Jeff Daniels is talking to a cameraman about (what else) lighting the driveway-parked pickup truck he'll be sitting in for the duration of this scene. Daniels's costar, the unfairly beautiful Kimberly Norris Guerrero, most famous for an appearance on *Seinfeld*, waits nearby with her unfairly handsome significant other. Michelle abandons our conversation and approaches Daniels, asking him timorously if he's "too overwhelmed" to sign an autograph. It takes Daniels a moment to look at her. When he does, his mouth is smiling but his eyes are cold and featureless. In a patient, considered tone, he tells Michelle he's *working* right now, and asks that she wait until he's done *working*. Michelle laughs in a nervous, humiliated way and hastens back to her husband's side. It is hard to fault Michelle much here, since I imagine that, in her mind, it was pretty damned generous of her to cede Daniels her home, but it is equally hard to fault Daniels's brusque reply, since he *was* in the middle of a conversation and child-proofing his personal space while on the job is something he shouldn't have to do. It is an all-around ugly scene that everyone pretends not to have noticed. Michelle and her husband soon join the phalanx of Escanabans watching safely from across the street.

Daniels climbs into the cab of the battered Ford pickup and Guerrero takes her place at the driver's-side window. Both suffer eleventh-hour preening at the hands of a makeup artist. Their conversation will first be shot from Daniels's perspective, and amassed on the Ford's passenger-side is a platoon of Movie People: the cameraman, the second assistant director, some gaffers, and the condenser mike operator, each frozen in a differently uncomfortable pose. Providing further distraction is the lights, all perched on thin metal stands called "lollipops," and a huge white deflector that resembles the screen upon which children are lobotomized by elementary-school filmstrips. Beneath this sensory ambush, Guerrero and Daniels are now expected to have a quiet, character revealing conversation. One does not need to see their awkward initial takes to grasp how ludicrously difficult motion-picture acting can be.

The Movie People will try to use as much native sound and dialogue as they can, since post-production redubbing is so expensive. It is therefore extremely important, Gary is explaining to the crowd, that everyone keep very, very quiet and very, very still while the cameras are rolling. The crowd is a cooperative of nods. Gary walks back over to the Movie People's side of the street, where he motions to a production assistant carrying a bullhorn.

A bullhorn-enhanced voice fills the air: "All right, everybody. No walking. Quiet, please." Although I am standing at least twenty feet away, the block is wreathed with such silence I can hear Guerrero and Daniels's conversation perfectly. Noah, the sound mixer, a lanky, longhaired young man in a white Irish sweater, sits nearby at his portable digital audio recorder, monitoring the sound levels over his headphones and minutely adjusting the console's numerous pots. Noah looks pleased until a neighborhood dog begins barking. The dog barks, in fact, through the entire take, and stops, with mysterious precision, the instant the take is complete. Gary motions for another bullhorned edict for silence, and Guerrero and Daniels begin anew. Five seconds in, the dog is at it yet again. Noah's eyes roll skyward, Gary is now helplessly scanning the neighborhood, and the production assistant is brandishing his bullhorn in a way that leaves little doubt of its canine-bludgeoning potential. When the dog's tireless larynx has spoiled the third take, another production assistant is sent on a door-to-door scour of the neighborhood.

A few minutes later, the production assistant, smiling and a little shaken, returns. The dog's owner has been confronted. Unfortunately, the man is not one of Northtown's finer citizens. This is not surprising, since finding an adult male at home at eleven o'clock on a Tuesday morning suggests dedicated unemployment. The man was unmoved by the production assistant's request that his dog be taken inside during the filming. The production assistant—wisely, I think—decided to leave it at that, and after everyone talks the situation over it is suggested that perhaps the bullhorn is the dog's Pavlovian trigger.

A fourth take is attempted minus the prefatory bullhorn. A weird, fretful aura descends upon the production. No one—not Gary, not Noah, not the crew, not the crowd—is listening to anything but this immaculate, fragile quiet. The dog's cue comes and goes, but we are no longer attuned to anything so specific. The late-morning twittering of birds all around us seems as raucous as a cocktail party. Footfalls register like exploding shells. It is pure aural anxiety. Near the end of the take, a crowd member's baby begins to cry. She turns and quite frankly *sprints* away from the crowd, her wailing infant mashed to her chest. It is as though she has just been gassed. At this, some more loutish crowd members begin to laugh. Gary stands there, tight-mouthed, while Daniels and Guerrero, wholly alone in the temple of art, finish their take with a soft, scripted kiss.

On the following take, a school bus grinds gears two blocks away. The take after that is made unusable by an inopportune car horn coupled with a rotten muffler. Several takes, in fact, suffer invasion by questionable mufflers. After what feels like the three-hundredth endeavor to film twenty seconds of human interaction without some spike of unbidden sound, Gary looks up with a beleaguered smile. "Are there any cars in this town," he asks no one, "that *have* mufflers?"

By now a small cadre within the crowd has openly turned against the Movie People. They are men, three of them, and their faint laughter is filled with hyenic contempt. They sport mullets, wraparound Oakley sunglasses, and shiny vinyl jackets with the names of local bars splashed across their backs. They are the sort of Escanaba he-men my friends and I, when in high school, approached outside of liquor stores and bribed to buy us cases of Milwaukee's Best. No one is paying these men much attention, though some members of the crowd have, in isolationist disapproval, inched away from them.

The battlements of filmmaking are moved from the Ford pickup's starboard side to that of its port. Daniels and Guerrero, their stand-ins in place, have taken refuge around a space-heater. Gary is on his cell phone again, probably thrilled that soon he will not have to endure such endless set-up and potential distraction. Tomorrow the production moves to a closed set in an abandoned health club just outside of town. The Movie People have constructed within the health club the simulated interior of a deer camp, and there the film's remaining scenes will be shot.

As I watch the laughing, truculent men, I remember a story

Gary told me a few days before. Last year, he directed a Visa commercial starring New York Yankees manager Joe Torre in Washington Square Park. Torre had, of course, just captained the Yankees to World Series triumph. Gary expected to do a good amount of Torre-shielding from gawkers, but other than a few raised fists and discreet hails, Gary's production was left unmolested. After Gary told the story, we exchanged some pleasantries of the Isn't-New York-Great variety. Yet I know that, for most of those New Yorkers, leaving Torre alone was striated with all kinds of apprehension, foremost of which is the New Yorker's singular desire to never *ever* seem eager or unguarded or gauche. I know, too, that these sneering Escanabans embody an exact inversion of that same desire. Why, then, do I *loathe* these men with such sudden intensity?

The lives of the laughing Escanabans are not too difficult for me to imagine. Their cars have shitty mufflers. They are smokers, drinkers, their romantic and occupational histories Iliads of woe. No doubt they have "some college." No doubt they've swabbed enough aircraft carrier decks to have decided that Escanaba isn't so bad after all. These upper midwestern Jukes and Kallikaks live in a culture which despises them, consume entertainment produced by people who mock them, and it is suddenly hard to fault their powerless laughter at a film in which they will find no representation, not even as tough-talking rednecks deodorized by horse-sense philosophy.

I realize, then, that this film is not intended for these men. Or for Escanaba. Or for any small town. It is meant, instead, for that know-nothing American monstrosity, the target audience. Although I understand the pressurized financial contingencies that make this necessary, I do not, at this moment, much care. Loyalty is the small town's blood, and assault from without is its transfusion. I work myself into such a lather it occurs to me only gradually that I am a potential bull's-eye in that target audience. My own private Escanaba shares some crucial denominators with the Movie People's: both are vessels of studied triumph over the inadequate past, both are backlit by the glow of the irrecoverable, and both are utter fabrications. Our Escanabas exist, but do not remain.

I abruptly thank the Movie People for having me and walk back to my father's truck. At the Second Avenue block-off stands a lone Escanaban. She is an old, old woman, thin in a nasty-looking way, with a nestlike white permanent.

"Dumbest thing I ever saw," she tells me, waving her hand at the distant Movie People. "I don't think it'll even be any *good*."

"Oh," I say, walking past her, "I think it will be."

Her look of cruelty softens into something hopeful, even tender, and she no longer seems nasty, but a confused small-town woman filled with doubt. "You think?"

—2000

GRIEF AND THE OUTSIDER

The Case of the Underground Literary Alliance

I suppose you want to become a success or something equally vile.
—John Kennedy Toole, *A Confederacy of Dunces*

Literature is always written by outsiders. Even lousy literature is written by outsiders. Everything from the artiest *Bildungsroman* to the most boldly ludicrous spy rhapsody to the Styrofoam drama of the lower science fiction was written by a person inclined not toward connecting with those around him or her but retreating into a world of nerdily private dream. But even within the outsider's own imagination, things do not much improve. The overwhelming majority of a writer's time is spent wondering why this world is not as vivid as he or she once—agonizingly, *deludedly*—believed. To write is to fail, more or less, constantly. Most writers are not garrulous people; those few who are can fall prey to substance abuse or behave in the uniquely alienating way of people who think they are celebrities but are not, actually, celebrated. There are reasons for this. Very little in our culture goes out of its way to reward good writing; as a profession, writing seems to interest people in the same exotic manner that professional whaling interests people. It is hard psychic work to feel professionally estranged. One explanation for why writers enjoy hanging around other writers is because writers often instantly forgive one another for being difficult or weird. In this way New York City is, for writers, a kind of literary sanatorium. I mean to imply in that equation some strong theoretical reservations about the sanatorium.

All the animals in Orwell's *Animal Farm* are equal, remember, but some are more equal than others. So, too, then, are some outsiders more outside than others. A few writers, such as Thoreau, seem for the sake of vanity or affectation to *will* upon themselves outsider status. Thoreau's friendship with Emerson, probably the most prominent writer of the day, indicates that he was something less than a solitary literary soul. There is the Clown Outsider, such as Whitman, who was not taken seriously until most of the insiders who despised him were dead. There is the Spurned Outsider, such as Melville, whose early success with *Typee* led him to believe that his skeleton key would forever provide entrance to the inside literary world; by the time *Pierre* appeared the locks had all been discreetly changed. There is the Outsider from Mars, such as Dickinson. There is the Outsider by Temperament, such as Jack London, who, however magnificent a man, was not actually a very good writer. There is the Square Outsider, such as Willa Cather, loved by readers but secretly loathed as a hopeless square by those on the inside. There is the Outsider Who Unexpectedly Finds Himself Inside, such as Jack Kerouac. There is the Nutcase Outsider, such as Hunter S. Thompson. There is the Geographical Outsider, such as the novelist Jim Harrison. (I once made the mistake of admiringly telling Harrison that I regarded him as the dean of Midwestern literature. His long career of being belittled by urban critics had acclimated him to regard that statement as a scatologically vivid insult. I am still apologizing.) There is the

Outsider Mistakenly Regarded as an Insider, such as John Updike, who is in fact so outside he does not even have an agent.

And then there is the True Outsider, the writer who believes, as he believes nothing else, that he has no hope of ever accessing the inner literary world. This conviction often sadly fulfills itself; people, artists especially, tend to internalize their fates. Nevertheless, not a few True Outsiders have met with literary success, though in many cases only when it was far too late to have any earthly benefit. The suicide John Kennedy Toole is probably the most famous True Outsider, though it pains me to admit that I regard *A Confederacy of Dunces* as one of the most overrated novels ever published. I am glad, all the same, that it *was* published, if only for the moments of reflection it caused those who rejected it to suffer.

Literature tends to maltreat outsiders more frequently than the worlds of music and film. Or so it is commonly supposed. Compared to the world's literal millions of unpublished novels, one hears relatively little of the numerous wrapped independent films that never see release. The logistical difficulties of mounting a film production surely have something to do with this, as does economics. Since movies made beyond the clutches of studios have been proven, at least in concept, financially viable, independent film has for the last decade been growing steadily less independent. The music industry, on the other hand, tends to mainline the energy of anarchic independence to such an extent that it packages even its grossly *mainstream* outfits in the roguishly tattered robes of the True Outsider. Given the considerable seductions of both industries, the successful True Outsider does not, as a rule, tend to stay True or Outside within them for very long.

The publishing industry, on the other hand, has little faith in and less regard for the True Outsider because it is difficult enough to make money on sure-thing *insiders*. It is a real challenge to come up with more than a tiny handful of self-printed novels of serious artistic intent published in the last hundred years that achieved even the mildest sort of cult status. (James Joyce's *Ulysses*, though not exactly self-printed, was a deeply homegrown publishing endeavor. A more modern example might be Arthur Nersesian's underground hit *The Fuck-Up*, though one could hardly claim it is well known.) In a weird quirk all but unique to publishing, even literary movements that furiously reject the mainstream—the Beats are the prime example—tend to be more or less gratefully published by traditional, mainstream houses. This is because traditional houses offer what are essentially the only means of widely dispensing one's work. This is also because the literary world is not usually regarded as spinelessly money-hungry as the worlds of film and music. In short, a different, less rapacious sort of person is attracted to the literary world, and the typical literary novel sells, if it is lucky, 5,000 to 10,000 copies. This is quite a bit less than one tenth of one percent of the American populace. The conglomerates could board up and soap the windows of literary publishing in a day, if they chose. People would complain, certainly. But would most Americans care?

Hence the problem the True Outsider has in the publishing world. The peddling of literature is itself an outside industry. So few literary movements have sought to destroy this fragile creature because without it, what on earth would they do? There is, however, one literary movement today that seeks to save the publishing industry by smashing it into a million genteel smithereens. They call themselves the Underground Literary Alliance. They also call themselves "the most exciting literary movement in America." They might well be, as I cannot really think of any other existing literary movement in America. This, they would say, is the problem. The system, as it currently exists, does not welcome movements or true independence, only perversely canny individuals who have figured out how to work that system as though it were an uncommonly prodigal slot machine. Here, perhaps, I should share another appellation the ULA has earned, this from an editor acquaintance: "The ghastliest group of no-talent whiners to have ever walked the earth."

The ULA's founding members first connected during the early to mid-1990s in what they themselves refer to as the "zine world." These writers read one another's zines and dispatched fan letters to the authors of the work they admired. Many of these letters were filled with complaints and jeremiads about what was currently being published, which makes them the least unusual writers in the history of American literature. (A quick scan of the letters of William Faulkner or Virginia Woolf will find them, too, railing against the perceived mediocrity of their contemporaries: in Faulkner's case, John O'Hara and James Gould Cozzens; in Woolf's far less happy case, James Joyce.) Nevertheless, in the summer of 2000 these writers decided to band officially together. Not to mention officiously together: theirs was a literary movement based not so much on some shared aesthetic or philosophy of generational focus but on the premise that just about every contemporary writer's work sucked.

The ULA has no apparent geographic center, and many of its members hail from faded industrial capitals such as Detroit and Philadelphia. If the ULA's own mythology is to be believed, Hoboken, New Jersey, became Bethlehem to its literary messiah. (This was followed, of course, by a three-day pub crawl.) Shortly after the group's launch, Michael Jackman, today the ULA's executive director, wrote the group's manifesto. Like most manifestos, it is neither punctilious nor especially logic-ridden, and it reads like the wail of True Outsider grief that it almost certainly is.

Why has the ULA been founded? "Because writing is being professionalized." (Yes, depressingly.) "Because professionalization initiatives push aspirants away from thinking in their own ways." (Probably yes.) "Because professionalizations enforces *a priori* prejudices of what 'good writing' is." (Possibly yes, but when has it ever been different?) "Because great writers must never be frightened that their 'credentials' may be revoked." (Absolutely yes.) "Because literature is elitist." (Yes—and it should be elitist, though *creatively* elitist rather than politically or socially elitist.) "Because literature is completely out of touch with the reality of contemporary life." (Whose literature? Which writers?) "Because literature has become just a tax deduction, mired in the upper class, written for readers isolated in their wonderful homes, who wish to believe that the world is filled with wonderful things." (Well, sort of, maybe, but mostly: huh?) "Because the literary lights of big publishing have nothing to be contentious about—they're sitting on top of the world." (*God* no.) "Because the literary establishment does indeed have an agenda, and the first point on that brief is that nobody criticize the agenda." (One whole agenda for everyone? A slightly *Protocols of the Elders of Zion*ish notion.) "Because literature must confront the evil and corrupt system of class, greed and exclusion that this country has been based upon from it's inception." (Sigh. And, guys: it's *its*.) "Because writers should see something wrong and denounce it, no matter how many friends it costs them." (Okay.) "Because style has become convoluted." (*Dude*. Whose?) "Because the literary establishment is corrupt to the core." (No.) "Because corruption, cronyism, nepotism, and cowardice are mixed into a toxic potation that poisons the soul of all who drink from it." (Come *on*.) "Because writers have become addicted to big words and stuffy syntax that puts the reader into a torpor, to the point where words clog up the pipes of the mind and produce a deadly sewer gas." (That's . . . that's just rich.) "THEREFORE, we renounce the professionalization of literary craft that has become part and parcel of the literary world." Well, they certainly renounced craft while writing this manifesto.

The ULA is the kind of group that boasts on its website not of any achievements but its protests. Thus one learns, in a long, exhaustive register, of the ULA's protestation of "millionaire socialite" Rick Moody's Guggenheim Award; of its protestation of a Best Zine prize awarded to *McSweeney's*, which the ULA regards as too "fancy" and "dandified" to be a zine, even though the entire operation is fronted with its own money and printed independently, which, at least as I understand it, pretty much defines a zine, but what do I know; of a purported victory at a debate between the ULA and the *Paris Review*, when, in fact, the *Paris Review*'s editor, George Plimpton, had gone into the debate with high hopes and fellow feeling but grew swiftly disgusted by the ULA's infantile antics; of its crashing of "an effete, boring reading" given by the novelist Elissa Schappell at KGB, where the ULA was thrown out after clapping inappropriately, and for which ejection the ULA's explanation is cast in the weaselly passive voice ("Alcohol was involved"); of its "Big Underground Invasion Reading in Detroit," the ULA's "first stop on its National Breakout Tour," where "Underground heroes read, rocked and revved up the crowd," which for all one knows they did; and of its "letters of challenge" sent "to many NYC publishers and writing programs," about which good luck.

With all this in mind, it will come as no surprise that occasionally—actually, way more than occasionally—the ULA is thuggish, cruel, and petty. Many of the writers on the receiving end of ULA vitriol have felt seriously threatened and, indeed, nearly terrorized. Many writers, including Dave Eggers (who at one time was sent poorly written mail from the ULA), were against the publication of this piece; their concern was that anything that might fuel the ULA's anger was a bad idea, as it might result in new eruptions and cause distress to fellow writers.

But the ULA seems worth examining, to me at least. In January of this year, the ULA turned up at a reading held at Housing Works, one of New York's most venerable used bookstores. The reading was intended to celebrate the alternative publishing community, embodied by the literary magazines *Open City*, *McSweeney's*, and *Fence*. By all accounts, including their own, the ULA made a thoroughgoing mess of the evening. In a report ominously titled "The Incident at Housing Works," which is posted on the ULA website, ULA founder (now publicity director) King Wenclas notes that the "crowd of several hundred was upscale and nearly all white." (I would be very curious to learn of the racial makeup of the average ULA reading.) Wenclas regards the event's audience as "pod persons with plastic smiles....The ULA was among a cultural aristocracy that evening, an aristocracy filled with smugness about their meaningless art." With the requisite ULA name-calling out of the way, Wenclas's more substantial gripe quickly surfaces: "Many things are happening outside the doors; a widening gap between America's classes; an approaching war. There was scarcely a vibration of any of this among the trust funders. Can our nation's most nurtured writers be so out of touch with their own country (or even their own city)?"

The readings that evening were given by Ben Greenman, a *McSweeney's* contributor and formidably clever, very funny satirist; Tina Brown Célona, a *Fence* poet; and Sam Lipsyte, an *Open City* fixture whose willfully slight but, again, extremely funny novel *The Subject Steve* had the unluck to be published on September 11, 2001. Whether these writers or their audience are "trust funders" is a little beside the point; my own experience with the youth demographic of New York City publishing leads me to suspect that most of them, in all likelihood, are not. (A quick résumé check of my closest publishing friends, admittedly not the most comprehensive portrait, reveals a young publishing world hardly born on velvet. One friend hails from a hardscrabble Mississippi background, another from upper-middle-class Brooklyn, another from rural middle-class Virginia, another from middle-class New Jersey. I myself hail from a lovely speck of a town in the Upper Peninsula of Michigan. I suspect our accumulated savings could probably cover a down payment on a nice apartment in the heart of Appleton, Wisconsin.) The only legitimate question, then, concerns the work the Housing Works readers shared. As Wenclas tells it, that night's offerings consisted of stories and poems about a "tree [Greenman], a cunt [Célona], and a candy bar [Lipsyte]." Wenclas wants to know, "Where were the current Balzacs, Zolas, Tolstoys?" (Maybe in France and Russia?) "We were accused," Wenclas notes of the hostile Housing Works crowd, "of wanting to inject politics into literature, because we asked for literature to be relevant."

Now, I have nothing at all against the writers who read at Housing Works that night, but I have been to enough such readings to have felt, from time to time, something of Wenclas's frustration myself. A fair amount of the work reaped in alternative publications such as *McSweeney's*, *Fence*, and *Open City* does seem only vaguely intended to be read. As for today's politically minded younger fiction writers and poets . . . Jesus, it *is* a little depressing. Wenclas is not wrong to want a stronger, more serious literature, especially during these sorrowed times, but his anger is more than slightly disingenuous if he expected to find an artist of Tolstoyan wingspan at a reading featuring the author of *Superbad*. If Greenman, the writer responsible for *Superbad* (which, let me say, is a pretty terrific book), had somehow fallen from the fold of serious fiction and embraced apolitical tomfoolery, then one could at least understand Wenclas's puzzlement. But Greenman is primarily a satirist, and Lipsyte is a comic writer.

That Greenman read a story about a tree and Lipsyte a candy bar is not surprising. Wenclas, surely, knows this. (I also imagine Greenman's tree story was a lot funnier than Wenclas lets on. I have seen Lipsyte read his "candy bar" story, and it is hilarious indeed.) To find fault with either for the reasons the ULA gives is a little like criticizing *The Producers* for not being more like *The Sorrow and the Pity*. Why are these writers not allowed to write what they want? There are, after all, other writers doing different things. And why, for that matter, should Tolstoy be the writer under whom we all fall into lockstep emulation? Tolstoy was a great writer, obviously, but if *every* published novel were Tolstoyan, I, for one, would be forced to kill myself. Most likely, Wenclas objects to the high-profile venue these writers were given. But as any writer who has given a reading knows, most readings are the precise *opposite* of high profile. They are almost exclusively attended by the assorted roommates, former roommates, girl- and boyfriends, former girl- and boyfriends, close friends, family members, and acquaintances of whomever happens to be reading. This leads to a certain insularity, but surely the ULA's readings are no less insular. Furthermore, in terms of the expected fun to be had at a reading, most place up there with trips to the Laundromat. People simply do not go to readings because they want to; they go because they *have* to. ("Ah, I can't tonight. I have this fucking *reading* I gotta go to.") I suspect that many of those who witnessed the ULA's Housing Works rampage—at one point, the fiction writer Thomas Beller and Wenclas nearly came to blows—found the disruption to be the evening's inarguable highlight.

The Underground Literary Alliance takes as its stated revolutionary mission the search for "America's great writers! If we don't do it, no one will." There are good, needed, and necessary revolutions, and then there are revolutions that upon successful completion require a new flag and lots and lots of tombstones. There is little doubt which type of revolution the Underground Literary Alliance has in mind: "The goal is to overthrow the literary establishment and get access for real writers. The public wants writing that's worth reading!" The sentiment behind the lattermost position is genuinely touching, even inspiring, and it saddens me to note that, in fact, the public does not want writing that is worth reading. By all available evidence, the public wants one novel after another starring Goodhearted Lawyers Fighting the System, Goodhearted Christians Battling the Antichrist, and Goodhearted Heroines Humped Silly by Manly Strangers Who Will Ultimately Leave Them but Damn, That Was Some Orgasm, Was It Not?

The ULA's other, less dismissible beefs amount to the following: "Put Populists on funding panels. Publish about real life. Support our starving real writers. Admit that today's system ruins art." Insofar as grants go, the ULA is probably correct to maintain that the grant system, particularly that which is overseen by the National Endowment for the Arts, is if not corrupt outright then at least hopelessly back-scratchy. The argument can be made, though, that the very nature of any funding scheme based on the decisions of self-interested judges, Populist or not, is itself corrupting. Is it not completely unrealistic to hope that the NEA behaves any less cravenly than, say, the Department of Defense when it dispenses its contracts? A truly revolutionary argument would be to oppose any and all government funding of individual artists. It is hard to seem rebellious, after all, while whining about who got Daddy's money. Alas, complaining about grants has led the ULA to some fairly appalling arguments, such as when they fingered fiction writer and "university professor" Josip Novakovich for receiving an NEA grant in 2002. It was, the ULA pointed out, his second NEA award in a decade: "Out of the many thousands of writers in America, should one of them receive TWO NEA awards? Is Professor Novakovich that outstanding a writer, or in that need of help? We think not."

I think so. Novakovich is a wonderful writer who would probably eat a bicycle to be published by a major house; I know, because I tried and failed to publish him when I was an assistant editor at W. W. Norton & Company. Novakovich (I do not think he would mind me saying this) also has a family; "university professors" do not, by and large, roll around in piles of money and typically see their writing time vacuumed up by teaching. The money was probably crucial manna for him and his writing life. That the ULA can take a fine, unsung writer such as Novakovich—a writer, moreover, hitherto neglected by the larger publishing world—and single him out for opprobrium is nauseating. He is exactly the type of writer whom the ULA should be championing, especially when Wenclas has claimed that the ULA is "a kind of advocacy group to stand up for writers."

Jackman has explained that the ULA does not stand up for writers who wish to work through the traditional publishing world simply because "we are not interested in trying to hype writers who doff their caps and meekly enter the offices of a major publisher. . . . Let them try their way; we'll try ours." Which would be fair enough if the ULA behaved with such fair-minded quietude in how they regard these meek, cap-doffing souls.

"Publish about real life," the ULA demands. William Goldman once wrote, with some rue, that the problem with novels is that they are written by novelists, all of whom necessarily share a basic similarity of foundational experience: bookishness, self-absorption, perceived alienation. Oftentimes, this can lead to shrunkenly personal work, something of which even Leo Nikolayevich Tolstoy was eye-crossingly capable. Recently, in *The Spooky Art*,

Norman Mailer made a point parallel to Goldman's. Not once in the twentieth century, Mailer noted, has a single politician, actor, athlete, or surgeon emerged as a first-rate novelist, despite the dismayingly huge breadth of experience each profession affords. For better or worse, and I am prepared to admit *worse*, writers are writers are writers. This explains why so many mediocre fiction writers sound the same, why there exist so many books about writers, and why many talented fiction writers seem to think that their best option to distinguish themselves is to flee the quotidian to explore more fanciful subject matter. The resulting work (novels about talking dogs, alternate-world fiction) can indeed grow wearying for those of us who read a lot of contemporary literature. Once again the ULA is not wrong in finding a large number of American fiction writers culturally remiss. The ULA solution is less appealing.

What the ULA is asking for is, in its own words, "writing . . . done in plain English about subjects that matter." What would such work look like? Steinbeck or, more likely, the interior of a Hallmark "Special Moments" card? The "plain English/subjects that matter" position reveals two things: 1) a perfect ignorance of the numerous novels—some would say *too* numerous—being written today that fulfill such a homely mandate; and 2) a stolid refusal to accept anyone who goes about his or her artistic life differently from the ULA. The ULA's habitual concern with "real writers" is abundant proof of this. Who are the "real writers"? "Real writers" are those who starve. Those who do not starve, it then follows, who have managed some level of professional success as writers, are not real writers. Success ruins art. The system ruins art. If this heartless dialectic makes it seem as though no one but the ULA could possibly win this argument, that is because no one but the ULA can possibly win this argument.

To anyone with a passing knowledge of Soviet history, such

histrionics for Realism! Relevance! and Politics! may seem strangely familiar. In 1917 the Bolsheviks picked up their power from the shattered streets of St. Petersburg and set out instantly to crush those journalists and writers in opposition to the new and shaky Soviet regime. Despite a long, pervasive, and decidedly un-European tradition of censorship in Russia, in 1906 the tsar freed Russia's newspapers to write what they pleased. This was to the short-lived relief of Russia's small intellectual class, as Lenin's very first public decree called for the suppression of all newspapers that did not recognize Bolshevik legitimacy. Lenin's edict met such widely felt derision that he had to abandon it until power—at least in St. Petersburg and Moscow—was fully consolidated, in 1918. Russia's hundreds of independent newspapers, some founded in the 1700s, were crushed over a period of mere days. Books, which enjoyed a comparatively smaller audience, were treated more leniently by the Bolsheviks, as they were by the tsars, but by 1922 all manuscripts were forced to go through the Main Administration for Literary Affairs and Publishing, otherwise known as Glavlit. Not surprisingly, the literary writers the Bolsheviks courted either rejected them outright or soon grew disillusioned with the regime's metastasizing totalitarianism. The poet laureate of the Bolsheviks, Vladimir Mayakovsky, a quasi-fascist Futurist whom Lenin privately despised for his "arrant stupidity," wrote gleefully of smashing the bourgeoisie. In one poem he speaks with chilling approval of killing the old men and using their skulls as ashtrays, and in another maintains that "he who sings not with us today / is against / us!" Mayakovsky's mono- and dipsomania grew as terribly as the Bolsheviks' power: his first volume of verse was titled *I!*, his autobiography *I Myself*. When Stalin tired of Mayakovsky in 1930, the poet did the world a favor and killed himself. The other notable Soviet poetaster was named Demian Bedny, a true literary butcher Trotsky commended for his "hatred." Bedny poems such as "No Mercy" and "Everything Comes to an End" were even worse than Mayakovsky's. Stalin tired of Bedny, too, though in an atypical show of mercy only forbade him from ever publishing again. But what of the truly significant literary artists living beneath the nascent yoke of the Soviet regime? What of Anna Akhmatova and Aleksandr Blok and Osip Mandelstam and Isaac Babel and Boris Pasternak? They were thought "corrupt," "fraudulent," "impure." They were not real writers. In a typically monstrous Soviet formulation they were, to the man, tarred as members of "individual nobility." That is, they had fancy educations. They did not write about the *correct* subject matter. They did not address what *mattered*. Soon Akhmatova was reduced to cleaning floors for a living. Blok, after publishing a few poems in praise of the Bolsheviks, gave up poetry altogether and died of tormented guilt in 1921. Mandelstam and Babel perished in the Gulag. Pasternak survived, but, in the words of the historian Richard Pipes, "had to bear humiliation . . . that [a] less stalwart soul . . . would not have endured."

I am not suggesting that the ULA wants to exterminate writers in a Stalinist burst of classocide. (Although who would know it when they say things such as: "These pretenders are in fact members of the cognoscenti: literary-bureaucrats-in-waiting. At best, they're Gorbachev-like reformers. But to the ULA, the mass media can't be reformed, only overthrown, destroyed, and replaced." Even the history in that statement is, in the politest possible terms, completely fucked. The putatively hapless reforms of Gorbachev restructured the Soviet Union right out of existence.) The point here is to call attention to the ramifications of the ULA's argumentatively reckless style. The Bolsheviks changed their names to reflect their personas ("Lenin" derived from the Lena River; "Stalin" derived from steel; "Molotov": hammer; "Bedny": poor), and many ULA members, such as "King" Wenclas, Wild

Bill Blackolive, Urban Hermitt, Crazy Carl Robinson, and Will Ratblood, seem to have indulged in similar nomenclatural baptisms. To rename oneself in such a way is a gesture both of concealment and aggression. The rhetoric one employs both fills out one's new persona and solidifies the always-hazy world into hatefully clear antipodes. In short, one simply cannot toss around such words as "destroy" and "overthrow" without their nasty energy bleeding right down into one's mental topsoil.

"One *must* avoid ambition *in order* to write," Cynthia Ozick once said. "Otherwise something else is the goal: some kind of power beyond the power of language. And the power of language, it seems to me, is the only kind of power a writer is entitled to." I suspect that the Underground Literary Alliance would vomit on that statement. And I suspect, too, that very few writers would want to live in a world in which the Underground Literary Alliance determined who could and could not write.

Reading through ULA agitprop, one is left with a persistent residue of the group's general cluelessness as to how the literary world actually functions. For one, it assumes that the literary world does, in fact, function. Yes, many literary people in New York go to too many parties. Yes, many have unfair social advantages—though just as many do not. Yes, personal connections account for a lot, but personal connections account for just about everything in any adult's professional life. Connections in this sense are, after all, just another word for luck. When someone within the industry likes one's work as a writer, it becomes a connection. When someone within the industry dislikes one's work, which is just as likely, it becomes another connection—a negative connection. This process is neither sinister nor corrupt. It is human and, for most editors, it is permeable and subject to unpredictable point mutation, not the least of which is when someone writes something someone else believes to be good. Connections are also rather defiantly not the final word. When I was an intern at *Harper's Magazine* in 1997—a position I lucked into with no connection whatsoever—I sat in on editorial meetings and watched in quiet awe as one Famous Writer's short story after another went down like Japanese Zeros over Midway. I would need several pairs of hands to count the writers, many of them excellent, wired for every connection one could dream of, whose novels and story collections continue to go unsold.

It is while attacking specific literary figures and organs that the ULA goes most woefully lost. The ULA speaks of the magazine *Open City* as a "well-hyped trendy NYC lit journal," and imagines its readers as "Binky" and "Bret." *Open City* is a fine journal but well hyped it is not, and I would be willing to wager my iBook that neither Amanda Urban nor Bret Easton Ellis regularly cracks open its issues. Similarly, the admirable, small circulation *Bookforum* is called a "mouthpiece" of "the literary establishment," which I imagine *Bookforum* longs were true for the sake of the ad dollars alone. The ULA impugns well-known fiction writers as merry Vichy collaborators when, in fact, many of them would cross the street to avoid one another. Other times, the ULA simply does not make sense at all. When the ULA challenged the Yale English Department to debate the future of American literature, a professor named Nigel Alderman kindly agreed, provided that the ULA read some books of his designation. "[I]n other words," Wenclas fulminated, "that we accept his premises; that we receive his indoctrination; that we THINK in roughly the same way he thinks—which would defeat the entire point." No, actually. The point is that Professor Alderman wanted to have a *debate*.

Finally, the ULA seems wholly ignorant of the Gissinglike toil faced even by "successful" writers with dozens of "connections." The ULA routinely refers to "cushy" university and editorial positions, when in reality these jobs are tenuous, difficult, and roughly as cushy as a six-foot-tall cactus. Many of the writers I know who work as college instructors or editors do it for the money, health insurance, and stability—realities that the ULA's studied blue-collar sympathies might be expected to accommodate. Working as a professional book editor today can be especially trying—it is certainly not financially rewarding—and not a few in my acquaintance belong on suicide watch. Being a writer, published or unpublished, is a life of frustration and rejection, which is why the dismayingly vast majority of writers who publish one book never go on to publish another.

Of the many words and phrases hip-hop culture has injected into the lexical bloodstream of America, few equal the brilliant definitional succinctness of "player hater." Player hating is not the same thing as jealousy, exactly, though jealousy obviously forms a keystone of the average player hater's emotional architecture. Player hating is less rational—not to mention less melancholic—than jealousy. This is not Shakespeare's "green-eyed monster" but a merciless, fire-breathing Godzilla. And the ULA takes player hating to a plane of Iagoan proportions. They are player haters who hate so purely and reflexively that they have run through all the players. Thus they constantly elevate non-players to player status, just so they can hate them, too.

One senses something of the ULA's transparent hunger for celebrity from the *kind* of the writer they consistently assail. All are young, thought to be wealthy, usually male, usually live in New York City or environs, and possess to the utmost that highly qualified species of fame known as literary fame. Rick Moody has been pursued by the ULA so ferociously he is probably checking his shirts for a stenciled-on "Valjean" by now. Jonathan Franzen is another target often fired upon, as is Jeffrey Eugenides. The ULA has virtually nothing to say about the actual *work* of the writers it hates, other than to point out that it is "much-hyped" or some similar approximation. The ULA's hatred of Moody appears largely centered upon the fact that Moody is independently wealthy (or that his family is—the ULA seems to believe this is the same thing, which maybe it is, but it is hard to see how this is the business of anyone whose last name is not Moody, or relevant to whether or not his work is any good) and that he accepted a grant. Franzen's doctrinal breach seems relatively minor: he accepted a grant after becoming unbelievably famous (though it was applied for before that crime). One of the more realish pieces of literary criticism to be found in the available ULA oeuvre concerns Eugenides's novel *Middlesex*. The review, written by Michael Jackman, concerns itself almost entirely with demolishing Eugenides's vision of "white flight" from Detroit, though it saves a little room to attack the use of "imagination" in writing. "Perhaps," Jackman writes bitterly, "I don't have the precious imagination that Eugenides seems to be blessed with. . . . Yes, writing can reach inside and find out what's within us. It certainly can cover what's happening inside the mind and below the belt. All I ask is that we turn that same scrutiny on the world around us, on the injustices and great crimes." Although it *is* nice to see a writer responding to a novel with something more potent than typical book-report musings, it would be hard to imagine a more ax-grindingly butt-headed reading of *Middlesex*. Dave Eggers, however, earns from the ULA a highly specialized anger—that of class betrayal. "The Dave" (in ULA parlance) emerged, after all, from a zine background similar to that of the ULA's founding members. What appears to bother the group most intensely is that Eggers is doing exactly what they would all like to doing, only much better. ULA contributor Steve Kostecke all but admits as much in the microessay about a *McSweeney's* event: "After [the reading] came a short play and, at a local bar, music performed by a band.... These things in combo *I myself had envisioned years ago* [emphasis most certainly mine].... The McSweeners understand ... that those who are easily bedazzled by the scent of things literary will react to them with hyperbole.... What they need ... is an injection of substance, of the writing that now only exists in the raw authenticity of the zine scene."

Perhaps now is the time to examine some of that raw authenticity.

It should immediately be said that the ULA has yet to find and develop its Jack Kerouac. Or its Lawrence Ferlinghetti. Or even its Ed Sanders. Nonetheless, though most of the work available on its website is bad, it is always bad in an interesting way. "Before You Know It," an essay by Emerson Dameron, contains several florid avalanches of prose that in some writers' hands are known as paragraphs:

> It's dangerous to play it safe. America is a
> powder keg of free-floating hostility. The upper
> class micromanages its chokehold on economic
> power, filling its media with vaccinations against
> the peons' sizzling discontent and pitting neigh-
> bor against neighbor like battling scorpions. It
> makes its lettuce sacrificing pawns such as you.
> And yet, among the plebes

and I have to stop, though Dameron doesn't. (Incidentally: *Emerson Dameron*. Anyone blessed with a name like that has no call writing so poorly.) Another essay, "Style vs Substance" by Chris Zee, argues against the workshop:

> How would people with the leisurely disposition to study "the craft of writing" explain their own privilege? If these writers held a mirror up to themselves and the world they enjoy, they might squirm a little at what they see.... It is no wonder that I've met more than one workshop writer who confided to me that they feel they have mastered the "craft" but they struggle in generating relevant subjects to write about.

Good points all, and these are points I have heard numberless editors and agents make. These are also points I have heard writers make. These are also points I have heard people who teach in workshops make. These are also points I have heard in workshops.

Prose that has passed through not a few of these ULA writers' minds does not always survive its transit. What does survive is usually trembling, starved, and weak. It subsists on a thin broth of cliché. Thus, any dash is a "mad dash." The past is inevitably the "not-too-distant past." We have "the daily grind," "the unwritten law," stories occurring in "a sterile laboratory." Things "cross the mind," get "stamped out," and are kept "under hats." One essay, its author an evident cruiserweight of cliché, ends with this left-hook, right-jab combo: "Because you only get so many chances. It'll be over before you know it."

One of the few pieces of fiction posted on the ULA's website is an excerpt from Michael Jackman's *The Corridor*. Jackman's is one of the more angrily eloquent voices within the ULA, and his pleas for honest, socially relevant fiction appear the most heartfelt. Thus, I read his fiction with great interest. What I found, though, was an artless ramble. I do not mean artless in the positive sense of seeming unforced or natural. I mean it in the sense of having no art. "I have always been a procrastinator," is how Jackman's narrator introduces himself to us, "and at the very last minute I had to get serious about finding a new place to live—I had told Henry I would be out of his apartment by the end of November, which was two days away. I needed cheap digs in a hurry." When Jackman's narrator suspenselessly opens the newspaper to find an apartment—its $200-a-month rent serves the same grandstandingly sociological purpose here as a Thomas Pink tie does in the work of Bret Easton Ellis—he decides to go have a look. ("I had no choice!") The apartment is in a bad neighborhood (barking dogs, trash, chain-link fences), details Jackman does not insert so much as rivet into his work. At least the apartment is not in the suburbs. All the same,

> "This place is a nightmare!" I thought. Still, I had to get out of Henry's hotel room, so I handed Stan [the landlord, who smells bad] the first and last months' rent. He wrote out a receipt on the back of an envelope, folding the keys inside. I drove downtown and requested juice at the utility office. They told me to expect to be on the grid within 24 hours. I drove to the record shop to go to work.

The excerpt staggers on, as though trying to defibrillate the suburban heart from its living bourgeois death: "When I had tossed the last of my boxes on the living room floor, I checked the power in the bathroom, but it wasn't on yet. I checked the stove. No gas hissed to life. I couldn't even boil a cup of tea!" Here we have fiction of negative perfection: so boringly real it *cannot* be read.

I held out greater hope for the work published in the ULA's

zine, *Slush Pile*. One of the writers the ULA hypes most sincerely in *Slush Pile* is a young woman—I am guessing she is young—named Urban Hermitt. A Hermitt story (or something) entitled "'I Don't Know'" is about a young woman named Urban Hermitt and her crazy adventures:

> When people say, "I don't know," i growl. "Whatta ya mean you don't know?" i retort. 'Cuz i always thought that people secretly knew why they did the things they did. Like you drink beer 'cuz you secretly can't handle reality and you wanna fuck. Like you avoid eye contact with a cutie 'cuz you secretly can't handle reality and wanna fuck. Well, i couldn't handle reality either and boy did i wanna fuck.

It is not that Ms. Hermitt is not able to write, or is not, often, sort of amusing. Of her crazy adventures in Mexico, she notes, "'Only eat food served to you in hotels,' the travel book on Baja Mexico says. 'And if you eat food from a street vendor, make sure you take pepto-bismol.' These travel books make all street vendors seem EVIL. And then they expect you to down this 'pink' liquid called pepto-bismol which is full of all this chemicalized crap!" Hermitt's problem is that she, like Jackman, has mistaken emotion and purity of intent for art. Wenclas has defended Hermitt's work by saying, "There can be no rewrites. . . . Attempts to impose order—grammar, spelling, and logic—would cause the fragile bursts of immediacy to fall apart." To that, one is tempted to argue that poiaurna fopiuay bnvmnnab.

Another story, "Weddings in Purgatory" by Cullen Carter (whose bio says, winningly, that he "likes beer"), has any number of paragraphs filled with writing like this:

But then Sofia took off her coat and introduced herself. There was a small spark of life in me when I noticed those firm breasts hidden underneath that tight black sweater of hers. I hadn't had any in a while, and I was feeling sex-starved. We ended up hooking up, and I was happy for a couple days, thinking I could maybe build a fire with that spark, thinking that maybe I could finally get on with my life.

And yet ULA members do not always write badly. One of the group's more prominent writers is Jack Saunders, a Santa Claus-ishly lovable sort who for years has been fruitlessly pestering the publishing world. I received a letter from Saunders in 2000, shortly after I published an essay in *The Boston Review* about the historical obtuseness of the publishing world's judgment, for instance its rejections of Melville and Whitman. Saunders's letter—angry but cheerful—contained excerpts of the many brush-offs he has received from editors, not all of them unkind. (It also, somewhat alarmingly, included a photo of him and a topless woman.) Saunders all but dared me to put my money where my essay was and publish him at Henry Holt and Company, where I then worked. I enjoyed what I read, but since I regarded—and regard—Saunders's work roughly as salable as a Hefty bag filled with used hypos, I was too depressed even to write him back. I also suspected that, if I did, I was going to get an extremely loquacious pen pal (and perhaps even increasingly nude photos). In an excerpted essay about the novel's future, Saunders writes:

> Anybody can become a writer if he ditches a perfectly good wife to marry one with a rich uncle,

leaves the kids with nannies—or puts them in
boarding school—and goes off on safaris, stabs
people who have helped him in the back....And
most of our writers have done things like that.
Even the ones I admire. If you're married and
have kids, you have to do your part. To be a good
father to your family. Only then can you write. In
the time remaining. No great novels are going to
be written that way. But you can become a better
human being that way.

Which may be dippy, and which may glisten with more than a
little old-coot-type treacle, but it is also pretty hard to argue and
bravely unfashionable to say. Especially for an author like Saunders, who has boasted of writing nine novels in six months. At
the very least, one senses a real human heart within this sentiment rather than the sort of sense-deadened literary adept whom
Borges once criticized as writing as though it were "a trick they
had learned....They know that when they have to write, then,
well, they have to suddenly become rather sad and ironic."

A 1997 essay by King Wenclas, "Living in the Real America,"
is equally worth considering. "Currently I work as a release
clerk/truck dispatcher for a customshouse broker at Detroit's
Ambassador Bridge," the essay begins, "the great commercial
NAFTA gateway of North America." The point here is thankfully
not trade-and-tariff politics but the plight of many Americans
to make what is sometimes cruelly known as a living. "When it
rains," Wenclas notes of his workspace,

the ceiling leaks. We have no place to hang our
coats, we have no lunch room, we grab food
when we can inbetween processing the unceas-

ing paperwork and dealing with the multiplying regulations of numerous government empires. . . . Phones constantly ring. "The container hasn't arrived." It's sitting in a railyard in Detroit.

What sort of people work these jobs? Well, Wenclas tells us:

> Young Latino girls, eastside ghetto blacks, down-river white trash, and broke losers like myself. The pay ranges between minimum wage and ten dollars an hour. We endure working conditions worse than those that caused Bartleby to go insane. How many hours do you want? 60? 70? 16-hour shifts? We work hard. . . . We have no rights, we have no unions, we have no time, money, or energy with which to enjoy any but the barest existence. We are the new American worker. . . . Amid the madness, on the dock[,] observing the activity[,] sits a four-month-old white baby strapped into a plastic seat. He's one of Tabitha's [a coworker's], who can't afford sitters. "Tabitha!" I yell. "You left your kid on the dock." "My mother's picking him up," she yells back. "I got drivers! Could you keep an eye on him?" The baby waves his arms. I wait with him, past and future[,] wondering what the world has in store for us.

It would be easy to assume that Wenclas is doing a lot of alienated socio-economic posturing here. I think it would be far too easy to assume this. The piece's early publication date and simpler, less hysterical tone suggests a writer whose voice has not yet been calcified by rejection and outside indifference, a writer who still had faith that the power of his human outrage, stated well, might allow him a way out of his desperation, that might make others *awake*. And yet, in his title, Wenclas has one thing wrong. The "real" America is not poor and desperate, just as the real America is not young and wealthy and hip. They are both America, and both can be written about in revelatory ways. Wenclas is living in Wenclas's America. It is his duty as a writer to convey that America to his reader, and here, at least, he does so well. I wonder how much work Wenclas has in this voice, and if it's as good. I wonder also if it would even matter, knowing too well the likely fate of even a superbly conceived piece of work dealing with the realities of our American underclass: regretful rejection and cheerful good wishes, followed, of course, by a completely understandable authorial despair. I then find myself thinking about the ULA's arguments even more, and I wonder if the fact that I am so surprised by how riled their arguments make me might not suggest that many of them have, in fact, an unpleasant tincture of truth.

Several people told me that any remotely personal dealings with members of the ULA uncovers not some secret cabal of literary anarchists but folk who are basically polite and, indeed, almost shy. One on one, I was told, ULA members come off less as fearless statue-topplers than maladjusted adolescents who have decided that the best way to get a pretty girl's attention is to snap her bra. It is when they gather that the problems begin (also like adolescents). The *Open City* poet (and lead singer and songwriter for the Silver Jews) David Berman learned as much when he sent a lacerating letter to Wenclas challenging the ULA to a "relevance readoff." Upon receiving Wenclas's sharp though polite reply, Berman shot back, "Look King, if you're going to be so civil about this then disregard my first letter. I thought you were hot-headed assholes looking for a fight.... Obviously I'm talking to the wrong guy. Who's the head asshole over there? Tell him to call me."

During an interview conducted over email, I asked Michael Jackman about this occasional severance between the ULA's spiteful tactics and the personalities of its individual members. He responded, "I think I know what you're getting at with this question. I can probably sit down and have a civil conversation with you. I can pass. I can even make my voice sound just like those voices on NPR.... In any event, sure, we're caring and decent people. I'd say that the most caring and decent people are belligerent when faced with injustice."

Although I can hardly claim to know him, I like Jackman. Possibly this is because I have a high tolerance for people who regard things that offend them as "injustice." I posed a series of fairly pointed questions and Jackman answered them quickly, intelligently, and well. When I asked if the ULA can appreciate how blatantly jealous it appears by attacking the writers it does, Jackman said my question reminded him of high school, in particular the timeless propensity of popular kids to look upon the actions of unpopular kids, no matter how innocuous, as an attempt to get the popular kids' attention. "How self-satisfied does somebody have to be to look at the opposition and simply see envy!" Jackman fired back. "What blind arrogance!" That his mind instantly retreated to the bivouacs of Phys. Ed. and prom is probably more revealing than he intended to be, but his point stands that fiercely opposing another person does not necessarily mean that all opposition is birthed in envy. "The 'big brainy writer's club' simply presents us with an appropriate target," Jackman went on. "They do an excellent job of representing everything we regard as foul. They are a smarmy, back-slapping network of people who have very little experience out there in the world."When I asked which writers Jackman admires, he mentioned Charles Bukowski. It is perhaps worth pointing out that Bukowski's experience with the world was largely consigned to seeing it through the bottom of a shot glass when he was not delivering people's mail. While this does not make him a bad writer, it certainly does not make him a good writer either.

I realized about here that Jackman was not actually criticizing these big-brained writers themselves, as writers. My secret suspicion is that he has probably read the writers he professes to loathe carefully and, somewhere within him, found at least something to admire. Otherwise they would not make him so angry. He was criticizing, instead, the image of these writers. In Jackman's mind, these writers have "very little experience out there in the world"—a ridiculous position in itself; *everyone* has experience out there in the world, seeing that everyone actually *lives* in the world—because, for him, these writers are only images. Images do not have experience. They are *images*. And this is the problem. It is an old problem, but it is still a problem.

If serious reading is in peril, and I believe it is—though I also believe that *in peril* may well be the default condition of serious reading—maybe it is because, for many, serious reading is increasingly revolving around nothing but image. Writers become brands or poses rather than individuals trying to communicate something human to their readers. What is particularly horrifying about all this is the fact that the writers themselves are rarely to blame for their images. To talk about books with many in the publishing industry, and God knows I have been as guilty of this as anyone, becomes less an occasion to discuss books than to conjure up some unreal quasi-world of byzantine intrigue and thrillingly naked literary Darwinism: Who is up. Who is down. Whose book sold. Whose book did not. How success has ruined A. How B is no longer in. How C never wrote anything good after the divorce. It is little wonder that the manner in which this gossipy system publishes many writers' work appalls those it excludes. I often find it appalling myself, and I used to do it for a living and might well, someday, do it again.

Literature is sacred. It is as sacred to me as anything I know. I suspect that most editors and agents feel the same way, if only during the quiet hours of the night. But there is always the issue of how one goes about selling the sacred without defiling it. There is the issue of how one goes about superintending the sacred when tens of thousands of fellow brethren, some of them abundantly insane but many of the truest sort of heart, want to add to its flame. What does one tell them? That they are not holy enough? However one personally and professionally elects to handle these troubling issues, a tiny piece of the sacred is ruined. For me, at least, all of this inevitably leads to a small, quiet grief. We would all like for our worlds to be bigger.

For Jackman and the ULA, however, it leads somewhere else. When I asked why the ULA does not attempt to call attention to the numerous published novels that disappear from public view so completely it is as though they were never published, he replied that the ULA is "not on a level playing field. We are engaged in a kind of cultural warfare here, and we're a small bunch of guerillas taking on a large opponent with vast resources. . . . If you're small and your opponent is large, attack—then the opponent has to devote resources to its defenses." He went on, "It's shocking to me how the ULA apparently believes in writers and believes in litera-ture more than the people who control the industry." I countered that the people who control the industry know horrendously well how poorly most books sell—even those that are "hyped." "I can't think of any other business that operates with that cata-strophic lack of vision!" Jackman responded. "Every business in this country tries to court success aggressively, it would seem, with the exception of literature."

It is sentiment such as this that makes me admire Jackman, even as I recognize that he does not always know what he is talking about, even as I suspect that, if *The Corridor* is any indication, he could not write his way out of an issue of *Ranger Rick*, and even as I believe his literary judgment to be basically not so good. He is a nobly unreasonable person leading an unreasonable group seeking to unreasonably alter the terms of a fundamentally unreasonable debate. Not only that of commerce versus art but art as it is enriched by ethics and ethics as they are challenged by social injustice. He is far from the only writer concerned with such matters, but he clearly believes he is. This strange, bug-eyed moral certainty is what is interesting about the ULA and what is repellent about the ULA. But it is usually more interesting than repellent. It is also more moving, especially when the ULA sucks the venom from its voice and speaks more to its very human concerns.

I wrote earlier of the sacred. Indeed, literary movements have a typical development not unlike that of religion. They begin in revelation, grow in consolidation, mature in strength, decay into complacent necrosis, suffer schism and partial inner destruction, and then are born anew. If the ULA follows this traditional arc, one of two things will happen. They will either grow frustrated, stop writing, surrender their faith, and disappear; or one of them, or two of them, possibly three of them, but no more, will publish or self-publish something that finds an audience large enough to move the traditional publishing houses and larger magazines to swing their censer before the ULA's eyes. Any such success will, no doubt, be a moment of some philosophical difficulty. The money will in all likelihood be convincing enough to allow these lucky ULA writers to swallow their rancor toward the system that shunned them, and with weighty hearts they will step into the bloody crossroads where art and commerce meet. Perhaps, then, the ULA will become the literary equivalent of, say, Episcopalianism. Suddenly, *they* will be the ones turning away expectant apostles. *Theirs* will be the door to which many will nail their bad-tempered theses. I personally hope for the latter, both because I believe that the ULA's movement is fundamentally one of hope and because I suspect that only success will convince the ULA that art, like death, is life's great leveler. We all grieve of it equally, and at no point can any of us expect to be treated fairly.

—2003

WRITING ABOUT WRITING
ABOUT WRITING

The first idea was not our own.
—Wallace Stevens, "Notes Toward a Supreme Fiction"

HOW-TO

To linger around the bookstore alcove dedicated to how-to-write books is to grow quickly acquainted with the many species of human expectation. One after another the aspirants come—the good-sport retiree who has decided to tell her life story, the young specter of manhood with scores to settle and truths to tell, the Cussler- and Patterson-overdosed executive aiming to blockbust his way to lakefront property and setting his alarm for ten—and shyly pull books off the packed shelves, level upon level of volumes promising to atomize the frustratingly numerous barriers between them and their dreams. Yet most of the people who frequent the how-to-write section will never become writers. It gives me no pleasure to make that observation, just as it gives me no pleasure to admit that I will never play swingman for the Indiana Pacers.

The question is whether these people will never become writers because they are not talented or because the books that congest the shelves of the how-to-write section are mostly useless. This sounds much sharper than I intend. Look around the how-to section. To your left: books on how to garden. To your right: computer programming. Down the way a bit more: *How to Play Five-String Banjo*. Most of the people who buy *these* books will not become professional gardeners or computer programmers or banjoists either. Would a successful computer programmer sneer at a person seeking to explore the pleasures of writing a few lines of code? Somehow one doubts it. Dreams, after all, are many, often mundane, and their private pursuit is the luxury of every dreamer.

But an even dustier (and probably unanswerable) question must first be posed: Can writing be taught? Both congratulation and flagellation tend to accrue upon the answers this question receives. Those who maintain that writing cannot be taught are in effect promoting the Priesthood Theory of Writing. In short, a few are called, most are not, and nothing anyone does can alter this fated process. Those who maintain that writing can be taught are, on the other hand, in grave danger of overestimating their ultimate value as teachers, though most of the writing teachers I know are squarely agnostic on the issue. My own view, if it matters: Of course writing can be taught. Every writer on the planet was taught, via some means, to write. Even those lacking the guildlike background of an MFA program or the master-apprentice experience of studying beneath an attentive teacher taught themselves to write—most likely by reading a lot of literature. To think about this question for more than a few moments quickly reduces it to the absurd. *All* human activity is taught. The only thing any human being is born to do is survive, and even in this we all need several years of initial guidance.

Harder to judge is the possibility of teaching a beginning writer how to be receptive to the very real emotional demands of creating literature. To write serious work is to reflexively grasp abstruse matters such as moral gravity, spiritual generosity, and the ability to know when one is boring the reader senseless, all of which are founded upon a distinct type of aptitude that has little apparent relation to more measurable forms of intelligence. Plenty of incredibly smart people cannot write to save their lives. Obviously, writerly intelligence is closely moored to the mature notion of *intellect* (unlike math or music, the adolescent prodigy is virtually unknown to literature) because writing is based on a gradual development of psychological perception, which takes time and experience. Writing can be taught, then, yes—but only to those who are teachable. Strong writers, especially, can be made, with sensitive guidance, even stronger. This is, in part, the service professional book editors provide. The problem is, truly fine writers have emerged from every cultural, sociological, and educational milieu imaginable. An even bigger problem is, at least for those who teach beginning writers, no one can predict who *is* teachable. Perhaps it is best, then, to teach them all.

ON BECOMING A NOVELIST

If any of this sounds familiar, it is because I am cribbing from John Gardner's *On Becoming a Novelist*, the book that did, in fact, teach me how to write. It is probably the most important book I have ever read—or rather the most important book ever read by the aspiring writer who became the person writing this sentence. Gardner, an erratically brilliant novelist, solid short-story writer, underappreciated critic, legendary creative-writing teacher, habitual animadvert, massive hypocrite, and awe-inspiring pain in the ass, died in a motorcycle accident at the age of forty-nine in 1982, having written more than thirty books; *Novelist* is one of the last he completed. With the exception of *Grendel*, his genre-shattering masterpiece, most of his books are, today, out of print. (I should disclose here that, as a young editor at W.W. Norton, I was behind *Novelist's* restoration to print. I tried the same daring rescue op with some of his fiction. That mission failed.) Why is *Novelist* so good? "Either the reader [of this book] is a beginning novelist who wants to know whether the book is likely to be helpful," Gardner writes in his preface, "or else the reader is a writing teacher hoping to figure out without too much wasted effort what kind of rip-off is being aimed this time at that favorite target of self-help fleecers." Instantly we see the many virtues of Gardner's approach: honesty, an up-front acknowledg-ment of the typical how-to-write book's worth, and a forgiving awareness of human limitation: "More people fail at becom-ing businessmen than fail at becoming artists." It was Gardner's unfakeable gift to write advice that feels laser-beamed into the cortex of each individual reader. *Me,* one thinks with amazement while reading. *He is talking to me.* Or so I felt, reading *Novelist* for the first time at a writer's workshop in Bennington, Vermont.

I was eighteen, had never been to a workshop before (and have, with a couple of exceptions, stayed away from them since), had never even been *east* before (I was then a community-college student in Michigan), and was surrounded, for the first time, by people crazy about writers and books. It was overwhelming, and after two days I wanted to go home. I did not have talent, was galactically outclassed by the Harvard students on their résumé-building summer vacations, and suddenly had no idea why I ever believed my deeply rural imagination would ever be capable of producing literary art. My teacher, sensing my distress, handed me *On Becoming a Novelist*, and by the end of the day I had nearly conked out my Hi-Liter. One paragraph in particular saved my literary life, as I was then struggling with the demands of telling "the truth" about the asses and idiots every young man imagines living all around him. I remember the passage so vividly I scarcely need to consult the source:

> One of the great temptations of young writers is to believe that all the people in the subdivision in which he grew up were fools and hypocrites in need of blasting or instruction. As he matures, the writer will come to realize, with luck, that the people he scorned had important virtues, that they had better heads and hearts than he knew. The desire to show people proper beliefs and attitudes is inimical to the noblest impulses of fiction.

Thunder! lightning! Read that again, please. These are the words of a fundamentally good man attempting to show the young writer one honest way in which to think, to *see*. (When I found out that the aesthetically conservative Gardner was actively loathed by many of his fellow writers—Joseph Heller called him "a pretentious young man"!—I loved him even more.) If I belabor the point with autobiography—and there will not be any more, or at least not very much—I do so to make a point. Most writers have thoughts about writing as an act, as a way of understanding oneself, or as a way of being, and they are often interesting. I have any number of thoughts about writing, all of which I find incomparably fascinating. How fascinating to others, though, might they be? A how-to-write book saved my life, then, but it did so existentially, not instructively. Many of the best books about writing are only incidentally about writing. Instead, they are about how to live.

USER'S MANUAL

There are several types of how-to-write books. The first is the rigorous handbook-style guide that does not concern itself with creating interesting characters or crafting exciting scenes. Rather, it concentrates on how to write a decent sentence that means what one intends it to mean: a User's Manual to the English language. The most famous is William Strunk Jr. and E. B. White's *The Elements of Style.* If one wishes to write *New Yorker*–style prose, this is the book to read. Of course, the *New Yorker* style is a fine style with which it is eminently worth getting acquainted, but it is not the only style. Nor is it, in every case, even the most preferable style. One truly interesting thing about the *New Yorker* style is that it can serve both as a hiding place for mediocrity and as the lacquered display table for masters rightfully confident in their powers. Used well, the *New Yorker* style is what one imagines the style of God might be, if there was any indication that God spoke English. Used poorly, the *New Yorker* style is all gutless understatement, decorous to a Fabergé extreme.

Composed of five parts ("Elementary Rules of Usage," "Elementary Principles of Composition," "A Few Matters of Form," "Words and Expressions Commonly Misused," and "An Approach to Style"), *Elements* is a handholding book, in the best sense. The first four parts are, as one might guess, almost ridiculously elementary, with brief and noticeably impatient advice as to how to punctuate ("A common error is to write *it's* for *its*," "do not use periods for commas") and employ basic literary logic ("As a rule, begin each paragraph either with a sentence that suggests the topic or with a sentence that helps the transition"). The last part, "An Approach to Style," opens with Strunk and White admitting, "Here we leave solid ground," and that "no key unlocks the door." It must surely rank among the most winning and incisive twenty pages on writing that have ever been published. "With some writers," *Elements* tells us, "style not only reveals the spirit of the man but reveals his identity. . . . The beginner should approach style warily, realizing it is an expression of self, and should turn resolutely away from all devices that are popularly believed to indicate style." In other words, when it comes to the most important stuff, kid, you are on your own.

Nevertheless, there is much within *Elements* to debate. Many have quibbled with Strunk and White's assertion to "Write with nouns and verbs, not with adjectives and adverbs." In fact, the passage in which this advice appears is actually an apologia for the much-maligned adverb. "Use adverbs *well*" seems to be the actual, hidden point of this initially restrictive diktat. "Avoid fancy words," Strunk and White tell us, and, if the wearisome battles I have had with copy editors and family members is any indication, the entire planet now agrees. "Anglo-Saxon," we are informed, "is a livelier tongue than Latin, so use Anglo-Saxon words." Well, according to whom? The "fancy words" Strunk and White unveil as examples—*beauteous*, *curvaceous*, and *discombobulate*—are less fancy words than incredibly dumb words. One thing a "fancy words" embargo does is squelch and stifle a certain kind of young writer—the kind of young writer who happens to love and cherish unusual words, and who can, more significantly, divine the appropriateness of a dumb word and a word of high contextual potential. "Do not inject opinion," *Elements* goes on. Dear Lord in heaven, why not? "We all have opinions about almost everything, and the temptation to toss them in is great. . . . [T]o air one's views at an improper time may be in bad taste." But good writing, like a good joke, is very rarely in good taste. It could be said—in fact, I will say it—that *all a writer has, in the end, is his or her opinions*. Hemingway believed that personal courage was the defining component of one's life; that is of course an opinion, and his entire body of work is shot to the core with it. "Do not inject opinion" is itself an opinion! This is not advice for a young writer seeking a stately style. This is advice one receives in a Toastmasters public-speaking class.

I do not really believe that Strunk and White thought opinion had no place in writing, or believed "fancy words" were inherently ill-advised. *The Elements of Style* is not proscriptive, despite its many proscriptions. It is suggestive, and wisely so. It has made and will continue to make many people write better, and more clearly. So shouts out. But it seems unlikely to help anyone already on his or her way toward becoming an artist. If even this most ideal of books is read at the wrong time, it may actually damage (or at least discombobulate) the young artist.

GOLDEN PARACHUTE

What of the how-to-write books with more financially liberating titles? I speak, of course, of Daniel H. Jones's *How to Write a Best-seller While Keeping Your Day Job*, Judith Appelbaum's *How to Get Happily Published*, James N. Frey's *How to Write a Damn Good Novel*, James N. Frey's *How to Write a Damn Good Novel II*, and so on. Quite a few of these Golden Parachutes are penned by people who have rarely written anything *but* how-to-write books. They are usually hack books for hacks. Most are fairly, and forgivably, straightforward about this. The self-aware hack is, after all, a pardonable literary colleague, largely because he poses no threat to an actual artist.

Artist. That is a grand word, and you might think that most of the Golden Parachute how-tos care little about the artier aspects of writing: integrity, truth, vision, and the like. You would be wrong. Many care deeply about art, as they care about advances and careers and publicity. Such books nanny every facet of writing equally, giving us a portrait of the artist as a fragile Hummel figurine.

Donald Maass's *Writing the Breakout Novel* is both a case in point and not. Maass, an established literary agent who, according to his biography, "is the author of fourteen pseudonymous novels," does not at first blush appear to be the most sensitive minister to the literary soul. Take, for instance, some of his clients, such as the novelist Anne Perry, one of the two girls whose real-life matricidal crimes were the subject of Peter Jackson's film *Heavenly Creatures*. Indeed, Perry provides the book's foreword: "Put yourself on the page and all that you think and feel about life, but do it with discipline; do it with skill. Then the good agents and the good publishers will get your work into the hands of the good readers." And then the good fairies and elves will approach your front door carrying bags of gold, and the leprechauns will come, and the gnomes, and the friendly talking monkeys will sing, oh sing! outside your window! Although Perry's is some of the most insincere advice I have ever read, it is not even her foreword's silliest moment. That would be: "Good luck. There's room for us all. They'll just build bigger bookshops!"

Maass is much shrewder than all that. *Writing the Breakout Novel* is about just what it claims: breaking out. Intended mainly for the already published novelist marooned upon the Isles of Midlist, *Breakout* is largely a fiduciary affair, as breaking out has little to do with art and much to do with sweaty calculation. Maass acknowledges this, more or less. He also acknowledges that people in the publishing industry, most often, "do not have the foggiest idea" why some authors break out and some do not. Authors who have broken out, Maass writes, "toss around wholesale numbers like baseball stats, and generally display the ease and confidence of someone who has made it big through long and dedicated effort." Such writers are often called assholes. However, these assholes have learned something, namely "the methods [of] developing a feel for the breakout-level story." The breakout-level story is one "in which lightning seems to strike on every page," written by authors who "run free of the pack." Writing a breakout novel "is to delve deeper, think harder, revise more, and commit to creating characters and plot that surpass one's previous accomplishments." But! "I am not interested in punching out cookie-cutter best-sellers, so-called 'blockbuster novels.'" Rest assured, "A true breakout is not an imitation but a breakthrough to a more profound individual expression."

Cynics would not be blamed for suspecting that Maass is sleeping in both bunks, as it were. But the fact is, agents are not the brainless dollar-zombies routinely imagined by lit-biz chatter-boxes. Virtually all of them know the difference between a work of art and a work of commerce, Maass included. Here is a man who can, in the space of one page, excerpt from and discuss the work of both Nicholas Sparks ("You have probably noticed from these excerpts that the prose and dialogue in *The Notebook* is rudimentary") and Colson Whitehead ("His fully developed premise meets all of my breakout criteria"). In his extremely good discussion of "Tension on Every Page" Maass holds up not, say, Robert Stone or Neal Stephenson, but John Grisham. Maass admits that "it is fashionable to put down [Grisham's] writing: *His prose is plain . . . his characters are cardboard cutouts.* There is some truth to those charges, but one cannot deny that Grisham compels his readers to turn the pages." I have read two Grisham novels, *The Firm* and *A Time to Kill*, and though my eyes rolled skyward several dozen times, I did, indeed, finish them both. In the case of *The Firm*, I could scarcely turn the pages fast enough. There *is* that to learn from Grisham, as Maass notes, "even in the absence of artistic prose."

But can one *learn* how to keep readers turning pages? Can one *learn* some magical method of "Building a Cast" of supporting characters, as one of Maass's subchapters is headed? "Needless

to say," Maass writes, "the more complex you make your secondary characters, the more lifelike and involving your story will be."
One can almost hear the scribbly note-taking accompanying that
insight. Maass is not wrong; it *is* needless to say. But seeking to
provide writers with some surefire method of injecting complexity into secondary characters seems rather difficult. How would
one do this, if not intuitively—if not *naturally*? Well, let us try. Say
I have just created a secondary character named Jake. Jake works
at a zoo. He is overweight, conscious of his body, and has no girlfriend. Okay. Complexity now. He was once kicked in the face.
By a zebra. That Jake, he hates zebras. This is pointless, of course.
Characters, along with their hang-ups and complexities, appear
in the mind of a writer and are honed or dispatched accordingly.
It is as simple and dreadfully complicated as that. Writers who
are able to summon up a lot of interesting secondary characters
have one of two things going for them: they have had a lot of life
experience and met many interesting people, or they are imaginative swamis.

Maass's book is at its best while destroying certain tightly
held notions of why writers do not succeed. Writers whose
books have not broken through, Maass notes, "would rather put
their faith in formulas, gossip, connections, contract language—
anything but their own novels." This is certainly true, but who can
blame them? The powerful counter-argument is that dozens and
dozens of writers (Joanna Scott, Brian Hall, Donald Harington,
Gary Sernovitz, Wilton Barnhardt) have written brilliant, exciting, innovative *breakthrough*-style books and not yet bathed in
the fountain of universal acclaim. I once asked a writer friend,
whose first book had won an important literary prize, what that
was like. He answered, "Like running around on a football field
with a hundred other people and being the only one struck by
lightning." *Getting Struck by Lightning* is an ungainly title, and its

premise is rather cracked. Ultimately, though, its premise is no more cracked than that of *Writing the Breakout Novel.*

Writing the Breakout Novel is published by Cincinnati's own Writer's Digest Books, possibly the most sinister malefactor of Panglossian expectations in the literary world today. Some of its books, like Maass's, are useful. Most are pandects of stupidity. From *The Insider's Guide to Getting an Agent* to *The Writer's Book of Character Traits* to *Fiction Writer's Brainstormer,* Writer's Digest Books preys on hopefuls' dreams. *How to Write & Sell Your First Novel,* by the literary agent Oscar Collier and the freelance writer Frances Spatz Leighton, is no doubt something of a landmark book for these aspirants, as it sells them a vision not of publishing but publi$hing: "Publishing has become a $32 billion industry in the United States, and authors are beginning to appear on annual lists of America's biggest earners." So quit your job and buy a boat, why don't you? "Writers," we are told, "are continuing to move away from the typewriter toward computers." And Model-Ts are beginning to roll down the cobbled streets of old Manhattantown. "A less promising development," Oscar and Frances tell us, "has been the appearance of novels devoted almost entirely to extreme violence." But first novels without such nasty bits still get published all the time. And what a feeling for the agent! "If I," Oscar confides, suddenly ditching poor Frances, "can get such a charge from merely *discovering* a new novelist, think how much more you can benefit from *becoming* one." Holy shit!

What does it take to write a salable novel? Let us see: "a feeling for characterization," "a passable plot," and an "interesting and well-detailed setting." What are the writer's chances at publishing his or her first novel? Oscar does some casual arithmetic and comes up with the following: "[Y]ou have a one in ten chance of getting published, unless you do it yourself." I would say that this is off the mark by a factor of, oh, two million or so. Oscar/

Frances then give us the success stories: "You couldn't get more obscure than John Wessel who worked in a bookstore." But Wessel sold his book to Simon and Schuster for $900,000. And since then Wessel has written . . . uh, let us move on. Tom Clancy! The admittedly interesting publishing history of *The Hunt for Red October* is addressed at length, and then: "Novels continued to explode out of Clancy." Alack, yes. But what *is* a novel, Oscar? "A novel is a story. It's just a story. It has a beginning, a middle and an end. That's all there is and you can handle it." This seems about as convincing and heartfelt as a Sigma Chi preparing a drunken coed for her first anal adventure. "Writing about what you know is fine, and writing what you only dream about in your mind is fine, too." Everything is fine, in fact. How do you make characters sympathetic? "In many ways." How do you make people sound natural in a novel? "How do real people talk? They talk like you. They talk like me." But what about finding the time to write a novel? "Steven Linakis worked full time as a book-keeper, commuted long hours on the Long Island Railroad and still managed to write a first novel that earned him more than $200,000." You know, Steven Linakis. He wrote . . . that book. That book that sold for $200,000.

NUTS & BOLTS, TEA & ANGELS

Probably the most well-known (and well-bought) species of how-to-write book is authored by someone who has published a few successful works of fiction or nonfiction and decided to share with the world his or her incunabulum of literary secrets. Such books are often aridly titled, highly theoretical, exercise-driven, and contain generous tissue samples of other writers' prose to be peeled and vivisected until the student-reader knows why the passage "works." Madison Smartt Bell's *Narrative Design* and Josip

Novakovich's *Fiction Writer's Workshop* are both fine and helpful examples, as is John Gardner's *The Art of Fiction*, an oak-solid Nuts & Boltser that is an interesting companion to his more philosophical *On Becoming a Novelist*. All of these books should be read, and not only by beginners. But this category breaks down into more Linnaean classification. Alongside the Nuts & Bolts how-to books of solidly accomplished writers, one finds what I will call the Tea & Angels how-to book. These are often deeply mystical affairs.

There is a place for mysticism when discussing writing, as much of the process is bloodcurdlingly strange. So many things happen in any given piece of writing that cannot be explained: hauntingly unintentional thematic echoes, unplanned characters who arrive as though by séance, moments all but impossible to describe to the nonwriter when one does not feel as though one is writing but *transcribing*. Amazing, all of it. But the majority of writing is not like this, and should not be discussed as though it is, or can be.

Natalie Goldberg's *Writing Down the Bones: Freeing the Writer Within* is more mystical than ten Sufis. Get the right pen, Goldberg advises, and the right notebook ("Garfield, the Muppets, Mickey Mouse, Star Wars. I use notebooks with funny covers") and just *go*. Keep your hand moving, she coaches. There is another activity that requires you keep your hand moving. The important things are not to cross out, think, or get logical. And keep a big wad of Kleenex nearby. "Lose control," she commands. Goldberg is St. Paul on the topic of the First Thought: "First thoughts have tremendous energy....You must be a great warrior when you contact first thoughts and write from them."

Goldberg tells us, "I teach the same methods over and over again." Unfortunately, she also makes the same points over and over again. "What is said here about writing can be applied to running, painting, anything you love." Indeed, writing is like cooking, she says at one point. Writing is like singing, she says at another. Writing is like running, she says (again). Actually, writing is like writing. Where did Goldberg pick up this breathtakingly inclusive view of writing? "In 1974 I began to do sitting meditation." Uh oh.

It is not merely that Goldberg is certifiable on the topic of writing; she is also a very cunning egomaniac, as when she describes with dewy wonder how a friend of hers once spent the afternoon reading over her (Goldberg's) old notebooks. "If you could write the junk you did then and write the stuff you do now," this friend tells Goldberg, "I realize I can do anything." Later on, she shares that she always brings a "date" to her readings: "I told the friend that as soon as I was finished reading, 'Come right up to me, hug me, tell me how beautiful I looked and how wonderful I am.'" Of course, nearly all writers are needy monsters, but that is no reason for Goldberg to unwisely encourage this lamentable condition. And yet some of what Goldberg says is beautiful:

> We are important and our lives are important, magnificent really, and their details are worthy to be recorded. This is how writers must think, this is how we must sit down with pen in hand. We were here; we are human beings; this is how we lived.

A lovely few lines of sentiment, and Goldberg is to be honored for sharing them. Equally salutary is her realistic appraisal of money and writing, so unlike Golden Parachutes and the troughs of lucre they promise: "I feel very rich when I have time to write and very poor when I get a regular paycheck and no time to work at my real work." One begins to like Goldberg—with qualifications, absolutely—but, all the same, one really begins to admire her spirit and goofiness and then she says something like "If you read good books, when you write, good books will come out of you" and you bow your head.

In *Bones*'s epilogue, she describes the day she finished writing the selfsame book and going to a local café: "I looked at everyone, spoke to no one, and kept smiling: 'I've finished a book. Soon maybe I can be a human being again.' I walked home relieved and happy. The next morning I cried. By the afternoon I felt wonderful." Reading this book feels a little like being in a long, doomed relationship with a manic-depressive. One also feels ruthlessly certain that, despite the fact that is has sold well over 150,000 copies, no one who ever read *Writing Down the Bones* became a writer by anything but sheer accident.

Of well-known how-to-write books by established authors, Anne Lamott's *Bird by Bird: Some Instructions on Writing and Life* is, despite her healingly mild approach, the most fun to read. The title comes from a story out of Lamott's childhood. Her brother, overwhelmed by a grade-school writing project on birds, despaired of his ability to finish it. Lamott's father put his arm around the boy and said, "Bird by bird, buddy. Just take it bird by bird." Perhaps one feels a small temptation to snigger at this advice—how easy it is to imagine these words stitched on a throw pillow—but this temptation should be fought, for a simple reason: like much of what is found on throw pillows, it is memorable and quietly true.

Bird by Bird's introduction offers a portrait of Lamott's father, himself a writer, who died early, of a stroke, at fifty-five. Lamott's first novel, published when she was twenty-six, concerned a family coming to terms with its patriarch slowly dying. Intended as a gift to the man, it was written as he succumbed. Not having read the book, I have no idea if it is any good. Having read Lamott's introduction, with its description of a dying father weakly raising his fist to his daughter as new pages are delivered, I can say I never want to: it could not be as good as that image, or as beautiful.

Like Natalie Goldberg, Lamott has a marked fondness for magical mystery tours ("December is traditionally a bad month for writing") but she is tougher, funnier, and more honest. Her admission of why she writes ("I am completely unemployable") may not be helpful, exactly, but it moved at least one reader to put down the book and laugh with warm recognition. Evidently, Lamott teaches quite a lot, and I was on guard for the moistly encouraging tone that I would imagine many career creative-writing teachers are, for their humanity's sake, forced to adopt. But getting published, Lamott writes, "will not open the doors that most of [her students] hope for. It will not make them well." (To indulge, briefly, in further autobiography, my first published book has just appeared in stores. The last year of my life—the year of finishing it, editing it, and seeing it through its various page-proof passes—ranks among the most unnerving of my young life. It has not felt good, or freeing. It has felt nerve-shreddingly dis-quieting. Publication simply allows one that much more to worry about. This cannot be said to aspiring writers often or sternly enough. Whatever they carry within themselves they believe pub-lication cures will not, I can all but guarantee, be cured. You just wind up living with new diseases.)

One learns many things about Anne Lamott in *Bird by Bird*. Quite likely, one learns far too much. We meet her friends Carpenter and the gay Jesuit priest Tom and Ethan Canin and a friend who died—far too young—of breast cancer. Lamott's son, Sam, keeps popping up, too, often to say something enchantedly cute, such as when he decides that night air "smells like moon." One or two instances of this would have been tolerable, but being held at paren-tal gunpoint by Lamott so many times grows irritating.

However, a good deal of what Lamott says is terrific; she rewards you for hanging in there. Much of the beauty of writing is, she writes, "the beauty of sheer effort." A whole chapter titled

"Shitty First Drafts" argues, hilariously so, for the necessity of such drafts. Another chapter, about her multiple failures to "fix" a novel that seemed obdurately resistant to fixing (meanwhile her money was running out) is not only useful and heartening but undeniably wrenching. "To be a good writer," she says, "you not only have to write a great deal but you have to care." Elsewhere she notes that writing "is about hypnotizing yourself into believing in yourself, getting some work done, then unhypnotizing yourself and going over the material coldly." In recounting a workshop that saw a good writer suddenly, viciously assault a bad writer after the class had offered the bad writer some patronizing praise, Lamott refuses any pat conclusions. Admirably refusing to criticize the good writer for her attack, she judges only that "you don't always have to chop with the sword of truth. You can point with it, too." She brilliantly and, I believe, accurately diagnoses the sort of student writer who routinely rips the spinal column from his classmates as a heathen seeking "pleasure that is almost sexual in nature." Less terrific is some of her advice:

> Write down all the stuff you swore you'd never
> tell another soul. What you can recall about your
> birthday parties? . . . Scratch around for details. . . .
> Write about the women's curlers with the bris-
> tles inside, the garters your father and uncles used
> to hold up their dress socks, your grandfathers'
> hats, your cousins' perfect Brownie uniforms.

There is such a thing as too-specific guidance, and I fear it will take some time for anyone who has read *Bird by Bird* to write about a birthday party *without* mentioning all the hair curlers and garter socks and Brownie uniforms. Lamott simply beats one to the writing. Also, for a writer of such shrewdness, Lamott allows herself to get lost among some awfully simple terrain. A longish section intended to inspire beginners who do not know what to write about sees Lamott throwing out suggestions as unpromising as school lunches and carrot sticks. Yes, an ode to the carrot stick will get one writing, but *Bird by Bird* is not, I don't think, intended for children but reasonably intelligent adults interested in writing. The whole question is beneath Lamott, and her suggestion is beneath her readers. Norman Mailer once said that, if a writer does not know how to get a character across the room, he is dead. I would append that: If a writer does not know what to write about, has no idea where even to *begin*, he was never alive to begin with.

OLYMPUS

"I do not think novelists—good novelists, that is—are altogether like other people." This insight comes fifteen lines into Norman Mailer's *The Spooky Art*, which was published on Mailer's eightieth birthday in January 2003. This sentence places us high upon the mountainside of a different sort of how-to-write book, the Olympus, which only rarely deigns to address the actual processes of solid fiction-making. Instead, it focuses on the philosophy of writing— again, how to live—enjoying frequent, rather stark expeditions into the joys and terrors of literature. Reading such books is not always easy; the mountain analogy is apt. One's pack is too heavy, the snow is thick, the guide is unforgiving, self-involved, but far too knowledgeable to ignore. One constantly feels as though one has to prove oneself worthy of his or her company.

The Olympus is always the work of a highly esteemed writer who has elected—perhaps for money, perhaps because the writer believes he or she has something interesting to say—to set aside the scepter for a short while and share with fans and hopefuls how and why he or she writes and what a beginning writer can do to improve him- or herself. With their mandarin tone and necessary overstatements, such books routinely annoy and worry beginners. Beginners are probably right to be worried and annoyed, and it is no coincidence that the typical Olympus is not usually read by aspiring writers but rather by their authors' fans and foes. The particles of their allure have altogether different electricity: the insights are less global and more personal, more spiritual and less emotional. Not surprisingly, the Olympus also tends to have a much longer shelf life than other how-to books, from E. M. Forster's *Aspects of the Novel* to Flannery O'Connor's *Mystery and Manners* to Margaret Atwood's *Negotiating with the Dead*. Joyce Carol Oates's recent (and excellent) *The Faith of a Writer* will, I suspect, outlast a good deal of her other work.

Mailer's *The Spooky Art* was greeted by notably hostile reviews. Many critics charged that it was simply one big microwaved potluck of Maileriana that contained only the stray spice of anything new. This charge was indisputably true, but some of us card-carrying Mailer fanatics are willing to read the man on topics as bleak as Madonna. (Indeed, some of us *have* read the man on Madonna.) Yes, Mailer devotees will be familiar with most of what appears in *The Spooky Art*. I will go perilously far out onto a limb, here, to say that, if only for its arrangement and augmentations, it is still very much worth perusal. Here is something:

> A man lays his character on the line when he writes a novel. Anything in him which is lazy, or meretricious, or unthought-out, complacent, fearful, overambitious, or terrified ... will be revealed in his book. ... [N]o novelist can escape his or her own character altogether. That is, perhaps, the worst news any young writer can hear.

This is a reversal of the mysticism one encounters in a book such as *Writing Down the Bones*, which promises that unlocking the inner writer will release only lemon-scented elation. Mailer suggests that the inner life of a writer is a vast, terrible ocean of doubt and despair. The former view will make for happier workshops and pleasanter emotional weather, certainly, but it is not likely to encourage a writer to "settle for nothing less than making a revolution in the consciousness of our time," as Mailer summarized his own goals in 1958. ("And I certainly failed," Mailer adds now, "didn't I?") There is much in *The Spooky Art* that few writers would be willing to say. "You can write a very bad book," Mailer tells us (and as anyone who has read *Marilyn* or *Ancient Evenings* or *Of Women and Their Elegance* or *An American Dream* can tell you, he would know), "but if the style is first-rate, then you've got something that will live—not forever, but for a decent time. . . . Style is half of a novel." Of writing in the first person, Mailer says, with his characteristic mixture of wisdom and buffoonery, "It is not easy to write in the first person about a man who's stronger or braver than yourself. It's too close to self-serving. All the same, you have to be able to do it." As for novel writing (I will hopefully assume he really means writing, as Mailer's chief accomplishment lies in nonfiction, which is no small thing, whatever he may believe or wish to believe), "It may be that [writing] is not an experience. It may be more like a continuing relationship between a man and his wife. You can't necessarily speak of that as an experience, since it may consist of several experiences braided together; or of many experiences braided together; or indeed it may consist of two kinds of experiences that are antagonistic to one another." If this sounds confused, one suspects it is supposed to, and it is inversely stirring to see a writer of Mailer's stature recklessly unable to come to terms with what, exactly, writing *is*.

In his bravely titled *How to Write: Advice and Reflections*, Richard

Rhodes takes an opposite tack than that of his Olympian colleagues: "If you want to write, you can. Fear stops most people
from writing, not lack of talent, whatever that is. . . . You're a human
being, with a unique story to tell. . . . We need stories to live, all of
us." Rhodes, the Pulitzer Prize–winning author of, among other
books, *The Making of the Atomic Bomb* (a great work of nonfiction
everyone should read) and *Making Love* (a queasy memoir of all
the sex Rhodes has had that I do not advise reading), has written a
decent, old-fashioned Olympus that honors writing and the writer
equally. That does not mean he will brook any of the self-delaying
measures to which writers routinely subject themselves:

> If you're afraid of what other people will think
> of your efforts, don't show them until you write
> your way beyond fear. If writing a book is
> impossible, write a chapter. If writing a chapter
> is impossible, write a page. If writing a page is
> impossible, write a paragraph. If writing a para-
> graph is impossible, write a sentence.

One is not likely to encounter any advice in a how-to book as
commendably intolerant of writerly self-delusion as that. One
will find in Rhodes, though, goodly helpings of advice that sound
awfully close to the advice of Natalie Goldberg and Anne Lamott
and any number of other Tea & Angels writers. To the stalled writer,
Rhodes offers this encouragement: "Everyone knows how to do
something: describe a process. How do you tie your shoe? How do
you brush your teeth? How do you plant a bulb, drive a car, read a
map?" Perhaps this K–8 tone can be traced to Rhodes's early career
as a Hallmark Card writer (about which he is unapologetic; he
considers all types of writing, no matter how cheap, another tool
in the writer's box), but I do not believe it should be. Rather, many

of these books sound so alike—from the atom-splitting concentration they bring to bear upon the minutiae of their authors' lives to their nakedly desperate implorations simply to write *anything*—because the questions the beginning writer needs answered are so depressingly similar: How do you start? What do you write about? How do you know if you are any good? Often you feel that these accomplished and famous writers are merely talking to themselves, since, in many ways, they still *are* that tremblingly starting-out scribbler. The how-to-write genre begins to feel less like an effort to instruct and more like a rear-guard action to reinforce the garrisons of their authors' own slaughtered confidence. Just about all how-to-write books have at least a little worth, and some, like Rhodes's, have great worth. For instance, Rhodes's discussion of the cardinal importance of "voice" in writing ("'Natural' is a hopeless word; it has always meant and continues to mean whatever the speaker wants to exclude from discussion") is as good as anything one can hope to find on the topic. But what begins to rise up from these pages is the iodine and lotions of self-healing. You start to wonder if you are responding not to the how-to writer who is least crazy, but the how-to writer who is crazy in the same way you are crazy. You want to be healed, too.

On its face, Stephen King's *On Writing: A Memoir of the Craft* is *primarily* about self-healing—written, as it was, in the wake of the nearly fatal accident King suffered while walking along a country road in the summer of 1999. (The man who ran King down, one Bryan Smith, was later found, in a very King-like twist, dead of undetermined causes in his trailer home.) Most of the how-to books I have elected to discuss in this essay are due to my familiarity with their authors' less subsidiary work. In King's case, I confess to having read everything from *Carrie* to *The Tommyknockers*. (The latter's demonically murderous flying soda machine made me realize, with what I can only call the shock of unwanted maturity, that perhaps I had outgrown this sort of thing. It comes as no surprise in *On Writing* when we learn that King wrote *The Tommyknockers* with "cotton swabs stuck up my nose to stem the coke-induced bleeding.") In other words, I have read, by quick estimate, about 15,000 pages worth of Stephen King's prose—and I do not regret one folio of it. Whether because of his success ("I've made a great deal of dough from my fiction"), his profligacy ("there's one novel, *Cujo*, that I barely remember writing at all"), or the simple likability of his voice ("Creative people probably *do* run a greater risk of alcoholism and addiction than those in some other jobs, but so what? We all look pretty much the same when we're puking in the gutter"), there are not many living writers whose views on writing will be as enthusiastically received by hacks, would-be hacks, artists, would-be artists, and civilians alike. On King's Olympus, God walks alongside man.

"This is a short book," King explains in the second of his three forewords, "because most books about writing are filled with bullshit." This is fairly representative of *On Writing*'s tone, though its anti-intellectualism is more akin to that of Abbie Hoffman than Rush Limbaugh. The approach results in some passages of wonderful bullshitlessness. For example, King's strident belief that a work of prose is about brutally controlled paragraphs rather than artful, free-flowing sentences ("If your master's thesis is no more organized than a high school essay titled 'Why Shania Twain Turns Me On,' you're in big trouble") seems that delightful thing: an insight that is both unexpected and true. His insistence that carefully placed fragments in a scene of action (King's example: "Big Tony sat down, lit a cigarette, ran a hand through his hair") nail down the writing, giving it a kind of vivid breather, is advice good enough to pay for. But King's dirt-plain line of attack also results in some massively wrong-headed counsel. "Remember," he writes, "that the basic rule of vocabulary is *use the first word*

that comes to your mind, if it is appropriate and colorful. If you hesi-
tate and cogitate, you will come up with another word . . . but it
probably won't be as good as your first one, or as close to what
you really mean." It seems to me that only willfully obtuse people
don't realize that the mind very rarely says what it means to say
in the heat of any given moment, writing included. One's first
word or thought is usually imprecise, muddy, and wrong. Writing
is seeing, but revision is reflecting on what one has seen. And the
first word that comes to one's mind when one is writing about
anything even remotely technical is all but *guaranteed* to be the
wrong word. The same goes for characters whose professions or
interests are unfamiliar to us: one *has* to go back and vivify those
"dogs" and "trees" and "wiry-type things" that, in every first draft,
exist lifelessly on the page. The many nuances of King's advice
will be teased out by more advanced beginners, but to the less
skilled one fears it will seem that King is giving prose permission to go AWOL from the interesting. "No one can be as intellectually slothful as a really smart person," King writes. No one,
perhaps, but an incredibly defensive dumb person. King is the
farthest imaginable thing from dumb, and it is unappetizing to
watch him pretend that he is.

But we quickly come back to the good King, St. Stephen:

> I am approaching the heart of this book with two
> theses, both simple. The first is that good writing
> consists of mastering the fundamentals . . . and
> then filling the third level of your toolbox with
> the right instruments. The second is that while
> it is impossible to make a competent writer out
> of a bad writer, and while it is equally impos-
> sible to make a great writer out of a good one,
> it *is* possible, with lots of hard work, dedication,

and timely help, to make a good writer out of a
merely competent one.

"Life," King writes elsewhere, "isn't a support-system for art.
It's the other way around." Of course, the world is filled with
those who will sniff at the notion of making good writers out
of competent writers, who will despair at the prospect of these
empowered good writers writing their good novels and stories
and filling the world with competent, interesting writing. That is,
in part, what I believe angers so many writers about the how-to-
write genre—and I would be fibbing greatly if I did not admit
to regarding it with a certain amount of skepticism myself. Every
writer's road is hard, and lonely, and forever covered by night, and
even the best how-to books splash the path with artificial spot-
light and claim it is the sun.

Nevertheless, one wonders. Just when was it that "competent" became such a terrible fate? Like "cute," it is a word that
has somehow culturally capsized and spilled its initial, positive
meaning. And since when have merely good writers been deserving of barbed wire and gruel? I, for one, am glad of the world's
good novels. I am reading a good novel right now. I hope to
write a good novel someday. (I have already written several bad
ones. That does not really seem such terrible providence either, in
the end.) Writers who fail are not pathetic; they are people who
have attempted to do something incredibly difficult and found
they cannot. Human longing exists in every person, along every
frequency of accomplishment. It is the delusions endemic to bad
writers and bad writing that need to be destroyed. Here are a
few: *Writing well will get you girls, or boys, or both. Writing well will
make you happy. Fame and wealth are good writing's expected rewards.
Writing for a living is somehow nobler than what most people do.* What
needs to be reinforced is the idea that good writing—solid, hon-

est, entertaining, beautiful good writing—is simultaneously the reward, the challenge, and the goal. Some of us will be great but, as King says, that will be an accident, and its determination is beyond our power, no matter how many books we read or write. Perhaps especially if those books are about writing.

A BEAGLE'S LAMENT

There is a final book about writing that I need to talk about. God help us, it is published by Writer's Digest Books, so allow me to encourage anyone interested to steal it forthwith, preferably from the warehouses of Writer's Digest Books. It is called *Snoopy's Guide to the Writing Life*, and forms a handsome collection of *Peanuts* Snoopycentrism. Snoopy, of course, is a long-suffering writer, and some of Charles Schultz's funniest strips have been devoted to his worthy beagle's literary frustrations; they are gathered here, in their glorious entirety. My second favorite strip gives us Snoopy in full profile, bent over his typewriter, diligently typing. "Gentlemen," he writes. "Enclosed is the manuscript of my new novel. I know you are going to like it." And in the final panel: "In the meantime, please send me some money so I can live it up." In my favorite strip, Snoopy gives Lucy van Pelt a draft titled "A Sad Story." "This isn't a sad story," Lucy complains. "This is a dumb story!" Snoopy takes back the draft and holds it close to his protuberant face. He thinks, "That's what makes it so sad."

That *is* what makes it so sad. That is also why we laugh. But it is a good laughter, a pure laughter, and not at all at Snoopy's expense. It is the laughter of necessity, laughter rich with the hope that, eventually, all of our stories will be happier.

—2004

NO DYING LIGHT

An Introduction to John Gardner's *October Light*

No major American writer wrote more frequently about dragons. Or seers. Or oracles. Even when John Gardner's fiction lacks literal dragons, seers, and oracles, there are always figurative versions of them skulking about. Gardner's imagination was a curiously premodern thing, as cryptozoological as a Yeti, as scaly as a sea serpent. He claimed the same amount of inspiration from Walt Disney as he did from Homer and Chaucer. Gardner's interviews—he granted 170 of them over an implausible ten-year period, which means he was interviewed once every 21.4 days—find this strange Merlin of a man conversing knowledgeably about Richmond Lattimore's translation of *The Iliad*, worrying over the finer points of the various librettos he wrote ("I'm really into opera now"), arguing for the centrality of Edgar Allan Poe in American literary history, attacking Bellow and Updike and Heller and Mailer and Barth and Gass and Elkin, praising Bellow and Updike and Heller and Mailer and Barth and

Gass and Elkin, admitting to his invention of words ("thestral," "hybreeding"), and, most notoriously, championing (and then recanting, and then championing again) his view of "moral fiction." Most writers unpack the better luggage of their lives inside their books. When one reads a biography of, say, Graham Greene or Dorothy Parker, one nods at the correspondences and rubs one's chin at the disconnects. With Gardner, though, one mostly wonders how he had time to write any of the books in the first place.

Before he became John Gardner, American Writer, he was John Gardner, Respected Medievalist, and as such was the author of two volumes of Cliff's Notes. He was an avid motorcyclist. He played the banjo and the French horn. He directed local theater and loved Stephen King. Through the years he taught Charles Johnson, Raymond Carver, and Ron Hansen. He was a talented womanizer—with a particular fondness for his students—despite looking like (in various summations) "a troll," "a rumpled gnome," and "a pregnant woman trying to pass for a Hell's Angel." Somehow (hubris? gin? Excalibur?) he managed to publish more than thirty books—five in 1977 alone—before his death, in 1982, at the age of forty-nine. The clear literary antecedent to the gunned-down yet ongoingly prolific hip-hop artist Tupac Shakur, Gardner was still publishing books years after he had died. He had sought nothing less than to change literary history, "to stand with Tolstoy, Melville, and all the boys," as Gardner himself once put it. At one point in his career he was a best-selling writer— "as famous as a novelist can be in America," in the words of his biographer, Barry Silesky—and Dan Rather announced his death on the *CBS Evening News*. In 1989, Vintage reissued a raft of Gardner's books. Within a few years, all but two, *The Art of Fiction* and *Grendel*, were lost at sea and declared out of print. The whirlwind that followed the man in life had, it seemed, finally spun itself into quietude, the grasses his fury had once bent all firmly sprung back into place.

Then, stirrings. The Stewart O'Nan–edited *On Writers and Writing*, an omnibus collection of Gardner's uncollected critical essays, appeared in 1994. As an assistant editor at W. W. Norton in 1998, I was able to buy the rights for the inexplicably out-of-print *On Becoming a Novelist*, which was reissued, and immediately sprinted through several printings, in 1999. Simultaneously, Basic Books reissued his both justly maligned and deeply underrated *On Moral Fiction*. In 2000, Susan Thornton, who attended Gardner's funeral on the day she was to have married him, published her strange, lovely, and spectral memoir, *On Broken Glass: Loving and Losing John Gardner*. In 2004, Barry Silesky finally brought out his long-awaited—and paceless, and insight-starved—Gardner biography. And now, twenty-three years after he died of internal injuries following a freak motorcycle accident in Pennsylvania, we have handsome new editions of John Gardner's major books, including the work at hand, *October Light*, the winner of the 1976 National Book Critics Circle Award and thought by a noisy minority of Gardner apostles to be his best.

I am afraid I disagree with that summation. *Grendel* is, and has to be, John Gardner's best work of fiction. It is the most sustained novel he wrote, the most freakishly unanticipated, and the work he had the most difficult time explaining. Although Gardner was always quick to blurt out dissertations on his own fiction, *Grendel* seemed to mystify even its creator. Gardner claimed to believe his late, fascinating, and fatally discursive novel *Mickelsson's Ghosts* was his best ("I think the fact is, it's a great novel"), but shortly after writing *October Light* he told an interviewer, "I do believe I am writing the best fiction that's being produced in America today." Gardner's critical judgments, however, at least those encountered beyond the sensible perimeters of *The Art of Fiction* and *On*

Becoming a Novelist, were rarely very reliable. He was right about much, but clearly and extravagantly wrong about Nabokov and Bellow (but then Nabokov was wrong about Bellow; Nabokov judged him a "miserable mediocrity"), wrong about Updike and Pynchon, wrong about the future of the novel. That he admitted as much later on ("Yeah, I grew up and began to understand Bellow. . . . Yeah, I'm comin' around to Updike. . . .") suggests his decency as a man as much as it does his occasional carelessness as a theoretician.

Nonetheless, *October Light* is very, very good—perhaps even great. Aside from *Grendel* it is easily Gardner's most singular novel. It is also his most densely realistic book. Since this is a John Gardner novel, that is not very realistic at all. It is finally not as haunted by obvious precursors as many of his other novels— with their galleries of monsters and philosophers—and was, one senses, his most happily written. (Every novel prior to *October Light* had been largely drafted by a man encountering difficulty getting published. *October Light* was written by a man first shaking hands with prominence. It shows.) *October Light* is also, somehow, Gardner's most American book. The novel's crafty colonial-era epigraphs suggest something of this. Gardner's politics, as best as anyone has been able to explain them, could be described as those of a Jimmy Carter Republican, and he believed that the United States, fresh from its tragic involvement in Indochina, was on the verge of cultural and artistic rebirth. In his shamelessly though qualifiedly patriotic essay "Amber (Get) Waves (Your) of (Plastic) Grain (Uncle Sam)," written during the composition of *October Light*, Gardner submits that "if the majority causes too much pain to the minority, the minority will scream (with the help of a free press and the right of assembly) until the majority is badgered or shamed into changing its mind." This is exactly the dynamic that plays out in *October Light*, when James Page, a majority man of dogged and inflexible rectitude, shotguns the television of his dis-satisfiedly minority sister, Sally, chases her up the stairs, and locks her in her bedroom.

Over-discussing a novel's plot in its introduction is akin to divining a fortune before breaking open the cookie that con-tains it. Those who have read this novel know that *October Light* is a strange, magical, and finally frustrating book. But it is only frustrating in the way that Gardner himself was frustrating. The surplus of ideas and charisma prove exhausting, just as one is exhausted by intense conversation or fervid exercise. Those who have not yet read *October Light* may find its opening stiff, some of its prose too caloric, and some of its characterization overly grotesque (Gardner had an acknowledged weakness for what he called "cartoon realism"). But not everything in a book that aims to be as humanly all-encompassing as *October Light* can be the best part, and the occasional inexactness of its art is quickly and decisively overthrown by its empathy and endlessly regathered energies.

On its face, *October Light* seems to be Gardner's least autobio-graphical novel. One finds here only the faintest imprint of the accidental death of his brother Gilbert, for instance, for which Gardner blamed himself, and which quasars throughout much of his work. But *October Light* can be seen in many ways to have eerie concordance to Gardner's life, if sometimes only prophetically. The novel-within-the-novel that Sally reads, the "black-comic blockbuster" *Smugglers of Lost Souls' Rock*, evidently grew out of the farm-boy despair Gardner felt while living in San Francisco, a city his wife Joan loved and never forgave him for forcing her to abandon; it is also the city in which *Smugglers* begins. (Joan, in fact, helped him write *Smugglers*, though it was begun on Joan's postprandial dare that Gardner write something that would make money.) James Page, like Gardner himself, is a man so convinced of his rightness that he hurts and torments those he loves. In 1978's *On Moral Fiction*, the book that hamstrung his career, Gardner chased half of literary America into the bedroom and tried to lock the door behind it. He ultimately relented, as James Page ultimately relents. As Gardner himself explained, "The overall effect of art is to say, one should have the noble ideals James Page has, one should do an hour's work for an hour's pay and so on, but one should also be aware that by being stern and rigid in pursuit of one's ideals, one can kill everybody around."

There is little point in revisiting the controversies of *On Moral Fiction*, but it seems certain that among the harmonies of complication that damaged Gardner's reputation and led, until now, to his wider disappearance from print, *On Moral Fiction* must be considered the most cardinal. His work is also, of course, inconsistent. In Gardner's artistic display case there are many diamonds (*Grendel, October Light, On Becoming a Novelist*, the short story "Redemption," *The Art of Fiction, Nickel Mountain*) but just as many cubic zirconias. His now well-documented hypocrisies have surely not helped his critical reputation. The champion of moral fiction had been known to hit his first wife, was an alcoholic, and occasionally dabbled in what a few regarded as plagiarism but which he himself impishly termed "borrowing." But within the general hypocrisies of a mortal life, of which we are all guilty, there are, many critics have charged, the deeper hypocrisies of his art. This aesthetically conservative artist who wrote movingly of the need to create "a vivid and continuous dream" in fiction habitually broke his own rules. (Nowhere does Gardner violate this diktat with more brilliant and calculated relish than in *October Light*.) "Believe it or not," Gardner once told an interviewer, "when I was writing *On Moral Fiction* I didn't consider whether or not my theory about what fiction ought to do applied to my own fiction." We believe it. In the end, there is much to be contemplated in such judgments of Gardner but little ultimate value in doing so. A novelist is more than her personal failures, hobbyhorses, and bugbears, as Gardner himself understood. When a young woman told him at a reading that she liked his work but did not like him, Gardner responded, "That's all right. I'm a much better person when I write." It would be pleasant to know that Gardner was not a tormented and complicated man, but he was. Understanding this may change how one reads his books, but it does not change the books themselves.

There is, finally, the vexing matter of Gardner's literary generation. The cutting-edge writers he believed he stood beside in friendship or opposition (or both)—William Gass, William Gaddis, John Fowles, Stanley Elkin, and John Barth—have not disappeared, certainly, but they have not endured in the Rushmorian way that Gardner was clearly expecting. "The only law I'm sure of," Gardner once said, "is the survival of the fittest." Gardner has certainly survived, but one wonders how many new visitors to *October Light* will be writers as opposed to readers. Most of those who today remember Gardner are writers, as he is sometimes said to have been the greatest teacher of writing who ever lived. Upon today's readers and critics, however, he throws down a far more diffuse shade. Yet during his life Gardner managed a rare artistic trifecta—simultaneously a campus favorite, a critical Helen of Troy, and a novelist of Dickensian popularity. Those who come to Gardner today usually enter through the portal of his books about writing. Has Gardner thus been doomed to the echo chamber of having an exclusively writerly audience? If so, this is a better fate than most writers enjoy, but it is also far from the fate he always imagined for himself.

It is the height of indecorousness to discuss oneself while introducing the work of another writer, but it was through *On Becoming a Novelist* that I discovered John Gardner, at nineteen, and why I read everything I could by him, and why I continue to hunt for him in indexes, and argue on his behalf, and think about him constantly, and have a hand-drawn portrait of his childhood home above my computer, even though I no longer regard him with the hero worship I once did. His opinions are no longer my own. I am much less sure about the *why* of literature than, under Gardner's spell, I used to be, but I am grateful to him, more than I can say.

I visited his grave in Batavia, New York, once, while driving across the country, and discovered not the artist or the critic or the beloved teacher but a man known to his family and friends as "Bud." When my (very patient) girlfriend and I asked for directions to the cemetery, people began discussing Bud as though, just last week, he had waved at them while mowing his lawn. Gardner is buried next to his brother, and nearby are his parents. Standing there amid the maple trees and sugary white headstones I felt pierced by an immediate and deeply cheated sadness. It was so unfair the way he died, so unfair we would never read the books he wanted to write. Shortly before the accident, he publicly claimed to have lost interest in fiction: "I'm sort of interested in politics now. I think that's what all of us writers should be interested in now." What might have resulted from this bizarre, imploded catharsis? We will never know. Of course, the great writer who never wrote the book he was capable of is not a new phenomenon. James Joyce is arguably one example; Norman Mailer is another. But Gardner is a different sort of beast than Joyce (who believed he succeeded) or Mailer (who seems to believe he has failed). Gardner simply did not know whether he succeeded or failed, and because of this his shadow is, for me, forever outlined in sorrow.

The first time I read *October Light* it changed my life, and few novels have ever meant as much to me. I reread it with delight and some pain, for Gardner, I think, despite his reputed conservatism, is a young person's writer, and while I cannot yet claim to be old I can say that a large part of Gardner's magic, his gravitational pull, depends on the certainty that, once you have begun to read him, you need to read all of him. I have now, largely, done so; my duty to him feels complete. For those who have yet to read Gardner, and especially *October Light*, I have envy and some pity. One day, you will be finished reading him, and the vectors of Gardner's life will seem doubly, triply unfair. Nor will your own feel quite the same. Whether the world's "arches and light," a favorite Gardnerism, will seem brighter or darker to you I dare not guess. But that seems like something. It seems enough. It seems like everything.

—2005

RULES OF ENGAGEMENT
The Iraq War and Documentary Film

I n the middle of Peter Davis's Vietnam War documentary *Hearts and Minds*, a large, pale, scarily eyebrowless face suddenly annexes the screen. It's the face of Colonel George S. Patton III as he describes his attendance at a memorial service in Vietnam for some fallen American soldiers. When he gazed upon the faces of the memorial's attendees, Patton says, "I was just proud. My feeling for America just soared. . . . They looked determined and reverent at the same time. But still"—and here Colonel Patton's abrupt, savage smile reveals a mouth packed with draft-horse-sized choppers—"they're a bloody good bunch of *killers*."

It is a moment you have to see to fully appreciate, which is to say it is a moment you have to see to believe. And it is the sort of completely defenseless moment you often see only in documentary films. No Hollywood dramatization could do justice to Patton's cheerful viciousness, and a print journalist would doubtless hoard Patton's words for some skeweringly perfect ending.

But Davis allows Colonel Patton and reverent killers to float through his film like stray pieces of the dreadful shipwreck that was American aspiration in Vietnam.

Hearts and Minds hit theaters in 1974. Columbia Pictures, *Hearts and Minds*'s original distributor, refused to release the film, and Walter Rostow, who had been national security adviser under President Johnson, sued to block its premiere. Warner Bros. eventually brought the picture out, and it won an Academy Award for best documentary—after which it was denounced by Frank Sinatra, the ceremony's next presenter.

Davis made his documentary with three questions in mind: Why did we go to Vietnam? What did we do there? What did the doing in turn do to us? "I didn't expect the film to answer these questions," Davis admits on the commentary of the recent Criterion Collection DVD edition of the film. "I expected it to address those questions." Explanatory impotence is not unique to the documentary but in some ways is abetted by the form. Inimitably vivid yet brutally compressed, documentaries often treasure image over information, proffer complications instead of conclusions, and touch on rather than explore. When a documentary film such as *Capturing the Friedmans* or *The Burden of Dreams* charts the mysteries of human behavior, an inconclusive effect can be electrifying. When a documentary film takes on the considerable subject of war, inconclusiveness can frustrate, though one's frustration is not necessarily with the film or its maker. Even *Hearts and Minds* acknowledges, in its closing scene, its limitations: "You were over there too," one man angrily says to the filmmakers at a stateside parade, "with your damn cameras."

The damn cameras have now been to Iraq and back. Few of the Iraq War documentaries offer such self-awareness, though, and most neglect to address the war as a result of choices that might have been made differently. The most ambitious and in some ways the finest documentary about Iraq is probably Stephen Marshall's *Battleground*. In showing us insurgents discussing their hatred of Americans while Humvees pass by, an Iraqi translator deludedly explaining that the invasion was due to the collapse of the American economy, a former anti-Saddam guerrilla reuniting with his mother after thirteen years of exile, and a U.S. soldier marveling at the fact that Iraqis wear blue jeans ("They could be anywhere in the United States"), *Battleground* provides a movingly human and admirably ambivalent portrait of the war. It is, however, more the exception than the rule. In the grunts'-eye-view offered by *Occupation: Dreamland* and *Gunner Palace*, the Iraq War functions as a savage reversal of American expectation. In *Control Room,* about Al Jazeera, which largely limits itself to Al Jazeera's coverage of the conflict, the war is a rough beast sprinting toward Bethlehem. In *The Dreams of Sparrows*, a film made by Iraqis, the war is a fiery doorway into a hitherto unknown reality. But in all of these films the war just is. Matthew Arnold famously said that journalism was "literature in a hurry." The analytic content of these Iraq documentaries sometimes feels like journalism in a hurry. These are partial maps drawn while still within the maze of war.

Traditionally, the wartime documentary dealt with the justness of the cause, like Frank Capra's Why We Fight series, made from 1942 to 1944. Such films, however artful or historically significant, are basically propaganda. The rise of the more questioning war documentary is a relatively recent development. Film provides audiences with a uniquely reactive vulnerability; a vivid description of a shrapnel wound can certainly be affecting, but a two-story-tall image of the same can move you to slam shut your tyrannized eyes. Thus it is not surprising that so many modern war documentaries look upon their subject with considerable jaundice. A time-tested way to turn against a war is to go have a look at it for oneself. "People want their steak," one soldier says in *Occupation: Dreamland*, "but they don't want to know how the cow got butchered."

Any honest documentary film about war must address the question of human suffering, given that human suffering is war's distillation. But whose suffering? In January 2004, we learn in Garret Scott and Ian Olds's *Occupation: Dreamland*, the U.S. Army's 82nd Airborne was living on the edge of Falluja in an abandoned Baathist resort officially called Forward Operating Base Volturno but popularly known as Dreamland. The 82nd's modest mission: "Maintain order and suppress resistance." The bloody Marine-led siege of Falluja in April 2004 would occur after the 82nd had been rotated out of Iraq. The film thus becomes a spooky exercise in prescience as well as an unlikely elegy, for the Falluja of *Occupation: Dreamland*, having been reduced to a Stalingradian ruin during its assorted American assaults, no longer exists.

The primary focus of *Occupation: Dreamland* is a handful of infantry troopers who occupy a single crowded room papered with *Maxim* pin-ups and scattered with spittoons. In their modest billeting these young men flex and pose in their mirrors, watch *Total Recall*, don their flak vests and goggles while listening to Slayer, mockingly read aloud from letters of stateside support, and heatedly argue politics until their staff sergeant reminds them of the camera. These soldiers' political diversity may—but should not—surprise many viewers. Last summer I spent a month in Iraq embedded with the Marines and found men and women of widely divergent opinions about the war. Some were thoughtful, others clerics of ignorance. Some believed the United States fought for liberty, others for oil. The soldiers in *Occupation: Dreamland* are equally afflicted and afflicting, and one quietly grieves for those soldiers given to more searching turns of mind: "I want some answers," Private Thomas Turner (an avowed Democrat) says early in the film. "I want some clarification of what we're doing. . . . I guess someone smarter than me knows what's going on."

A good deal of the film serves up what are by now many visual commonplaces of the Iraq War, in particular the chaotic nocturne of American soldiers on insurgent sweeps, bashing down Iraqis' doors and screaming at people who do not speak English. The familiarity of these scenes makes them no less disquieting. "That might not look all that great," an officer admits, "but it's a necessary evil that's inherent in war. People are going to be inconvenienced and pissed off. If their husbands weren't trying to kill us, we wouldn't be there."

Soon enough the mood turns ominous. One suspected insurgent explains to an American through a platoon interpreter: "I'm not opposed. Do you understand me? I'm not opposed." "Fuck this guy," the soldier responds. "Zip him up." The Iraqi is next shown being hooded and cuffed and pushed into the back of a truck while nearby some young Iraqis watch mutely. Later, while an outraged Iraqi buttonholes the camera about the "indecent" actions of Americans taking Iraqi women from local homes, a nearby soldier explains where he is from to two supremely unmoved Iraqis. "What is 'California'?" one Iraqi asks the other in Arabic. The soldiers themselves realize these pathetic public-relations attempts are scarcely worth the oxygen, yet one of the film's most heartbreaking scenes—filmed in night-vision-goggle green—shows an American soldier stopping to make small talk with an Iraqi man near Dreamland's perimeter. An effortful, translation-error-ridden conversation ensues, and one senses that this soldier is so urgently attempting to communicate because he feels his very humanity is at stake. Many of the soldiers, to their credit, acknowledge the legitimacy of Iraqi anger and fear. As one says, "If this was home in Chicago, and there were some Iraqi soldiers shovin' up on my door, I'd be running up there with a couple guns myself." Sergeant John Blyler, one of his platoon's most outspoken Republicans, says, "When I first got here, I wanted to help these people. But now after my old squad leader got killed . . . I just don't really care about these people." A few scenes later, Sergeant Blyler is wounded in an IED blast, which quickly serves to underscore the mindless retributive logic of war. One of the soldiers present at the blast later regrets not gunning down an Iraqi who, understandably, began to run away: "I should have fucking killed him. I hate these people." None of these moments—and there are several—are played for "gotcha" effect. Although their film occasionally feels like an elongated *20/20* segment whose profanity has been left intact, Garret and Olds are sensitive without being credulous and unimpressed without seeming cynical.

The overall atmosphere in *Occupation: Dreamland* is churchy, Skoal-drooling, almost exaggeratedly heterosexual, and not quite Southern so much as southern Indianan. In *Gunner Palace*, the overall atmosphere is pass-the-mike ebullience. Several soldiers freestyle some not-too-swift rhymes ("We live from Baghdad / Man, it's so sad") and another plays the "Star-Spangled Banner" on his electric guitar before a molten Baghdad sunset. Narrated by its whiskey-voiced director, Mike Tucker, *Gunner Palace* takes a markedly different view of the war from *Occupation: Dreamland*. In *Gunner Palace* the war is presented as deadly but vaguely ennobling. Gunner Palace itself, a ruined and colonnaded home that once belonged to Uday Hussein, is described by its commanding officer as an "adult's paradise." Tucker never really steps back to examine the wisdom of American soldiers locating themselves in the opulent mansion of a murderous regime they came to depose; instead he employs his most pointed ironies by overlaying Donald Rumsfeld saying things like "Baghdad is bustling with commerce" upon scenes of a Baghdad bustling with flying lead. Which is not to say that *Gunner Palace* lacks a moral measuring tape. In the film's most moving interview, a young Army intelligence analyst, clearly frustrated by the war, says, "I don't think, anywhere in history, somebody has killed somebody else and something better has come out of it."

Many of the subjects in *Gunner Palace* talk about how no one can understand what they are going through, how to their friends back home Baghdad is one big action film. "For y'all it's just a show," Specialist Richmond Shaw, the "palace poet," tells the camera. "But we live in this movie." Tucker's narration also addresses this existential quandary: "Unlike a movie, war has no end." But by the end of the film one is fairly sure that viewing the Iraq War as a movie is less our problem than that of these soldiers. Enriched by its metal-and-hip-hop soundtrack and littered with dramatic comeuppances, *Gunner Palace* feels just like a movie, and moreover appears to know it: one of its wittier touches updates the famous "Ride of the Valkyries" scene from *Apocalypse Now*. What is strangest about *Gunner Palace* is its appeal both to the ardently pro-war and militantly antiwar. No doubt this is due to its obvious affection for its subjects alongside its unblinking portrayal of what they are forced to do.

There are only a few species of American soldier to be found in *Control Room*: shouting brutes, grinning rationalizers, and incompetent morons. The brutes all come to us through third-party footage, the rationalizers through intimate interview, the morons from behind press-briefing podiums. Directed by Jehane Noujam, *Control Room* is a sleek inquiry into the nature of media in a time of war, and what Noujam discovers amounts to a murky casserole of McLuhanesque ingredients. Unlike the makers of *Occupation: Dreamland* and *Gunner Palace*, the makers of *Control Room* were never in actual physical danger, which probably explains its icier gaze. But in telling the story of the Iraq War through the prism of Al Jazeera Satellite Channel (with 40 million Arab viewers, the largest and most influential media force in the region) and CENTCOM (specifically the American military's wartime information clearing house, located in Doha, Qatar), *Control Room* achieves a tone as apocalyptic as that of *Gunner Palace* and *Occupation: Dreamland*, but in a far quieter key. It is an assassin to their blundering grunts.

Donald Rumsfeld groused that Al Jazeera "has a pattern of playing propaganda over and over and over again. What they do is when there's a bomb that goes down, they grab some children and some women and pretend that the bomb hit the women and the children." At one point in *Control Room* the winningly bitter Al Jazeera producer Samir Khader, who appears to have had a cigarette surgically attached to his finger, points to a television screen which holds the image of a wounded Iraqi child. "Rumsfeld called this incitement," he says. "I call it true journalism."

In most of the Iraq War films this is as close as we get to the victims of American violence and insurgent terror. The war Peter Davis filmed in *Hearts and Minds* is not the sort of war American filmmakers in Iraq are privy to—at least, not without risking their heads. Davis could, and did, talk to average Vietnamese who had been bombed and maimed. Such victims are virtually absent in *Occupation: Dreamland* and *Gunner Palace*, and they are footage of footage in *Control Room*.

What *Control Room* seeks to illuminate (where truth devolves into propaganda, and where war and media join hands) is much less interesting than its incidental illuminations, among them the ineptitude of the U.S. military's press office, such as when an American press officer obliviously attempts to interest a roomful of hostile Arab reporters in the story of Jessica Lynch's rescue.

"We're not here to give coverage to the press," announces a U.S. Navy press officer giving coverage to the press. "We're here to liberate the people of Iraq." It all builds into a frieze of cluelessness.

Noujam's method is to wait around long enough for something to happen. Her patience is both dreadfully and movingly rewarded. An Al Jazeera reporter is killed by American forces, perhaps intentionally, and an unlikely friendship develops between Hassan Ibrahim, a portly Al Jazeera producer, and Lieutenant Josh Rushing, a handsome and sensitive Marine Corps press officer. Rushing's moral awakening provides *Control Room* with much of its arc. Routinely slaughtered by Ibrahim in conversation, Rushing struggles with his memorized talking points and the reality of what he sees, ultimately recognizing that Fox News and Al Jazeera are simply two sides of the same cathode and deciding that improving Arab-American relations is the duty of his generation. (Rushing now works for Al Jazeera.)

The Dreams of Sparrows, Iraqi director Hayda Mousa Daffar's account of life within the occupation, opens with a reenactment (the film's only obvious fictional interlude) of a mother giving birth during the U.S. invasion; she dies. "This movie," Daffar tells us, "is about what happened to that child, to the new Iraq." The new Iraq is not of much interest to Scott and Olds, Tucker, or Noujam. Nor are they much interested in the old Iraq. They are concerned with the minute-to-minute Iraq, which their cameras devour. Through the eyes of Iraqis, in *The Dreams of Sparrows*, we can finally divine what really emerges from the war's digestive tract.

Daffar notes that, before the invasion, filmmaking in Iraq was completely controlled by the Baathists, and one can sense not only his excitement but also the unfamiliarity of his excitement

("I couldn't believe I was finally making a documentary about Iraq!") at being able to drive around Baghdad photographing everything from smiling American soldiers to fly-covered dog carcasses lying roadside amid empty Pepsi cans.

If *The Dreams of Sparrows* has a fault, it is that it too consciously addresses Western viewers, and too reductively assumes the worst of those viewers. But it is when Daffar is thinking less of his presumed audience and more of his subjects that his film stuns. Perhaps most notably, *The Dreams of Sparrows* suggests an emotional complication about the war that few Americans, whatever their feelings, appear willing to entertain. Daffar's sweet, huggable, pro-America cameraman, Hayder Jaffar, carries a picture of Bush in his wallet: "I love him as much as I love my father." Khariya Mansour, a red-haired Iraqi filmmaker, tells Daffar, "The occupation is bad, and Saddam is bad." Daffar asks her about the portrait of Bush in her living room. "I like Bush," she says. "I like him so much I am in love with him. I love him because he gave us freedom."

Much of what Daffar shows us is revelatory. From Baghdad's necropolis of slums and nightmarish refugee camps we travel with Daffar to middle-class apartments, artists' hangouts, mosques and the headquarters of the Communist Party. This is a city of armed men and of stylish women nervously chain-smoking in their apartments; a city where children studying in a private school hold up crayon drawings and say, "Here the tank is aiming at the helicopter, and they exchange shells and rockets." Some Baghdad taxi drivers complain about the Americans ("God willing, [Saddam] will come back and will bring peace to the country"), while former Iraqi soldiers trained to kill Americans are interestingly divided. One calls America a "by the book" terrorist state, while another says, "Saddam's party was a terrorist regime. He was strangling us. It was an unbearable regime." Daffar does not soft-peddle on the issue of Baathist brutality. "Do you have any cases affected by the regime?" he asks a doctor at an insane asylum. "They are all affected by it" is the response. Here Daffar's moral vision is unassailable, and one realizes the truly flea-market nature of American anti-Baathism.

When asked if cinema is necessary for Iraqi society, Daffar's cameraman Hayder Jaffar says, "Cinema is very necessary. Cinema is language . . . the fastest way to reach the people." One suspects the makers of *Occupation: Dreamland*, *Gunner Palace*, and *Control Room* did not have "reaching the people" in mind while cutting together their footage, and, perhaps consequently, around the edges of their films lingers a grim irrelevance. *Control Room* in particular is so resigned to its futility it achieves a kind of depressed self-hypnosis.

In the closing minutes of *The Dreams of Sparrows*, the lovable Hayder Jaffar tells us that, because of a checkpoint misunderstanding, a friend of his and Daffar's has been killed by American soldiers, who accidentally pumped more than a hundred bullets into the friend's car. "He was," Jaffar says of his dead friend, "the first one to be happy at the fall of Saddam's regime." The film cuts to Daffar, who is smoking, raccoon-eyed, wearing a tank top, and addressing the camera directly.

"Baghdad," Daffar says, "Baghdad is hell, really is hell." He laughs bitterly. "U.S. troops and government of U.S.A. is very dirty here. In start, when Baghdad is fall, when Saddam is gone, I am very happy. Not just me. Believe me. All Iraqi people. . . . U.S. troops is very hard-hearted." This shattering film ends with Daffar shaking his head, unable to remember his English. His despair does not come off as predatory but personally and harshly earned. Very few of us live in *this* movie.

—2005

EUPHORIAS OF PERRIER

The Case Against Robert D. Kaplan

[A]n embattled democracy . . . soon becomes the victim of its own war propaganda. It then tends to attach to its own cause an absolute value which distorts its own vision on everything else. Its enemy becomes the embodiment of all evil. Its own side, on the other hand, is the center of all virtue.
—George F. Kennan, *Russia and the West Under Lenin and Stalin*

Throughout his long career Robert D. Kaplan has consistently benefited from the fact that no one has any idea what, exactly, he is. A humble travel writer? A popular historian? A panjandrum analyst of developing-world politics and personalities? The 2001 reissue of Kaplan's *Soldiers of God: With Islamic Warriors in Afghanistan and Pakistan* (1990) tried to settle the matter. The back-cover copy refers to Kaplan, pretty much definitively, as a "world affairs expert." Kaplan's prolific writing would appear to bear out such stature. The subtitles of his eleven books mention twenty countries or regions. The Mediterranean? Check. Kaplan has even lived there. Central Asia? Too late. Kaplan covered it. Southeast Asia? Nope. Annexed by Kaplan. North Africa? Kaplan. *West* Africa? Sorry. South America? What do you think?

During his often brave and occasionally astounding career of peregrination, Kaplan has earned an influential readership. Not many authors can expect blurbs from senators, former Department of Defense secretaries, the Director of Central Intelligence, or Tom Brokaw, but Kaplan can. Despite (or perhaps because of) Kaplan's polarizing worldview, he has been embraced by the administrations of both Bill Clinton and George W. Bush, and to American civilian readers he has become one of the most prominent lay voices on issues surrounding American foreign policy. Of late, however, there have been alarming indications that Kaplan has undergone some sort of imploded political transformation. His books have grown more vague but also more strident; angrier, but also more complacent. He has, in short, begun to write like a man who knows his audience, with a correspondingly fatal confidence that his words will be contemplated in high governmental and military aeries indeed.

To be sure, there has been previous unrest in Kaplanistan. In 2000, the historian Robert Kagan noted Kaplan's "cheap pessimism," his indifference "as to whether societies are governed democratically or tyrannically," and his "weak" grip on history: "Just about every historical event or political philosopher he discusses he gets at least half-wrong." In 1993, the Balkans expert Noel Malcolm gutted Kaplan's *Balkan Ghosts* for its many errors of fact and judgment; Kaplan's hapless response earned this rejoinder from Malcolm: "The basic problem, I think, is that Mr. Kaplan cannot read." Kaplan's new book, *Imperial Grunts*, in which one cannot be sure whether the latter word is a noun or a verb, has unleashed a new offensive. Writing in *The New Republic*, David Rieff takes Kaplan to task for his "boneheaded nonsense." In the *New York Times Book Review*, David Lipsky laments that Kaplan "appears to have become someone who is too fond of war." But these traits have been visible in Kaplan since his first book, as has his love of intellectual shortcuts and invincible humorlessness. Kaplan's real problem, which has become growingly evident, is not his Parkinson's grip on history or that he is a bonehead or a warmonger but rather that he is an incompetent thinker and a miserable writer.

Kaplan came to my attention while I was researching my first book, an account of my travels in the former Soviet republic of Uzbekistan, in 2001. I believed then and believe now that the travel genre has much to answer for. Travel writers are seldom scholars. They are, by inclination if not definition, transients and dilettantes. All that can save the travel writer and redeem his or her often inexpert perceptions of foreign people and places is curiosity, a willingness to be uncertain, an essential emotional generosity, and an ability to write. Even travel writers well equipped in all of the above are inevitably attacked for missing the point, getting all manner of things wrong, and generally mucking about in questions of history and scholarship to which they—at least when compared to experts or specialists—have only lightly exposed themselves. This does not mean the travel writer is incapable of insight, to say nothing of entertainment, and in some cases the travel writer's fresh-eyed unfamiliarity with a place can be made a virtue. As Lord Palmerston once said, "When I wish to be misinformed about a country, I ask the man who has lived there thirty years."

While reading up on the available English-language literature concerning Central Asia, I came across Kaplan's *The Ends of the Earth: A Journey to the Frontiers of Anarchy* (1996), which features a long section on Uzbekistan. Until Kaplan reaches the Uzbek capital, I read *The Ends of the Earth* more or less attentively. While Kaplan's prose was usually peahen drab and his use of illustrative detail unimaginative, the man was certainly intrepid. He wanders from Sierra Leone to Iran to Cambodia, all the while splattering the reader with regurgitations of various scholarly research: where the word *Turk* comes from, a pocket history of the Iranian city of Qom, the "deceptive" nature of the term *Indochina*. I did not mind Kaplan's cribs; I have done the same, as has every travel writer. Kaplan's tone, however, often troubled me. The disintegrating, anarchic world he conjures in *The Ends of the Earth* is irradiated with tribalism, fanaticism, and stupidity, but since I had no first-hand experience with the places Kaplan was writing about, I swallowed his essential points even as I grimaced at the castor-oil hectoring that accompanied them.

Then Kaplan arrives in Tashkent, Uzbekistan, a city filled with what he calls "the most hideous and alienating example of Soviet design I had seen. It cried out, *We crush the weak*." I actually find Tashkent lovely. But then there was no accounting for taste. Once ensconced in Tashkent, Kaplan regards a Russian-Uzbek marriage he encounters there as "potentially dangerous." His visit took place in 1994, only three years after the Soviet collapse. My first visit to Tashkent was in 1996, and Russian-Uzbek intermarriage, at least in Uzbekistan's cities, was common enough, though perhaps in 1994 these issues were still smoldering. He then moves on to Samarkand, the noblest and most famous city in Central Asia. The bus ride from Tashkent to Samarkand provides some spectacularly rocky and mountainous scenery, but somehow Kaplan notices only "high weeds" and an "achingly flat, monochrome landscape." Once he reaches Samarkand he remarks on the "battered automobiles, and people in unsightly polyester clothing." Battered automobiles? Most of Uzbekistan's people are poor, and this seemed needlessly petty. As for people's clothing, I have never found Uzbekistan's city-dwellers to be anything but maniacally fastidious about their appearance. (Shoe-shining is practically the Uzbek national pastime.) He gets wrong the 1994 exchange rate of the Uzbek currency by a factor of one hundred. He visits the tomb of the fourteenth-century despot Tamerlane, known as the Guri Amir, which he spells Gul Emir. He says the word *uzbek* means "independent" or "free." It doesn't. His translator, Ulug Beg, a young Uzbek, claims to be "ashamed" in Samarkand because it has so many Tajiks. "How can I like them?" Ulug Beg asks Kaplan of the Tajiks. "We must settle Uzbeks here. We must settle many, many Uzbeks in Samarkand." Problem: Samarkand, though a Tajik-majority city, *has* many, many Uzbeks. He writes that Samarkand is a "would-be Bangkok," with its "army of whores." I asked a friend who lived in Samarkand for years if that description at all rang true to him. My friend was still laughing when I hung up the phone. When Ulug Beg slurps as he eats Kaplan calls him "crude" and wonders if Ulug Beg's manners might be explained this way: "Could these be *pre-Byzantine* Turks? Could this be what Turks might have been somewhat like before the great Seljuk and Osmanli migrations to Anatolia?" The Seljuks migrated to Anatolia around nine hundred years ago. That Kaplan does not understand how offensive such eugenic explanations are for one young man's eating habits is appalling. That he does not recognize *the basic implausibility* of such an explanation is beyond reason. This is to say nothing of the fact that, in Uzbek culture, slurping one's soup is considered neither crude nor uncouth.

Kaplan's big thesis in *The Ends of the Earth* is that "ethno-cultural tensions" are leading to a world in which "national borders will mean less, while political power falls increasingly into the hands of less educated, less sophisticated groups," in whose dim minds "the real borders are the most tangible and intractable ones: those of culture and tribe." Like every nation, Uzbekistan has its "ethno-cultural tensions." But a race riot here or there, especially in a nation faced with Uzbekistan's crushing Soviet legacy, is hardly indicative of a globe trending toward disaster. Kaplan claims to give us the gristly stuff of what he calls "tragic realism," to show us how the world works, and how it will likely fracture. Was it thus a coincidence or something far uglier that the

Uzbekistan Kaplan describes is unrecognizable to me but happens to align perfectly with his grand thesis?

How to deal with this fractious world is Kaplan's great question. Some years ago, he has written, after a conference where "intellectuals held forth about the moral responsibility of the United States in the Balkans," he took a cab back to the airport and was asked by the cabbie, "If there's no oil there, what's in it for us?" This was, Kaplan says, "a question none of the intellectuals had answered." And shame on them, because "thousands of words and a shelf of books in recent years about our moral interest in the region do not add up to one sentence of national interest.... It is only from bottom-line summaries that clear-cut policy emerges, not from academic deconstruction." Kaplan once believed that something called "amoral self-interest" should be the defining aspect of American foreign policy. His hope for the Clinton administration was that it could "condense" a justification for Balkan intervention "into folksy shorthand," because "speaking and writing for an elite audience is not enough." Robert D. Kaplan, meet George W. Bush. The writer who could once argue that "the world is too vast and its problems too complicated for it to be stabilized by American authority," has found his leader in a man who in the 2000 presidential debates proclaimed that the job of the military was "to fight and win war," not toil as "nation builders." Kaplan is said to have briefed President Bush in 2001, and today finds these protean gentlemen in a surlier and far more interventionist mood. They have fused an apparent personal fondness for strutting machismo with a fetishized idea of simplicity's value. Both have willed into unsteady reality extremely forced senses of personal identification with the common American, whose imagined need for that which is clear and cut trumps all other moral and political considerations.

Bush has gone from an isolationist to an interventionist minus the crucial intermediary stage wherein he actually became interested in other places. Kaplan has traveled from the belief that America should only "insert troops where overwhelming moral consider-ations crosshatch with strategic ones" to arguing that "September 11 had given the U.S. military the justification to go out scouting for trouble, and at the same time to do some good," seemingly without understanding that he has even changed. Doubtless both men would sit any skeptic down and soberly explain that Septem-ber 11 changed everything. What September 11 changed, however, was not the world itself but their understanding of America's role in the world. For President Bush and Robert D. Kaplan, Septem-ber 11 primarily seems to mean never having to say you're sorry.

Carl von Clausewitz famously wrote that war is the extension of politics by other means. Bush and Kaplan, on the other hand, appear to advocate war as *cultural* politics by other means. This has resulted in a collision of second-rate minds with third-rate poli-cies. While one man attempts to make the world as simple as he is able to comprehend it, the other whispers in his various adjutants' ears that they are on the side of History itself.

In *Mediterranean Winter: The Pleasures of History and Landscape in Tunisia, Sicily, Dalmatia, and Greece* (2004), we learn a bit about Kaplan's background. He began his career as a small-town news-paper journalist in Vermont, after which he attempted to get a job with "wire services, the television networks, and over a dozen large metropolitan newspapers." Because of his "forgettable" résumé and education at a "non-prestigious college," Kaplan believes, he was unable to find work. So he went traveling. A graceful man might recount his early, humbling attempts to become a writer with, well, grace. Kaplan, however, has hewn from this block of youthfully ordinary frustration a chip he has spot-welded to his shoulder: "Like so many other free-lance journalists I would meet over the years, I was never to enjoy the social and professional status—or the generous travel budgets—of foreign correspondents for major media organizations." *Never?* This man has written for the *Atlantic Monthly* for twenty years. His books have been bestsellers. He has briefed two American presidents. It is either comical or pathetic or both that a writer so disdainful of "elites" and their fancy educations can write, "Just as military officers who have known war first-hand can grasp more fully the meaning of Thucydides, only after I married and had a family would I grasp what Virgil, Homer, Tennyson, and others meant by the hardship of travel." The classics, that most elite form of moral instruction, are for Kaplan a Casaubonian key to experiential enlightenment. They allow him to pretend he's Ulysses.

In all of his books, but especially in *Mediterranean Winter*, Kaplan is incapable of making a point about the past without pointing a finger at the present. To wit: "Carthage's defeat in the First Punic War—like Germany's in World War I—led to anarchy at home." But how is the 2,200-year-old First Punic War *at all* otherwise comparable to Weimar Germany? (In another book he again rolls out this hot rod, slightly modulated, and writes how the Second Punic War has "many resemblances to World War II that seem to warn against the hubris of our own era.") He also connects, preposterously, a fourth-century BCE Athenian invasion of Sicily with "President Lyndon Johnson dispatching half a million American troops to South Vietnam." Of course he acknowledges the differences, but they "seemed less interesting than the similarities." That is because Kaplan is addicted to similarities and blind to differences. "One can write endlessly about the differences between the first and twenty-first centuries A.D.," he writes in another book. Yes. One *can*.

Kaplan's bibliographies are usually anchored with fiction and poetry, and he can write how an iron balustrade reminds him of a line from Wallace Stevens. All of which makes the damage he has done to literature unforgivable. Kaplan's "Euphorias of Hatred: The Grim Lessons of a Novel by Gogol," an introduction to the Modern Library edition of Nikolai Gogol's short novel *Taras Bulba,* is a bracing case in point. "The signal error of the American elite after the end of the Cold War," Kaplan writes, "was its trust in rationalism, which, it was assumed, would eventually propel the world's people toward societies based on individual rights, united by American-style capitalism and technology." Again, this is by way of introducing a novel by Gogol (1809-1852). "The work has a Kiplingesque gusto, too, that makes it a pleasure to read. . . . We need more works like *Taras Bulba*, to better understand the emotional well-springs of the threat we face today in places like the Middle East and Central Asia."

Taras Bulba is about a few things—Ukraine in the seventeenth century, the Russian ideal of the romantic, a guy named Taras Bulba—but it cannot, under any reasonably sane reading, be said to warn us about Wahhabism or the Taliban. Late in his life Gogol himself abandoned rationality, burned the second volume of *Dead Souls*, surrendered to Christian mysticism, and starved himself to death. The original draft of *Taras Bulba* was written early in Gogol's career, when he was gleefully strip-mining his exotic Ukrainian homeland to the delight of parochial Moscow's literary circles, about which Kaplan has exactly zero to say. Kaplan's take on *Taras Bulba* is so absurd it is amazing that when his introduction arrived at the Modern Library's offices, the pages were not locked in a lead-walled time capsule.

* * *

What happened to this man? Kaplan's early books suggest a clue. His first, *Surrender or Starve: Travels in Ethiopia, Sudan, Somalia, and Eritrea* (1988), an account of the famine that devastated Ethiopia in the mid-1980s, is not a bad book. "Drought," he writes, "according to those first, memorable media reports, was the villain, and if anyone was to blame, it was the overfed West." In fact, as Kaplan tells it, the famine was a neo-Stalinist device used by Ethiopia's Marxist and politically powerful Amhara minority against their rebellious, also largely Marxist, and more numerous Eritrean and Tigrean fellows. His grief at the major media's inability to grasp the famine's classically Soviet character is compelling and convincing, and his account of traveling with the region's Eritrean rebels is terrific. Even if the Ethiopian famine did not turn out to have the global ramifications Kaplan projected—wherever Kaplan travels, we are assured that whatever is happening there is going to have vast consequences—his attempt from within one of hell's inner circles to make others take note of the suffering he has witnessed is salutary, and even moving. For once this monopolist of doom was looking around him rather than only forward and back.

Soldiers of God, his next book, concerns Kaplan's travels with the mujahideen during the Soviet-Afghan war. He admits in the foreword to the paperback version that he "was caught up in the struggle to liberate Afghanistan, and my lack of objectivity shows; nor was I fair to some people, or as critical of others, as I should have been." Actually, Kaplan is fairer and more objective in this book than anywhere else. Nonetheless, he still defends his "brutal, tragic" position that U.S. policy in Afghanistan was morally appropriate: "The United States, in the 1980s, was doing what great powers have done throughout history. . . . A state that neglects the projection of power has little chance of spreading its values." But surely foresight is called for while the great power in question is spreading its values. American "policy" in Afghanistan consisted mainly of throwing guns and money at whichever nationalist, religious psychopath, or "commander" Pakistan's secret service put forth as a slayer of Communist infidels. To be sure, the Soviet disaster in Afghanistan was well deserved and did help hasten the collapse of the Soviet regime, but many CIA agents on the ground and even many Afghans warned the State Department that it was financing its own assassins. As is now abundantly clear, the United States' Afghanistan policy did not spread its values but undermine them.

Nevertheless, *Soldiers of God* is Kaplan's most well written book, his most empathetic, and his most humane. An early description of Kaplan's waltz through a Soviet minefield is a model of descriptive writing. His take on Afghan's guerrillas, while somewhat naive (as he himself admits), is, all the same, winningly honest: "Sympathizing with guerrilla movements is an occupational hazard of foreign correspondents everywhere, but the Afghans were the first guerrillas whom journalists not only sympathized with but actually looked up to." The other Kaplan, however, shoulders his way forward from time to time, as when he condemns "the elite establishment media and the new brand of 1980s foreign correspondents who stocked their fridges with Perrier water and talked incessantly of their computer modems."

In *Soldiers of God* one finds what is surely a partial source of Kaplan's later unhingedness: "Away from Pakistan and Afghanistan, I could barely speak about the war. When I told people where I had been, their blank expressions indicated I might as well have been on the moon. Of the few who were truly interested in what I had to say, the retort that often greeted me was: 'Really? Well then, how come we read so little about it in the newspapers?'" Never again, he surely decided, would people doubt why being concerned with strife in faraway places is important. Kaplan would make it important, even if that meant being disingenuous and, indeed, often wrong about the places and conflicts he covered. Even if it meant *Balkan Ghosts*.

Although it was widely acclaimed when published in 1993, *Balkan Ghosts* (called by Kaplan "an idiosyncratic travel book") has over the years been savaged by many Balkan experts, and Kaplan himself has been blamed for President Clinton's hesitancy to intervene against the Serbs' slaughter of their Bosnian Muslim countrymen. Clinton, according to the political journalist Elizabeth Drew, used Kaplan's dour, hopeless portrayal of the region to justify American inaction. Kaplan laments this in a new foreword to the most recent paperback edition: "That policy makers, indeed a president, might rely on such a book in reaching a momentous military decision would be frightening, if true. My personal suspicion is that back in 1993, at the beginning of his term, Clinton had so little resolve that he was casting around for any excuse not to act." This is doubly unfortunate, Kaplan writes, because "I myself have been a hawk on the issue" of intervening militarily in the Balkans.

One can tell the charge has stung him. "Neither Martians nor President Clinton killed Bosnians," Kaplan writes. "Other Bosnians did." This is a perfectly reasonable thing to point out. What is less reasonable is his belief that Bosnians killed other Bosnians because they had been programmed to do so by history and ethnicity. Kaplan can complain about the unwarranted aftereffects of *Balkan Ghosts* all he wants, but he is the man who salted his book with statements such as, "while the Greeks and the Macedonian Slavs despise each other, as Orthodox Christians they equally despise the Muslim Kosovars." The metaphysics of what makes people suddenly garrote and rape their neighbors can be debated from now until the end of time, but to generalize so complacently gives hatred a mask that too many can hide behind. In Kaplan's telling, Balkan mass-murder was inevitable and unsurprising, given the region's history. One wonders why, then, those who were slaughtered did not see it coming, and get out. "Nevertheless," Kaplan writes in *Balkan Ghosts*'s new foreword, "nothing I write should be taken as a justification, however mild, for the war crimes committed by ethnic Serb troops in Bosnia, which I heartily condemn." Here is a writer reassuring us that he does not think genocide is justifiable, and that he condemns it. Any book written in a way to require such a statement is on thin moral ice.

Once the book proper begins, Kaplan tells us, "The Balkans produced the century's first terrorists." That is pretty definitively untrue, but at any rate terrorism is at least as old as warfare itself. Who gives a shit which region introduced it to the twentieth century? "Even the fanaticism of the Iranian clergy has a Balkan precedent." It also has an American, English, Russian, French, and Spanish precedent. "Twentieth-century history came from the Balkans. Here men have been isolated by poverty and ethnic rivalry, dooming them to hate." In Carinthia, Austria's southernmost province, Kaplan notes that "a shop sold women's undergarments from Paris that were as expensive as they were naughty. The perfume worn by the blond shop girl had a sweaty, animal scent." Could this be a quirk of Kaplan's inquisitive sniffer? No. You see, "The offspring of the SS have become expensively groomed, performing tigers, safely tucked away in middle-class box houses... Carinthians have become a tamed species." It takes a special kind of man to waltz into a foreign city, tar the entire populace as recessive Nazis, and then refer to them as animals.

This is to say nothing of the book's prose, which is incurably bad, as in this barroom scene: "Men had their arms around the oily backsides of women." Arms around their oily backsides? How does that work, exactly? "There were shouts and laughter, and almost every one of the red velvet chairs was occupied. A massive wall-to-wall mirror reflected the filmy bath of cigarette smoke." Filmy bath of cigarette smoke? "I felt an intensity of emotion, a fleshy intimacy, that seemed to be based on confinement and therefore could never be duplicated in the West." So: he is having an orgasm? "While extramarital affairs in the West were mainly a result of middle-class boredom, here I felt they served deeper needs. With politics and public life so circumscribed, there was a huge well of authentic emotion that even the most ideal of marriages could never consume." I have no idea what this passage even *thinks* it means.

When he reaches Greece, where he lived for several years, Kaplan chides scholars for ignoring "the most recent 2,000 years of Greek history...in favor of an idealized version of ancient Greece, a civilization that had already died before Jesus' birth." But this is precisely Kaplan's technique in looking upon the rest of the world: Find one epoch, fixate upon it, project outward in the most intellectually irresponsible method imaginable.

Some truly nutty books followed *Balkan Ghosts*, among them *Warrior Politics: Why Leadership Demands a Pagan Ethos* (2002) and *An Empire Wilderness: Travels into America's Future* (1998). What *Warrior Politics* really gives Kaplan is the chance to show what he and a bunch of geniuses have in common. First, Churchill, whose "unapologetic warmongering arose not from a preference for war, but from a breast-beating Victorian sense of imperial destiny— amplified by what Isaiah Berlin calls a rich historical imagination." That sort of sounds like someone we know. Onto Livy, whose "factual errors and romantic view of the Roman Republic should not dissuade us from his larger truths." Sound familiar? Then Hobbes, whose "concepts are difficult to grasp for the urban middle class, who have long since lost any contact with man's natural state. But however culturally and technologically advanced a society is, it will endure and remain civil only so long as it can in some way imagine man's original condition."What original condition might that be—throwing spears at woolly mammoths? Kaplan does not understand man's original condition any better than this so-called "urban middle class," which is just a bit more diverse than Kaplan imagines. Malthus, then, who "was humiliated by the literary elite of the day, including Wordsworth, Coleridge, and Shelley." Did Malthus go to a "non-prestigious" college too?

Along the way Kaplan writes, "The short, limited wars and rescue operations with which we shall be engaged will . . . feature warriors on one side, motivated by grievance and rapine, and an aristocracy of statesmen, military officers, and technocrats on the other, motivated, one hopes, by ancient virtue."What ancient virtue is that? Achilles disfiguring Hector? Consulting a haruspex about whether to invade Syria? Using an executioner class of soldiers to slaughter men who have surrendered, as was the rule of ancient warfare?

At the end of the book, he imagines a "nontraditional American-led empire," which would mean . . . what? "The power of this new imperium will derive from it never having to be declared. . . . Joseph Nye Jr., dean of Harvard's Kennedy School, speaks of 'soft' American hegemony." But if men are essentially and savagely unchanged, if we need to know about our elusive mammoth-hunting "original state" to understand how craven people are, what possible guarantee is there that this American hegemony *will* be soft? That Kaplan can quote John Adams saying that "there is no special providence for Americans, and their nature is the same with that of others," shows something quite distressing: Not even *he* understands what he writes.

Amazingly, *An Empire Wilderness* is even worse. This book followed *The Ends of the Earth*—Kaplan's account of a world riven by

ethnic tension and unstable governments—and describes his jour-
neys around the American West. What does Kaplan find? Ethnic
tension and unstable governments, what he calls the "coming
medievalization of the continent." Renaissance fairs and President
E. Gary Gygax? No, he means the "globalized settlement" like the
one he finds in Kansas City, with its "cappuccinos, French pastries,
and designer seafood in the midst of the formerly beef-eating prairie." *Designer* seafood? The prairie itself ate beef? He has dinner at a
"Eurobistro," and wonders "if traditional patriotism may become a
waning formality. . . . How much longer, I wondered, will the patriotic marches of John Philip Sousa move America's inhabitants?"

On he goes, antennae bristling for all indications of the
deSousafication of the American landmass. In a Los Angeles restaurant, he finds a crowd that is "young, heavily Oriental, and fiercely
middle-class. . . . I sat down at an outdoor Thai-Chinese restaurant
for an early dinner. The manager was Japanese, the hostess Iranian,
and the other help Mexican immigrants." He walks into a Chinese
grocery and says, "I could have been in Hong Kong or Taiwan."
If he had continued and said, "or in a Chinese grocery in Los
Angeles," he might have been onto something. He goes to Orange
County, which he "was prepared to hate," but his visit to the
Fashion Island Mall in Newport Beach leaves him "as impressed as
I had been when I had seen the great squares of medieval Bukhara
and Samarkand," and God help him. In Orange County, however,
he has one big question: "Will this place fight for its country? Are
these people loyal to anything except themselves? . . . Rather than
citizens, the inhabitants of these prosperous pods are, in truth, res-
ident expatriates, even if they were born in America, with their
foreign cuisines, eclectic tastes, exposure to foreign languages, and
friends throughout the world." Friends! How dare they.

Kaplan then surveys the Arizona-Mexico border. On the
Mexican side are a bunch of Mexicans. On the American side

people are speaking Spanish, "but to me they might as well have been speaking English. Whether it was the high quality of their leisure clothes, their purposeful stride—indicating that they were going somewhere, rather than just hanging out—the absence of hand movements when they talked...they seemed to me thoroughly *modern* compared to the Spanish speakers" over in You Know Where. (The italics, I swear, are his.)

At a basketball game in Tucson, Kaplan notices that "the entire crowd, as well as every cheerleader, was white, in many cases with honey-blond hair, while almost everyone playing on the court was black. Wasn't this a bit like ancient Rome, in which the gladiators were often from 'barbarian,' that is, subject races?" I recall having a similar realization of this "blunt racial fact," in Kaplan's words, at about twelve years of age at the Mecca in Milwaukee, Wisconsin, watching the Bucks lose to the Cavs. I have to admit, though, I never took it this far: "The shrieking blond crowd and the sweating black players may indicate a society's way of coping with racial tensions rather than dramatizing them." Or it may indicate Robert D. Kaplan's racism as he thoughtlessly compares perspiring black Americans to barbarians.

On a Greyhound bus this man who survived Ethiopia and Afghanistan nearly goes to pieces among what he calls the "Greyhound underclass." They are fat, and loud, and Jesus Christ, could someone please shut up those bawling kids? "Can democracy flourish among people like this?" he wonders. When he gets near Canada, he makes a startling discovery: "Canada can't hold together," he for some reason quotes a former mayor of Missoula, Montana, as saying. Kaplan agrees that things look pretty bleak for Canada, and writes, "So far, most Americans have not thought much about the psychological effect of the peaceful disintegration of an entire Atlantic-to-Pacific middle-class nation on their northern border." There is at least one obvious reason why they have not much thought about this. In Vancouver, Kaplan writes, "we may be seeing something else, too: the erotization of race." The reader leans forward; this will surely be priceless. "As another Vancouverite told me, if you walk down the street and look at who's holding hands with whom, you'll observe that whites find Asians, particularly Asian women, with their small-boned symmetricality, highly desirable." I hear they have tiny little snatches, too. "Still," Kaplan says, "Vancouver has something special, a cohesiveness evinced by the never-empty streets and interracial couples: people would fight for this, I thought." Great. But are they not Canadian? And isn't Canada doomed? What if they fight us?

Never fear. Kaplan has found our saviors. They are called the American Military.

Imperial Grunts, Kaplan's gritty account of life among America's front-line soldiers in the War on Terror, is the first of what he promises, ominously, will be several books. Kaplan had the full cooperation of the Department of Defense while researching this alpha volume, and despite being treated by the military like "an oddity, a threat, and a VIP all at once" Kaplan grew close to the soldiers. He tells us how this was possible: "When the battalion found out there would be a journalist among them, there were rude complaints, *another fucking left-wing journalist.* Then an 18 Delta medic...used the NIPRNET to check me out online. He downloaded some of my articles and pronounced me 'okay' to the others."

Kaplan describes receiving a "command briefing" that began with an Orwell quote: "People sleep peaceably in their beds at night only because rough men stand ready to do violence on their behalf." *Imperial Grunts* is that peaceable sleep's lullaby. The book is not merely an account of twenty-first-century soldiering; it is also

Kaplan's attempt to define, defend, and justify American "imperial-ism." On this point *Grunts* is a thesaurus of incoherencies.

"Indeed," he writes, "by the turn of the twenty-first century the United States military had already appropriated the entire earth, and was ready to flood the most obscure areas of it with troops at a moment's notice." To say the least, the notion that the United States effectively rules the planet is an emaciated one. Does Kaplan not remember the endless haggling the United States was forced to do on the eve of the Iraq War to enable its use of other nations' airfields? Do other nations' desires and integrity really mean so little to Kaplan? But at the Pentagon, we learn, Kaplan gazed upon a Mercator Projection of the U.S. military's areas of responsibility and saw a planet chopped up into jagged rectangles of supposed command (CENTCOM, EUCOM, PACOM, and so forth). He "stared at it for days on and off, transfixed. How could the U.S. not constitute a global military empire?"

In an interview, Kaplan has said, "our challenges abroad are exactly like those of other empires in history. . . . You don't like the word 'imperial' for America? Tough luck." So what is Kaplan's understanding of imperialism? "Imperialism is but a form of iso-lationism, in which the demand for absolute, undefiled security at home leads one to conquer the world." Okay. But then: "The grunts I met saw themselves as American nationalists, even if the role they performed was imperial." Got that? And: "America's imperial des-tiny was to grapple with countries that weren't really countries." It is? They *aren't*? "Imperialism was less about conquest than about the training of local armies." Oh. "All America could do was insert its armed forces here and there, as unobtrusively as possible, to alleviate perceived threats to its own security when they became particu-larly acute." But didn't you just say that—oh, wait. He's still going: "The Americans wanted clean end-states and victory parades. Imperialism, though, is a never-ending involvement." Before long you're wondering if taking a good old-fashioned American dump in a U.S.-dug latrine in Yemen is not also "imperialism."

The ideas in *Imperial Grunts* are garbage, but the book is often absorbing. Here credit goes to the spectacular locales (Colombia, the Horn of Africa, the Philippines, Mongolia, Afghanistan) Kaplan visits, though they are usually described in incompetent études such as, "to the north loomed a *Planet of the Apes* landscape." Once he reaches the Philippines, things get interesting. With some Green Berets Kaplan goes to a restaurant, where he describes the local women, whom he calls "girls," as "typical *Filipinas*: small-boned, symmetrically featured [again!], and walnut-complexioned beauties, with twangy, mellow Spanish-style voices and subservient oriental manners, a devouring mix of South America and Asia." But for one Green Beret vanishing "for an hour with a girl into the darkness of the beachfront," the evening is, Kaplan assures us, "innocent." U.S. military personnel are forbidden from fraternizing with local people, in my view wisely. Kaplan, though, writes, that this forbiddance was "a shame. . . . Had this been the old Pacific Army, some of these men would have taken some of these girls as mistresses." And then gotten them pregnant, and left, and reduced them to pariahs within their culture. Soon enough the horny Green Beret returns to their table. "Driving back," Kaplan writes, "someone joked about smelling his finger to see where it had been." That needless "to see where it had been": pure Kaplan. The man's cluelessness is equally apparent at a funeral for a slain soldier in Afghanistan, where Kaplan describes the "thumping, rousing song" that is played: Barry E. Sadler's Vietnam-era chestnut "The Ballad of the Green Berets." It is not a thumping, rousing song. It is kitsch as surely as the old Soviet sing-along "The Internationale" is kitsch.

The soldiers themselves like the song, however, and that is enough for Kaplan, who goes gaga for nearly every soldier and Marine he meets. ("He seemed to have a somewhat cold and surly nature" is about as negative as Kaplan gets about a soldier. He does note, however, that many soldiers' inability with foreign languages is "where the American Empire, such as it was, was weakest." Solution: more imperialism.) The problem with loving every soldier he meets is that the soldiers themselves, in Kaplan's hands, quickly shed their individuality. The loss of individuality may be the necessary point of military indoctrination, but a writer has no such excuse when writing about them. While Kaplan is always careful to provide us with *Stars and Stripes*–style enumerations of their ages and hometowns, they are but in a few cases allowed little texture or eccentricity.

Why does Kaplan so adore these rough men? Because they "had amassed so much technical knowledge about so many things at such a young age." He refers to their "brutal, refreshingly direct" manner. One soldier in the Philippines, Kaplan writes, "made snap cultural judgments of the kind that would burn an academic's reputation, but which in the field prove right seven out of ten times." And that's 70 percent! ("The Afghans are just great," one soldier says. "Yeah," says another. "They love guns and they love to fight. All they need are trailer parks and beer and they'll be just like us." These are presumably the kind of snap cultural judgments that have thus far served us so well in the War on Terror.) "Nobody," Kaplan writes fondly, "is afraid to generalize in the bluntest terms. Thus, conclusions do not become entangled in exquisite subtleties. Intellectuals reward complexity and refinement; the military, simplicity and bottom-line assessments." But rest assured they are scholars, too: One soldier is reading "Cervantes in the early-seventeenth-century original text," while another is "dipping into the complete works of James Fenimore Cooper." "Bad things happen in the world," Kaplan is told by a soldier. "You do the best you can, and let the crybabies write the books." The soldiers' and Marines' various thoughts and feelings, as transcribed by Kaplan, are rarely more complicated than this gunky self-congratulation.

"The American military is a worldwide fraternity," Kaplan writes, filled with "singular individuals fronting dangerous and stupendous landscapes." The soldiers "talked in clichés," he informs us. "It is the emotion and look in their faces—sweaty and gummed with dust [gummed with *dust*, you say?]—that matters more than the words. After all, a cliché is something that only the elite recognizes as such." That is surely why, Kaplan says, "these guys like George W. Bush so much.... He spoke the way they did, with a lack of nuance, which they found estimable because their own tasks did not require it." Besides, those cliché-conscious elites are yellow anyway. As one soldier tells Kaplan, "I believe character is more important than education. I have noticed that people who are highly educated and sophisticated do not like to take risks." Kaplan himself seems to have come to share this harsh essentialism. One Marine, Kaplan notes, "was not interested in what was interesting, only in what mattered." In an earlier book, Kaplan could write: "*Such interesting objects, I had told myself, each separated from the other by centuries, could be connected only through a lifetime of study, and what could be a better way to spend a lifetime?*" He could also write that a traveler is "an explorer of everything interesting." No longer.

There is at least one problem with this dismissal of the interesting, seeing that what is interesting, when dealing with foreign cultures, *is* very often what matters. "We need people who are quick cultural studies," an Army major general tries to tell Kaplan, which Kaplan deduces not as "area expertise; that took too many years to develop," but as "a knack ... a way of dealing with people.... The right men would find things out and act on the information they gathered, simply by knowing how to behave in a given situation." Sounds easy enough. And what kind of soldier would be least equipped, emotionally speaking, to deal with vexed, confusing matters of religion and culture in nations understandably sensitive to foreign occupiers? If you said, "Evangelical Christian soldiers," well, you could not be more wrong. Kaplan argues that Evangelical soldiers, whose entire worldview is founded upon accepting that everyone who is not a Christian will roast on Beelzebub's spit, is in actual fact the U.S. military's strongest asset, seeing that "morale could not be based on polite subtleties or secular philosophical constructions, but only on the stark belief in your own righteousness, and in the inequity of your enemy." God will just have to sort them out.

As a journalist I have spent some time around Marines and soldiers, both within and without war zones (my father is a former Marine and a Vietnam veteran), and I have found as much political and intellectual variance among them as one might find among the occupants of an F train into Brooklyn. Deployed soldiers do indeed tend to be good at their jobs, and since their jobs are often irreducibly technical, it is no surprise that their expertise can seem mind-boggling to outsiders. Kaplan is never quite clear whether it is the culture of the U.S. military—egalitarian, clear-eyed, unsentimental, decisive, and, sometimes, despite all that, completely nuts—that attracts such men, or that produces them, but he has some thoughts.

Writing that he "happily admitted guilt" to the charge of having "lost [my] professional detachment and begun to identify with the troops [I was] covering," Kaplan claims a unique understanding of American soldiers. After all, "I was a citizen of the United States and a believer in the essential goodness of American nationalism." His argument is that "the objectivity of the media was problematic" because journalists "were global cosmopolitans," whereas the "American troops I met saw themselves belonging to one country and one society only: that of the United States." This is delusional. For one, are there really American journalists who do not think of themselves as American? I would very much like to meet one. And does Kaplan really think it is unusual that American soldiers view themselves as American soldiers? He does. The military, he writes, "is part of another America, an America that the media establishment was increasingly blind to, and alienated from." This Perrier-quaffing media establishment cannot hope to understand this "vast, forgotten multitude of America existing between the two coastal, cosmopolitan zones, which journalists in major markets had fewer and fewer possibilities of engaging in a sustained, meaningful way except by embedding with the military."

In *An Empire Wildnerness*, Kaplan voiced disgust with America's "Greyhound underclass," but in *Grunts* the "country-slash-southern-slash-working-class version" of that underclass is America's very heart and soul. "The American military . . . was composed of people who hunted, drove pickups, employed profanities as a matter of dialect, and yet had a literal, demonstrable belief in the Almighty," which he later calls an "unapologetic, literal belief in God absent for the most part among the elites." But why would a literal belief in God be anything *but* unapologetic? And what do the elites have to do with it? Kaplan uses some tough, pretty-sounding words to conjure up these soldiers, but one scratches at Kaplan's prose just a little to find a nasty little drummer boy incapable of addressing any matter without going after those elites who denied him a job so long ago. He sees the world so relentlessly in terms of class, tribe, and race because he himself is unwilling to see the world in any other way.

"I wish people in Washington would totally get Vietnam out of their system," a soldier tells Kaplan. He translates this sentiment thus: "[I]t was the politicians who were afraid of casualties, not the American military." Similar callousness about the lives of the men he lionizes and lauds are strewn throughout the book: "The working class's attitude to casualties was fairly tough . . . It was the elites that had a more difficult time with the deaths of soldiers and marines." The Marines, you see, "were an example of how government channels the testosterone of young males toward useful national ends." Like, say, dying. "If the military were much smaller than it was, the result might be only more gang violence within the homeland," I guess because soldiers are borderline criminals? Along these lines the book reaches its disgusting crescendo:

> The grunts' unpretentious willingness to die was
> also a product of their working-class origins. The
> working classes had always been accustomed to
> rough, unfair lives and turns. They had less of an
> articulated and narcissistic sense of self than the
> elites, and could subsume their egos more easily
> inside a prideful unit identity.

Kaplan is equally coldhearted about civilians' lives. When a Marine kills an Iraqi civilian, Kaplan writes, "I felt bad for the marine who had fired the shot—any civilian would have felt bad for him, if he or she had experienced the complexity and confusion of this urban battle space." As for the dead Iraqi—tough luck, Ali. Next time don't be so pretentious.

Here we see a writer effectively lapped by his subject matter, yet still believing he is in first place. After quoting one National Guardsman as saying, "We're like tourists with guns," Kaplan writes, "While the media was filled with lugubrious stories about the great sacrifices being made by reservists in Iraq and Afghanistan, these guys were having the time of their lives." Last summer I was embedded with the Marines in Iraq, and I certainly noticed some of soldiering's satisfactions, even a few of its hard-won joys. I also saw men and women tensely grinding their dinner between molars and crying while talking to their loved ones back home; I saw equal amounts of frustration and confusion, and, in one particularly awful occasion, some wounded Marines brought into a surgical ward. A screaming, burned Marine is not having the time of his life, and neither are his friends. I am sure the U.S. military has its share of cheerful characters—the burned Marine may have been having a ball until the day our paths crossed—but Kaplan continually, and in my opinion criminally, refuses to dig beyond his baseline feeling that soldiers are super. It is both a literary and moral failure.

Who, then, are Kaplan's books for? The liberal elite he lectures as being too pampered and cosmopolitan to understand his Manichean world? An untraveled American reading public looking for reassurance that the nations beyond their borders are hostile, crumbling, and in need of some harshly applied American elbow grease? Right-wing think tanks in search of on-the-ground folderol? Policymakers casting about for some troublesome new chimera to chase along the crags before the next electoral cycle? One wonders if Kaplan himself knows the answer to this question. He has been so content to wander from his beloved quasi-isolationist "tragic realism" (the world is harsh; people behave abominably; war is terrible, and should only be waged when there are obvious and overwhelming strategic benefits to be reaped) to pounding a bloody-minded drum of imperialism largely because he enjoys the sound it makes, with no secondary recognition that "tragic realism" and soldiers having the time of their lives is, in fact, a profoundly self-contradictory notion.

Kaplan is worse than a bad writer or thinker. He is a dangerous writer made ever more dangerous by the fact that he is taken seriously. Even his most hostile reviews have treated him as though his arguments are still within the pale. His worldview is, in many ways, that of the current administration, and shared by many Americans. These are people for whom the wider world means only acrimony to be dismissed and obstacles to be knocked over. People who care not for "exquisite subtleties" when it comes to matters of force and occupation. People who do not think in human terms, except insofar as those terms reflect their own beliefs, which are supremely correct. People, in short, who have no use for people, except as cannon fodder—lives whose passing they dutifully mourn on their side and gleefully celebrate on the other. "Kaplan is America's Kipling," reads one of *Imperial Grunts*'s blurbs. This is to slander Kipling, who nevertheless did write one Kaplanesque sentence: "All the people like us are We / And everyone else is They."

"Lying awake," Kaplan writes in *Imperial Grunts*, "as Indian Ocean breezes raced through my mosquito netting... I thought that if you were a male of a certain age during World War II and had not served in some capacity, you were denied the American Experience." Not some part of the American Experience, mind you, but the American Experience. Let us, please, reflect on this. If you have not killed a fucking kraut or zipperhead with your own two hands, you are not a real American. "Now I realized that many of my own generation had been denied it as well. . . . Perhaps it was a safer, more enriching global experience that we were having, but whatever it was I knew now that it was not fully American." So what is this American Experience? It was "exotic, romantic, exciting, bloody, and emotionally painful, sometimes all at once. It was a privilege, as well as great fun, to be with those who were still living it." I do not doubt that it was great fun for Kaplan to play soldier, but he is apparently unaware that he is celebrating the taking and loss of life in this leprous book—though, given the current state of our nation, perhaps he is the writer we deserve.

Travel, Kaplan has written, "is where we truly meet ourselves." Unfortunately, this has proved to be his one most accurate articulation.

—2006

STILL RISING

The possibility that becoming the most distinctive American prose writer of the twentieth century would have its considerable drawbacks probably did not occur to the twenty-seven-year-old author of *The Sun Also Rises* when it was published in 1926. Despite some powerful literary advocates, Hemingway's first two books had flopped; copies were not even available in Hemingway's hometown of Oak Park, Illinois. His third book—a cocky, strutting, elliptical novel about British and American expatriates behaving as badly as their times (and Hemingway's censors) allowed them—changed all that. As Lionel Trilling wrote only thirteen years after *Sun's* publication, Hemingway, "more than any writer of our time . . . has been under glass, watched, checked up on, predicted, suspected, warned." The book's much-heralded style, as liberating as a magic spell for its author, eventually became a kind of aesthetic stockade. By 1961, serial shock treatments at the Mayo Clinic had left the arch mage depressed, unable to write, needlessly lecturing his wife about her "expenses," and convinced that the FBI was reading his mail and wiretapping his phone. Hemingway's suicide of that year was not only an act of escape from the various furies, real and imagined, in steady pursuit of him; it was the explosive period to the only sentence he could bring himself to compose. For this reason any writer who has been compared to Hemingway feels a certain clammy shudder. As it turned out, not even Hemingway could survive the comparison.

The bright student who picks up *The Sun Also Rises* today cannot be wholly blamed for finding its opening pages somewhat cinched and joyless, in the manner of a man playing badminton in a tuxedo. We should be glad that Hemingway, on F. Scott Fitzgerald's suggestion, dumped *Sun*'s original and singularly leaden opening: "This is a novel about a lady. Her name is Lady Ashley and when the story begins she is living in Paris and it is Spring." An assumed conservatism is the fate of nearly all books that become classics, though few are less deserving of that fate than *The Sun Also Rises*. The opening Hemingway ultimately went with ("Robert Cohn was once middleweight boxing champion of Princeton") ranks among literature's great misdirects. *The Sun Also Rises* really *is* a novel about a lady. Cohn is merely one of her four suitors, though he suffers the most because of it.

Lady Brett Ashley, recently divorced, presently engaged, frequently drunk (or "tight," in Hemingway's parlance), and doggedly promiscuous, is one of American fiction's more striking heroines. Like Hamlet, she controls the action even by her absence. The novel's narrator, Jake Barnes, loves her, but cannot consummate their relationship due to an undisclosed war wound. ("Of all the ways to be wounded," Barnes thinks before falling asleep. "I suppose it was funny.") Brett's bankrupt fiancé, Mike, loves her, but is sickeningly aware of her infidelities. Rounding out the cast are Bill Gorton, Barnes's viciously funny writer friend from New

York, who alone among the novel's men pulls back before succumbing to Brett, and the Spaniard Romero, a teenage bullfighter whose relatively late introduction results in the multilateral ruination of Hemingway's characters.

What begins as "the chaps" jaunting down to Pamplona to watch bullfighting during *fiesta* season quickly, and unforgettably, becomes an occasion for a more human form of blood sport: Cohn is chronically humiliated, Barnes is beaten, Mike is destroyed, countless bottles of wine (I lost count at fifty) are imbibed, and the slaughter of the bulls themselves becomes merely dramatic counterpoint. Here Hemingway has few peers. Yes, the descriptions of Paris, which Hemingway worried were too satirical, are lovely, and the several dozen pages lavished upon Barnes and Gorton fishing for trout along a lonely Spanish river are more or less unimprovable. But in depicting the toxic interaction between scarred and broken people who love and hate both one another and the lives of threadbare glamour they have found themselves trapped inside—"a wonderful nightmare," Gorton quips—Hemingway invented a new way to write about women and men and the world Americans found themselves forced but not yet ready to confront. *The Sun Also Rises* has now been with us for eighty years. What one imagines seemed irrepressibly fresh to its readers then feels deathlessly relevant now, but its brokenhearted tenderness and savage skepticism know no expiration date, and need no renewal: We are all a lost generation.

—2006

THE SECRET MAINSTREAM
Contemplating the Mirages of Werner Herzog

Truth is always concrete.
—Hegel

O f that time, there is still much we do not know. Although answers exist to the basic questions—how they fought (viciously), how they governed (variously), how they worshipped (combatively)—there are those among us who warn that no real comprehension of twentieth- and twenty-first-century civilization is attainable, much less advisable. But those who attempt to hold knowledge back can only lose ground.

What caused this remarkable civilization's collapse is now generally understood. There are controversies, naturally, about the precise nature of its collapse, foremost of which is the extent to which this civilization destroyed itself. Most of us believe that, given the way its constituents lived, the annihilation was inevitable, even if the overwhelmingly thorough nature of the annihilation was not. We need not delay ourselves debating these issues yet again.

It is here where the recent discovery of the films of Werner Herzog provides us especial aid. The extraordinary circumstances of the Herzog archive's survival have been amply celebrated and documented elsewhere, but that does not mean we can forget how objectively precious these films are. An entire civilization's most popular form of art also proved one of its least durable. The expected deterioration of their film stock took most of the earliest films, and the fragile nature of their digital storage systems, which was apparently unanticipated, resulted in the loss of many of the rest. The relatively few films that have survived do not always provide the most culturally revealing portholes through which we can today peer. We all exalt in the survival of Kurosawa's *The Hidden Fortress* (1958), but the cultural significance of Carpenter's *Escape from New York* (1981) has proved difficult for many of us to articulate (though it does have its champions).

The work of Werner Herzog presents a different case, as it offers us the only instance of a single filmmaker's entire corpus surviving until our time. His numerous films—so heterogeneous in technique, genre, and breadth—scarcely seem the work of one man. Indeed, some of us have doubted that they *are* the work of one man. Thankfully, we have been able to put such fanciful conjecture to rest. Unfortunately, that is where our agreement concerning Herzog's work ends.

> *"[W]hen you think about people four hundred years from now trying to understand civilization today, I think they will probably get more out of a Tarzan film than out of the State of the Union address by the President that same year."*
> —Werner Herzog

What, indeed, would future historians make of our civilization if the frustrating, beautiful, always mesmerizingly strange films of Werner Herzog were their primary cinematic witnesses? Would they be seen as damage inspection of a civilization at horrifying odds with nature and itself? As documents so fiercely visionary they often come within millimeters of insanity? Would they be seen as mirrors or warnings? Symptoms or cures? Herzog himself has explored this question, using a similar science-fictional conceit to frame several of his ostensible documentaries, the genre in which he has done his most singular and protean work. *Fata Morgana* (1970) is nominally a film about mirages in the Sahara Desert. The film's narration, read by the German film historian and Herzog mentor Lotte Eisner, offers long recitations from a Mayan creation myth: "Therefore the creatress and the creator essayed once more to build living beings, to make moving creatures." Early in the film, a long tracking shot offers some windblown orange dunes, across which sail tiny whirlwinds of sand—a bizarre, almost Martian vision. This, in fact, is part of the point. While the film has been called "a cosmic pun on cinéma vérité," Herzog has said that his "plan was to go out to the southern Sahara to shoot a kind of science-fiction story about aliens from the planet Andromeda, a star outside of our own galaxy, who arrive on a very strange planet. . . . The idea was that after they film a report about the place, we human filmmakers discover their footage and edit it into a kind of investigative film."* This conceit, barely evident in *Fata Morgana* itself, announces itself more clearly in Herzog's other "science fiction" films, namely *Lessons of Darkness* (1992), which features putatively "alien" narration over apocalyptic footage of the oil fires in Kuwait ignited by retreating Iraqi forces at the end of the first Gulf War, and *Wild Blue Yonder* (2005), which stars Brad Dourif as an embittered alien narrating the story of an unwelcome Earthling mission to his home planet

---

* This Herzog quote, like many others throughout this piece, comes from the invaluable *Herzog on Herzog*, edited by Paul Cronin.

over actual—and hilariously mundane—footage of NASA astronauts floating around their space-shuttle living quarters.

Fata Morgana marked Herzog's first overt confounding of the feature film/documentary boundary. Like *Lessons of Darkness* and *Wild Blue Yonder*, it is not a narrative film, but neither is it strictly factual. Rather, it uses factual images to tell a fictional story the images do virtually nothing to suggest. Like his late countryman W. G. Sebald—who admired Herzog's films and referenced them in his equally fact-blended fiction—Herzog makes stylized use of the factual and, through its valence with the invented, pours "the facts" from their test tube of the verifiable. This is what gives these films their grandeur and brilliance as well as their occasional yet distinct undertow of unease. At the German premiere of *Lessons of Darkness*, Herzog claims to have been spat upon for its contextless, highly aestheticized images of an entire ecology dying in a fiery, petroleum-fueled Revelation. A brief but notably grisly sequence, furthermore, presents us with a deranged Kuwaiti woman whose sons were tortured and killed in front of her, and an unforgettable pan of the still-bloody implements within a Republican Guard torture chamber. The matter of torture is quickly dropped, and although Herzog later introduces us to a young boy who was left mute after a beating by Iraqi soldiers, he is clearly more interested in beautiful images of flaming oil wells than in testaments of human suffering. Thus there arises, in some viewers at least, the sense that Herzog has made these "documentary" films under false pretenses. The rulers of Kuwait agreed, and when they realized Herzog was not making a film about the heroic men and women fighting Kuwait's oil fires, as he had initially claimed, but rather something of his own devising, they expelled him from their kingdom.

Herzog, however, is an artist, not a journalist. An artist can respect the backfield of fact before which every human being stands and choose not to address those facts. Obscuring another's history is not necessarily a hostile act, and arguments that Herzog has responsibilities to his subjects overlook the fact that even though Herzog may be filming under false pretenses, he is not presenting his films under any pretext but that of art. We know, after all, that the tortured Kuwaitis are not actually aliens. Herzog's conceit does not undermine their suffering, for what conceit, short of outright denial, could? Any art form that incorporates the experience of real people will inevitably result in accusations of distortion. The question is not whether Herzog has shaped his subject matter but why.

Despite Herzog's notoriety (this is a man who publicly ate a shoe after losing a bet to the documentary filmmaker Errol Morris), his formal accomplishments (more than fifty films, fourteen of which are features), and his acclaim (both Miloš Forman and François Truffaut have deemed Herzog the world's greatest living filmmaker), he is relatively obscure when compared to directors of equal stature. (His most vocal American champions—Errol Morris, Francis Ford Coppola, Harmony Korine, Zak Penn—are usually filmmakers themselves rather than critics.) His films were most widely discussed during the 1970s and early 1980s, when the antipodes of film criticism, with *Film Quarterly* in one hemisphere and Pauline Kael and Andrew Sarris in the other, had less ocean between them than do their rough equivalents today. At that time Herzog was typically linked to the New German Cinema, which grew out of the poisoned artistic lacunae of Nazism or to some greater dirigible of European cinema as a whole. In many ways Herzog has outgrown, and even outlasted, such categorizations. This is to say nothing of his films themselves, which, however difficult to classify, tend to be fairly straightforward.

Indeed, Herzog often hurls into the last few minutes of his films some wizardly curveball. *Stroszek* (1976), for instance, ends with a several-minute-long sequence of a dancing chicken. A favorite Herzog gambit is to give his characters lengthy concluding speeches that have little apparent connection to anything else in the film. These are not the coyly "experimental" touches typically associated with non-American filmmaking. They are, rather, exceedingly weird touches that come off as though one were entering a stranger's REM state. Herzog refers to such devices as "moments of special intensity when suddenly you hear something that rails against the most basic rules you are accustomed to."

Born Werner Stipetić in Munich in 1942, Herzog grew up in a lonely mountain village in Bavaria with a doting Croatian mother and absent father. He assumed the name Herzog, or "duke," as a totemistic way of protecting himself from what he has called "the overwhelming evil of the universe." Herzog has claimed that his solitary wanderings in the mountains of Albania at age fourteen made him into a filmmaker. A fifteen-page encyclopedia entry on filmmaking gave him "everything I needed to get myself started," and a pilfered 35mm camera from the Munich Film School gave him the tools, a theft he has since justified on Nietzschean grounds: "I know it was not theft. I had a natural right to take it." He would make his first seven films with that camera.

Herzog came of age among West German artists and intellectuals who were discouraged from calculating the extent of their parents' capitulations to Nazism and disgusted with their divided nation's unfamiliar servitude to outside powers. Unlike many of his contemporaries, Herzog did not become a political radical. Instead he became a visionary, aesthetic radical. His first feature-length film, *Signs of Life* (1968), tells the story of an injured German soldier recuperating in Greece during World War II—a conflict to which the film, rather curiously, makes no reference. Herzog's German soldiers are barefoot existentialists who rarely salute and go shirtless for much of the film, which, as Herzog acknowledges, "certainly has nothing to do with the Third Reich." After receiving considerable accolades for creating the first Third Reich layabouts in film history, Herzog noticed his fellow West German artists discerning the brighter side of Maoism and equating the American misadventure in Indochina to Hitler's revanchism. Herzog responded to such revolutionary bromides with *Even Dwarves Started Small* (1970), a bizarre and, to my mind, nearly unwatchable film about the revolt of a platoon of little people against their institutional masters. Parabolic, nasty-minded, and thoroughly ugly in its evocation of rebellion, the film leaned hard into the prevailing winds of the late 1960s. Jean-Luc Godard, whom Herzog has condemned as "intellectual counterfeit money," had famously declared that "Photography is truth. The cinema is truth twenty-four times per second." Herzog spurned such sentiment, believing that photography created its own kind of truth, the idea that *Fata Morgana* strove so powerfully to explore. Many critics, particularly German critics, were unmoved.

Herzog, undaunted, kept making films, becoming something like the Updike of contemporary cinema. Only eight of the last thirty-eight years have gone by without a new Herzog film, and in a few years there have been as many as three. Some of these films have been commercially successful (for instance his moody and terrifying 1979 remake of F. W. Murnau's *Nosferatu*, which features the most memorable use of Wagner since *Apocalypse Now*), but most have gained their audiences long after the fact. This time-lapse appreciation suits his work, for to become interested in Herzog is akin to initiation into some rite- and secret-handshake-filled cult. The mark of most cults is a wide range of interests coupled with a circular series of obsessions, and no filmmaker is more greatly afflicted with this syndrome than Herzog. While his films take place *everywhere* (Germany, the United States, South America, Africa, Southeast Asia, Australia, the Middle East) and are about *everything* (adventure, courage, madness, failure, death, time, space travel, nature's indifference), his imagistic obsessions (auctioneers, flight, monkeys, chickens,* ski-jumpers, dwarves, bears, boats, wind, roosters,† midgets, mountains, windmills, hens) reappear again and again. Herzog's work is marinated in cross-reference: more than one of his films features an enchanted waterfall, others turn upon ghostly visions of jellyfish, several characters wear nearly identical aviator goggles, other characters' names recur, dialogue is often resuscitated from film to film. In *Grizzly Man* (2004), Herzog's documentary about a well-meaning amateur filmmaker named Timothy Treadwell, who met his end at the hands of the very grizzlies he sought to photograph and protect, Herzog pauses to admire one of Treadwell's most beautiful shots: an empty windblown field in the Alaskan outback. The longtime Herzog viewer can only smile. The shot is nearly identical to an early image of his 1974 film *The Enigma of Kaspar Hauser*.

In the mudslide-plagued, brushfire-prone, yet somehow still exceedingly desirable hills above Sunset Boulevard, where Herzog

---

* Chickens (and roosters, and hens) are Herzog's objective correlative and play some role in dozens of his films. A film as early as *Even Dwarves Started Small* contains a disquieting sequence in which a chicken eats a dead mouse. "Look into the eyes of a chicken and you will see real stupidity," Herzog has said. "It is a kind of bottomless stupidity, a fiendish stupidity. They are the most horrifying, cannibalistic and nightmarish creatures in the world."

† Herzog: "Years ago I was searching for the biggest rooster I could find and heard about a guy in Petaluma, California. . . . I went out there and found Ralph . . . who weighed an amazing thirty-two pounds! Then I found Frank, a special breed of horse that stood less than two feet high. I told Frank's owner I wanted to film Ralph chasing Frank—with a midget riding him—around the biggest sequoia tree in the world. . . . But unfortunately, Frank's owner refused. He said it would make Frank, the horse, look stupid."

has lived for six years, sidewalkless roads turn and twist beneath a canopy of copiously weeping willows and improbably tall palm trees. Many of the pale, pastel homes seem 80 percent garage, the remainder of their mishmash architecture largely hidden behind parapets of shrubbery, curtains of vine, and thick walls of fructiferous trees. It was here that I thought of Herzog's famous soliloquy about the Peruvian jungle in Les Blank's documentary *Burden of Dreams*: "Nature here is violent, base. I wouldn't see anything erotical here. I would see fornication and asphyxiation and choking and fighting for survival and growing and just rotting away.... The trees here are in misery. The birds are in misery. I don't think they sing; they just screech in pain.... Even the stars up here in the sky look like a mess." Occasionally the foliage broke enough to allow me to spy some copper-skinned human presence shearing away at a property-marking topiary wall. Dusty Jaguars and Mercedes Benzes were parallel-parked adjacent to bespoke little mailboxes and actual picket fences, and the films of David Lynch (an admirer of Herzog) made sudden, visceral sense to me in a way they had not when I woke up that morning.

Herzog greeted me in a white soft-collar shirt and biscuit-colored slacks. He led me into his white-carpeted living room, which was as sun-drenched as a greenhouse and filled with over-sized photography books and various relics from his travels. For much of his career Herzog sported a thick neo-Prussian mustache and the shaggy brown hair of a Seventies-era Munich soccer player, resulting in the type of face that *looked* famous even if one did not know who Herzog was. A few years ago Herzog shaved off the mustache; his shaggy hair, which had abandoned Herzog on its own accord, survived only in smooth gray recession, revealing a prodigal forehead as well as a remarkable resemblance to the philosopher Thomas Hobbes. As we began to talk Herzog seemed somewhat exhausted—I would later learn he was experiencing severe appendix pain that day—and his overall mien was akin to that of a dissident from a nation whose regime refused to fall. Herzog's voice—raspily forceful and marked by a slight tendency toward sibilance—was his most distinctive feature. Coming in at a close second were his eyes, which Herzog has claimed not to know the color of, and which sat unknowably deep in cavernous sockets. But when he laughed or smiled his eyes glowed with fallout, and there they brightly were: grayish blue, like fog over the ocean.

It was suddenly very hard to imagine this calm, quiet man, around whom more legends had accrued than Excalibur, directing his actors at gunpoint (a false legend), being shot during a televised BBC interview (true), depriving Peruvian Indians of their civil rights (false), rescuing Joaquin Phoenix from a car crash (true), faking a supposedly pro-Sandinista documentary (false), or voluntarily swan-diving into a cactus field to prove a rather ineffable point (true).

"It's a natural phenomenon in the media that things like this happen," Herzog told me when I brought up the legends. "Partly it's just sloppiness. I have a very good example. As a young man I learned of a producer in Cleveland who was planning a series of NASA films on advanced rocket-propelled systems. So I went to Ohio, but since there was a high-security atomic reactor there as well, I found out that I was not allowed to enter. Now, a lot of reports say that I made films for NASA, or abandoned a promising career as a NASA scientist in order to become a filmmaker. So, it's sprouting. It's okay. I let it sprout."

I hoped—in retrospect, stupidly—to impress Herzog by pointing out a continuity error I had noticed in one of his films. I had believed this would impress him because of his many pronouncements unfavorably comparing how a "bureaucrat" made films to his own more instinctual method. These pronouncements ranged from cinematography ("I hate perfectionists behind the camera, those people who spend hours setting up a single shot") to storyboards ("storyboards remain the instruments of cowards who do not trust in their own imagination") to continuity itself ("The continuity girl kept bothering me by asking over and over, 'How many shots are we going to do now?' I kept saying to her, 'How would I know?'"). Herzog, however, leaned back and looked at me in horror. "In the thirty years that this film exists, you are the first one to mention something like this. I would have to check into it." While he fretted, I stammered something about how I had assumed such trivial matters meant little to him. But Herzog shook his head. "It *does* matter because it has to do with flow of storytelling. It has to do with the inner structure and inner emotion of narration; it has to do with the inner movement of an audience."

In an interview given during the filming of *Nosferatu*, Herzog had spoken of a wish to make a film in the vein of Akira Kurosawa, a director whose calibrated sensibility and operatic visuals seemed rather distant from Herzog's more chaotic aesthetic. When I wondered if he still had that ambition, Herzog smiled. "I've never made a film of complete balance like Kurosawa. I've never gotten close to it. But so be it. May Kurosawa rest in paradise. But *The White Diamond* has something close to a real balance."

The documentary subject of *The White Diamond* (2004) is Dr. Graham Dorrington, a British researcher who wants to photograph the wildlife in the jungle canopy of Guyana from an experimental low-flying zeppelin of his own design. An archetypal Herzogian figure—the dreamer plagued with bad luck—Dorrington is haunted by the death of a cinematographer friend, killed a decade ago in one of his earlier zeppelins. Although the death was an accident, Dorrington cannot forgive himself. When Dorrington finally gets up into the canopy, a scene most filmmakers would have chosen to shoot as a moment of glorious transfiguration, Herzog uses it to create a monster-movie fresco: tree frogs with huge paddle-sized suckers on their long fingertips; millipedes covered in seemingly weaponized spikes; an evil-looking and empty-eyed sea-green lizard. *The White Diamond* becomes truly remarkable, however, with the introduction of Mark Anthony Yhap, a diamond-mining roughneck whose bizarrely moving predicament all but hijacks the film midway through. (There is also a long sequence involving a rooster.) Released shortly before the publicity-hoarding *Grizzly Man*, *The White Diamond* is among the most beautiful and unusual documentaries ever made, and it is something akin to a crime that it is not at least as well known. On this point Herzog agreed, saying, "*The White Diamond* simply has more depth than *Grizzly Man*."

Given that Herzog had made a film about the first Gulf War, and given that, on the evidence of *Grizzly Man* and *The White Diamond* alone, his documentary powers have never been more burnished, I asked whether he had any interest in making a film about the current Iraq War.

"No," he said quickly. "That is something Americans are doing. And there are very, very good films emerging. And all of the sudden I hear cries of, 'Move away from *cinéma vérité*!' *Cinéma vérité* is the accountant's truth, cinema's answer of the Sixties. Look out now for different voices for imaginative films. And they are coming in throngs." In 2006, Herzog was honored with an Outstanding Acheivement Award at a documentary film festival known as Hot Docs. Eight years ago, he said, only six films were submitted to the festival. "All were shown and all got an award. This year sixteen hundred films were submitted, and one hundred were selected. And there are formidable films there. They are coming from all over the place. I am not alone anymore."

I asked if that was a good feeling.

"Oh, sure. Thank God! But it's not because I raised my battle cry. It's because there is now such an incredibly momentous assault on our perception of reality as immense and of the same magnitude as firearms confronting the medieval knight. But all this is not that interesting. Neither facts are that interesting nor is reality that interesting. Somehow in all of this we are still capable of finding some illumination, some truth, some place where we step out of ourselves, where we are ecstatic, where we have an ecstatic, visionary realization."

When I wondered if Herzog had plans for another documentary, he shrugged and said it was impossible for him to anticipate what his next documentary would be. By way of illustration he brought up *Grizzly Man*. "When I came across Treadwell's story, I knew, simply knew, that it was big, really big, and I had to tackle it and I had to do it no matter what. I started to watch Treadwell's footage, and that resulted in nine days of editing. And then I shot my half of the film. And while I was editing that, I wrote the commentary, recorded the commentary, and did the pre-mix. But we didn't have music yet, so I had to wait until I had the musicians together and record the music and then mix that into the film. But in principle, from the day I received Treadwell's footage until the delivery of the film took twenty-nine days."

Although Herzog has spent years making certain films, he rarely takes more than a few days to write a script; *Woyzeck* (1979) was shot in eighteen days and edited in four. "That's how films should be made," Herzog told Roger Ebert. "That was perfect." Nonetheless, less than a month to make a film as nearly perfect as *Grizzly Man* struck me as almost impossible to believe. It *was* possible, Herzog said. "I saw it so clearly. There was not one moment of thinking."

* * *

Herzog's world is not thoughtful. It is reactive, lined with thorns, and frequently blown through by ill winds. One of his most striking films, *The Great Ecstasy of the Woodcarver Steiner* (1974), about competitive ski jumping, gives us replay after replay of ski jumpers landing badly, their scissoring skis explosively shed, followed by a final image of unconscious jumpers sliding to gentle stops in the snow. Just as often, though, Herzog's ski jumpers succeed. Action is neither rewarded nor condemned but rather enacted within a vacuum emptied of everything but its potential poetry. No filmmaker is better at evoking the curious beauty of our indifferent universe.

What is surprising, in light of this, is how tender Herzog can be—but it is a cunning tenderness. One of his first documentaries, *Land of Silence and Darkness* (1971)—Herzog's favorite of his films—opens with the voice of its deaf-blind subject, an elderly woman named Fini Straubinger, who went blind at fifteen and deaf at eighteen as the result of a nasty fall. "When I was a child," she says over a blackened screen, "before I was like this, I watched a ski-jumping competition. And one thing keeps coming back: those men going through the air." Herzog archivally obliges Straubinger's memory with gorgeous silent footage of ski jumpers soaring off their slopes and alighting upon the snow with physics-defying lightness. But this is not Straubinger's memory; it is Herzog's. In fact, he wrote the lines for her. Straubinger did not mind, believing that the sequence was representative of her experience, whatever the literal content of her few remaining sighted memories was.

Later in the film, Straubinger and some of her deaf-blind friends visit a zoo, where they play with a recalcitrant monkey. The monkey, who undoubtedly has a greater awareness of the fact it is being filmed than most of Herzog's deaf-blind subjects, reaches out and yanks the lens's casing off Herzog's camera. This is a moment many filmmakers would have elided, but Herzog keeps it in, as though reminding us of his camera's presence. Herzog's films are filled with similar breaches, both explicit and implicit, and viewed in the aggregate his work becomes a way of thinking about mediation: between viewer and image, between fact and fiction, between the real and the unreal. *Grizzly Man* may be Herzog's best-known (and most commercially successful) film, at least of recent years, but it is also his most straightforward and unmediated, which is to say, his least representative.

In *Little Dieter Needs to Fly* (1997), Herzog's astonishing documentary about the escape and survival of a German-American pilot named Dieter Dengler from a Pathet Lao prison camp in 1966, Herzog shows us Dengler entering his San Francisco home, whereupon he opens and closes the front door several times before entering. "Most people," Dengler explains, "don't realize how important it is, and the privilege that we have, to be able to open and close the door. That's the habit I got into, and so be it." Dengler did not actually have this habit. In fact, it was Herzog's idea. While it embodied a real feeling Dengler had, it was not a real activity. Assigning to Dengler an activity he did not engage in is what Herzog has called "the ecstatic truth," wherein literal accuracy cedes its ground to emotional accuracy, a subjective realm entered through manipulation and fabrication. Consider a disquieting sequence later in the film, in which Herzog takes Dengler to the Thailand-Laos border, hires a group of Thai villagers to tie Dengler up, and runs the former captive through the jungle much as he had been run through the jungle three decades before. "Uh oh," Dengler says, as he feels the binds bite around his wrists, "this feels a little too close to home." Herzog narrates, "Of course, Dieter knew it was only a film. But all the old terror returned, as if it were real." Here the manipulation is blatant, if profoundly unsettling. Later, when Dengler uses a Thai villager to reenact a notably awful story involving Dengler's stolen engagement ring and the Viet Cong's machete-based method of dealing with theft, the villager becomes visibly upset. Dengler notices and hugs the man. "Don't worry," he tells him. "It's only a movie." It is as though Dengler, in simply telling his own story, has become the filmmaker.

Herzog's ecstatic truth finds its way into his feature films as well. *The Enigma of Kaspar Hauser* fictionalizes the real story of an eponymous young man who turned up in a nineteenth-century German town with scarcely any speech and no experience with the outside world, for he had been kept chained in a cellar, by unknown parties, for the first two decades of his life. In the role of Kaspar, Herzog cast a nonprofessional actor, the incomparable Bruno S., who was in actual fact a prostitute's son who had spent twenty-three years in various mental institutions, where he was often beaten and kept in deep isolation. In *Stroszek* (1976), the story of a luckless German street musician who travels to the American Midwest to improve his life, and fails miserably, Herzog uses Bruno S. again. The film's most disturbing scene involves Bruno S.'s character being beaten by pimps in his apartment, which Herzog chose to film in Bruno's actual apartment. This sequence, Herzog has admitted, "pains me so much because it was probably the kind of treatment that had been doled out to him for years when he was a child." (Bruno S. told Herzog right before they shot the scene, "I'm going to be a good soldier, and I've been hurt much worse before.") Two other sequences offer equally startling but far less brutal ecstatic truths: a scene in which Bruno talks to his prostitute girlfriend about life in America (under the Nazis, Bruno says, they beat you and cursed you, but in America, "They do it ever so politely, and with a smile") was improvised, reflected what Bruno S. himself felt upon his first trip to the United States, and results in what is perhaps the most moving, intimate moment in the film. For another sequence, Herzog flagged down two Wisconsin deer hunters and asked them if they would agree to be filmed while one of his elderly German actors spoke to them in German. They agreed, and Herzog turned on his camera. After listening for a few moments to this strange little German discuss the power of "animal magnetism," the deer hunters look at each other, laugh, get into their car, and quickly drive away. Herzog never saw the deer hunters again. It is one of the funniest sequences in any of Herzog's films.

For *Aguirre: The Wrath of God* (1972), a violent, troubling film about a breakaway expedition of Spaniards searching for El Dorado along the Amazon River while gradually going mad, Herzog filmed on the Amazon River with a cast and crew who nearly went mad. The reality of the shoot constantly intrudes into *Aguirre*'s story. When the raft he was filming on developed a mouse infestation, Herzog filmed the mice. When part of the raft was in danger of being sheared off by low-hanging branches, Herzog scrambled for his camera, captured the collision, and incorporated it into the film, which ends with the megalomaniacal Aguirre (played by the megalomaniacal Klaus Kinski) coming to grief on a raft crawling with spidery little monkeys. The end of *Aguirre*, Herzog says in the film's DVD commentary, is "so strange and so real at the same time." While Aguirre wanders about his raft, his comrades dead, his mind slipping past the final checkpoints of sanity, he delivers a mad speech—parts of which Herzog says incorporate an equally mad speech delivered by the Zanzibari revolutionary John Okello—while the monkeys skitter around him. After pointing out in the commentary that it was nearly impossible to choreograph the monkeys (and Herzog received dozens of monkey bites to prove it), Herzog says, with a laugh, "You just have to follow the monkeys."

In *Fitzcarraldo* (1982), Herzog again tells the story of a dreamer searching for salvation in the Amazon. Fitzcarraldo's doomed quest to bring opera to the Amazon requires dragging a 340-ton ship over a mountain in order to reach another, inaccessible river; Herzog naturally decided that he would actually drag the ship over the mountain. The film thus becomes an allegory of itself. Herzog spent three years in the jungle making *Fitzcarraldo* and in the process had to deal with scrapping everything halfway through when his original star, Jason Robards, fell ill with dysentery and was forbidden by his doctor to return to Peru; plane crashes; a border war between Peru and Ecuador; Herzog's arrest (twice) by the authorities; several crew members' injuries (including one man chainsawing off his own foot after being bitten by a poisonous snake); and attacks by hostile Indians (one of which resulted in two members of the production undergoing eight hours of surgery). When the time came to recast *Fitzcarraldo*'s leading man, one might have expected Herzog to opt for an actor with peace at the center. Herzog, however, cast the miracle of ill temper that was Klaus Kinski,* even though Herzog knew Kinski "would freak out" and "go totally bonkers" in the jungle. Kinski did not disappoint.

Yet Herzog kept working with Kinski—they eventually made five films together—and in this, one can detect something of the perversity that impelled Herzog to drag a boat across a mountain in the first place. Herzog has never really been able to provide full

---

* In an outtake of Les Blank's *Burden of Dreams*, a documentary about the making of *Fitzcarraldo*, we witness one of Kinski's Pompeiian outbursts as he screams at Herzog's production manager, Walter Saxer: "You can lick my ass! I'm going to smash your face!" This was nothing, as Herzog himself points out. During the filming of *Aguirre*, Kinski opened fire with his Winchester rifle on some extras. Herzog says it was a "miracle" no one was killed. Elsewhere Herzog has said, "Kinski was probably the most difficult actor in the world to deal with. Working with Brando must have been like kindergarten compared to Kinski."

accounting for his and Kinski's twisted reliance upon each other. He did pull from Kinski some astonishing performances—particularly in *Woyzeck*, a film basically composed of several long one-take sequences—but their working relationship involved serial pledges to kill each other. Kinski, who died in 1991, wrote in his autobiography that "I absolutely despise this murderous Herzog. . . . Huge red ants should piss into his lying eyes, gobble up his balls, penetrate his asshole, and eat his guts!"*

Herzog avoids filming in studios. His films, he has said, are "killed stone dead without the outside world to react to." He resists resolutely such elementary film devices as the freeze frame or zoom. His camera is largely stationary, and he holds on his images with vulturous patience. These are traits Herzog developed by necessity. *Aguirre*, for instance, was filmed with only one camera—the camera he liberated from the Munich Film School—and Herzog's view of much of modern filmmaking's "flashy tricks" and "excess of cuts" is predictably dour: "This kind of filmmaking . . . gives you a phony impression that something interesting might be going on. But for me it is a clear sign that I am watching an empty film." For Herzog, emptiness is analogous to the devices most of us associate with film. Kinski, then, illustrates what it is about Herzog's films that is simultaneously real, unmediated, and manipulated. While his actors deliver crazed, scripted speeches days after taking crazed, unplanned potshots at extras, and his non-actors are asked to reenact their most painful life experiences and then to engage in unusual behavior that will be portrayed as characteristic, we can see Herzog's films as an

---

* Herzog maintains he helped Kinski write many of the book's anti-Herzog diatribes, and Herzog's take on their relationship, the documentary *My Best Fiend* (1999), is notable for its searching tone and gentle touch. The last minute or so of the film, which shows an outtake (shot by Les Blank) of Kinski playing with a butterfly, rates among the loveliest sequences to be found in any of Herzog's films.

ongoing attempt to illustrate the porosity of the barrier between fiction and nonfiction. What is any film, after all, but a series of images burned onto celluloid?

"When I see a great film," Herzog has said, "it stuns me, it is a mystery to me." Images, Herzog's films repeatedly suggest, have their own mysterious reality that, finally, cannot be codified, only beheld. His strength as a filmmaker is certainly not psychological, and often his fictional characters behave inexplicably. Thus his tendencies toward halos of imagery, as though to fill in the motives his screenplays refuse to provide. This can sometimes amount to a kind of idolatry of composition. Herzog has not helped himself when he speaks of film as being the "art of illiterates," or when he repeatedly expresses disgust toward film criticism. As one of Herzog's more eloquent critics once wrote, Herzog and his "celebrants" believe that "there are more things in heaven and earth than are canvassed by our dictionaries. Most of us, I think, would assent to this." But Herzog is not being mystical as a means toward will-to-power supremacy. His films are too overwhelmingly concerned with the vagaries of human experience, which is different from human behavior, to allow him such easy metaphysics, especially when the types of experience he is most interested in fall beyond the parameters of the imagination. Fini Straubinger is real. Don Lope de Aguirre is not. Neither is a typical human being. Their realness is of only incidental importance when one attempts a full understanding of what Herzog has spent his career attempting to achieve. His films are the alembic through which life itself is distilled—not explained but *distilled*—and we are his fellow alchemists. Upon seeing the boat in *Fitzcarraldo* finally inch over the mountain, Herzog says this on his DVD commentary: "I always knew it was a central metaphor of this film, maybe even of life. And I can't even say [a] metaphor of what. I can't even name it." A critic, perhaps, could. But in presuming to name it she, too, will have become an artist.

* * *

For the final-stage edits of his new film *Rescue Dawn*, Herzog was working out of a suite of soundproof rooms in a gated building in an indistinct Los Angeles neighborhood, the nearby streets of which were lined on one side with tattoo parlors and the other with "laser tattoo removal" specialists, among whom one Dr. Tattoff stood out.

After introducing me to Joe Bini, his editor on his last nine films, Herzog sat down and prepared himself for yet another round. At this late stage editing seemed to involve watching slightly different versions of the same take, discussing the microscopia of what made them better or worse, and after a semiautomatic flurry of Bini's mouse clicks judging the results of their decisions, at which point they either moved on or started over.

Rescue Dawn is Herzog's attempt to retell the story of Dieter Dengler, the captured pilot of *Little Dieter Needs to Fly*, who died in 2001. It is the first time Herzog has fictionalized one of his own documentaries, and during a lull I reminded Herzog of his statement, "I have never made a distinction between my feature films and my 'documentaries.' For me, they are all just films." If that was the case, why did he feel the need to remake what had already been recognized as one of his most extraordinary films?

"It's basically the same story," he said, "but it's unfinished business. Much what you see in *Rescue Dawn* is something you do not see or hear in the documentary. So there's a huge amount of story that is untold." When I asked if he approached representing the story differently now that it had assumed explicitly fictional form, Herzog shook his head. "I do not fear representation. I represent at the personal level. That's what Dieter himself understood. When I said, 'Dieter, I'd like to shoot a scene where you are opening and closing your front door,' he said, 'That might look funny—my friends will think I'm bonkers.' And I said, 'No, you have to understand this gives a deep insight into who you are.' He looked at me and said, 'I think I understood you.' And he did it. He did something staged and scripted for the sake of truth, the deeper truth, something that is deeply embedded in his soul. You cannot make it visible otherwise. Of course, it depends on what you're doing. Timothy Treadwell in *Grizzly Man* had been dead almost a year when I got his footage. And you do not invent around his material. You respect it. You don't fool around with it."

I thought of the sequence in Zak Penn's agreeably minor, frequently amusing fictional documentary *Incident at Loch Ness* (2004), in which Herzog plays himself making a documentary film about the Loch Ness Monster. Penn, who has great fun playing himself as Herzog's producer, stages repeated Nessie sightings until Herzog threatens to quit. The aggrieved Penn says to Herzog, "You once said to me, 'Cinema is lies.'" Herzog's response: "There's a distinction. If you can't make the distinction, if you just can't make the distinction, why don't you become a talk-show host?" The scene's intention is comic, but the point it makes is a serious one. There *are* distinctions to be made. Herzog's distinctions about when to mingle fact and fiction may appear to take place within a corona of nebulousness, and may even appear self-justifying, but then so do most matters of human morality, which in all but a few extreme cases are fluid rather than fixed. The morality of narrative art, whether fictional or fact-based, hinges upon knowing when the additives one injects into representation begin to poison rather than fortify the narrative—knowing, in other words, what to include and what to leave out. Every artist will judge differently, but these are judgments that must be made—even by those who fanatically insist that any fabrications, however small, inserted into what is intended to be "real" result in fiction—and they implicate even such elementary decisions as choosing where to begin telling a story. Yet is not choosing where to begin a story so subjective it amounts to a lesser brand of fabrication?

Herzog went back to observing Bini, whose round face was lit with the glow of the three flat-screen monitors off of which he worked. The left screen held a tabular file listing of all of *Rescue Dawn*'s catalogued shots and takes. The center screen was where useable shots were stored before their transfer into the final cut. The right screen held the ever-mutating film itself, and on it I watched Christian Bale (playing Dengler) and Steve Zahn (playing Dengler's doomed friend Duane Martin) wander, shoeless and bloodied, through some Thai jungle, which stands in for Laos.

Herzog described for me his typical process. Shortly after a film wraps, he and Bini view all the rough footage, which in optimal conditions they can do in one or two long sittings. While watching the footage Herzog takes notes. These notes, he said, can be very cryptic—Bini smiled in apparent agreement—often amounting to nothing more than "!!" for takes he particularly likes. Herzog assured me he did not need to take extensive notes. "I remember everything, even the tiniest shots." To illustrate this he asked Bini to call up a just-completed scene near the end of the film in which Dengler is signaling the spotter plane that ultimately summons a rescue chopper. While editing this scene Herzog remembered, for instance, exactly how long the spotter plane hangs behind some treetops, for it was a moment he wanted to elongate as much as possible. He also remembered a certain look on Bale's face from a previous discarded take, and made sure to insert it right after the plane reappears. Watching the rough cut again, though, Herzog seemed suddenly unsatisfied, and told Bini, "Probably we'll need his face once more." He then turned to me, as if in apology. "This is a *very* rough version."

Herzog's elephantine memory is necessary for several reasons, among them the fact that he does not watch dailies. Instead he knows "in my stomach" if a scene is strong or not. This is good and even noble, though only to a point. Occasionally in Herzog's work, though usually in his feature films, there occurs some moment of inexplicable clumsiness. A key scene in *The Enigma of Kaspar Houser*, for instance, in which the hero is attacked by his former captor, is so poorly filmed that what should be a frightening moment of reckoning instead looks like something out of a home movie: *America's Funniest Assaults*. A look at that day's rushes might well have prevented it. But what Herzog often lacks in elegance he more than makes up for in the unusual ferocity of his vision. The critic Clive James once wrote that today's blockbusters, "despite the technical bravura of their components, rarely strike us as being very well put together. . . . The special effects leave NASA looking underfunded, yet the general effect, despite oodles of expertise, is one of a hyperactive ineptitude—of the point missed at full volume." Herzog has never had in his films much by way of special effects, though his film *Invincible* (2001) had some digital effects, as will *Rescue Dawn*. While making *Fitzcarraldo*, Herzog needed to send his three-story barge down rough, dangerous rapids. He did not use a model. He and his crew and actors climbed aboard the ship and filmed it themselves. At one point the vessel almost capsized. The footage Herzog and his crew shot from on board is uniquely jarring, and the actors themselves look appropriately terrified.* It is not a bludgeoningly impressive sequence when judged alongside the sinking of James Cameron's *Titanic*, say, but what Herzog captured has to it a dreadful intensity altogether lacking in the more expensive film.

---

* Thomas Mauch, Herzog's cameraman, split his hand down the middle while filming the sequence and had to undergo some impromptu thatch-hut jungle surgery without the benefit of morphine.

Rescue Dawn's budget is around $10 million, some of it Hollywood money. Thus I asked Herzog if this meant *Rescue Dawn* qualified as a "studio film." Herzog laughed and shook his head. He has never made a studio film, and probably never will. He does not like to be edited, proudly maintaining that every one of his films is a "director's cut." He then informed me that *Rescue Dawn*'s financiers are "newcomers from different professions." One is the Los Angeles Clippers forward Elton Brand, whom Herzog deemed "the most reliable investor in the whole thing." Another is a man named Steve Marlton, a former businessman and nightclub owner whose lapses, both financial and aesthetic, during the filming of *Rescue Dawn* resulted in the dismissal of several of Herzog's longtime collaborators and no small amount of trouble with the Thai authorities. (As Daniel Zalewski wrote in his 2006 *New Yorker* profile of Herzog, Marlton, at one point, suggested to his director that a recent adventure film starring the Rock would be a useful model for *Rescue Dawn*.) But of Marlton Herzog had nothing bad to say. "What endears to me to him," Herzog said, "is that he gave up a college career, quit everything, went into foosball, and then twice became the world champion foosball player. Of course, we ran into trouble on this film because he was too inexperienced. But that's okay. That happens. The film is in the can. I am very close to finishing it now, even though there was a six-month hiatus because there were no funds for post-production. We were in limbo for a while. Which also is okay. It will not damage the film."

"Money," Herzog has said, "has two qualities. It is stupid, and it is cowardly." Later he would admit to me that he was preemptively planning on not showing up at various film festivals if his film was edited without his permission, and that Christian Bale had also promised to boycott any showing of a bastardized *Rescue Dawn*. In the end, Herzog was allowed the cut of the film he wanted. The man's determination to work solely on his own terms struck me as personally inspiring and profoundly depressing. The filmmaker who made *Fata Morgana*, *Aguirre*, *Fitzcarraldo*, and *The White Diamond* deserved some late-career fate altogether handsomer than this.

Bini and Herzog were now working on *Rescue Dawn*'s final sequence, when, after weeks of wandering and hopelessness, Dengler is hauled into the rescue chopper. There were four versions of this scene, all of which had tiny variations of timing and tone, though the basic sequence of movements was the same. One man pulls Dengler aboard while another riffles through his doleful little satchel. Dengler then crawls for a figure who can be seen only from the waist down, whose khaki-uniformed legs he wraps his arms around. This embraced figure is Herzog himself. The chopper was too small for him to be elsewhere, and Herzog insists on being close to his actors as they perform.

The first take Bale plays grimly, almost emotionlessly. The next take Bale plays with smiling relief. In the third take Bale holds on to Herzog's legs with childlike tenacity, and in the fourth he looks up at Herzog and grins. All of the takes conclude with Herzog handing Bale a Butterfinger. Only two of these takes have good sound. In every take the soldier going through Dengler's satchel finds a half-eaten snake, yelps, and falls back. Unfortunately, this gentleman's performance is the worst thing about all four takes. Sometimes he takes too long to find the snake, other times he is too clearly "acting" when he finds it. The man was not a professional actor but rather a tourist a member of Herzog's production found in Bangkok.

The other problem with this scene—the film's emotional climax—is that Herzog, as usual, filmed it with only one camera. ("The rhythm of a film," he said once, "is never established in the editing room. The directors who rely on editing are cowards.

Rhythm is made in the shooting—that is filmmaking.... Editing merely puts it all together.") There was but one opportunity to cut away, when the pilot announces over his radio that they have Dengler. Bini opted to jump into the scene relatively late when Herzog noted how much he liked the manner in which the man who pulls Dengler aboard stomps his boot down next to Dengler's head. (The soldiers are not yet sure if they have an American or a Viet Cong insurgent on a suicide mission.) The decision to go with the boot stomp locked Bini and Herzog into a take that otherwise had a few imperfections, which they minimized by cutting away to the pilot earlier than they had planned. This left them with the decision of which take to use when they cut back to Bale holding Herzog's legs. Herzog was most fond of the childlike take, if only for the knowingness of Bale's smile when he accepts Herzog's Butterfinger. While Bale's expression fulfilled its dramatic function (*I have been rescued!*), it had some other strangely private glimmering.

Much of *Rescue Dawn* was filmed in sequence. In many ways it had been a difficult shoot, and Bale, along with everyone else, occasionally lost his composure. On this day of shooting in particular, Bale and Herzog argued about Bale's safety concerns, with Bale reportedly yelling, "I'm not going to feckin' *die* for you, Werner!" What I was seeing on Bini's screen, then, was a perfectly Herzogian paradox: the scripted film based on the documentary that contained fabrications had come down to a moment in which I was no longer sure if I was watching Dieter Dengler accepting a candy bar or a great director attempting to apologize to his leading man.

Herzog walked me to the door. I had spent only a few hours with him, but I had spent many weeks watching his films, and somehow I knew they had changed me. I wanted to tell Herzog this but was not sure how. Instead I asked him if he was ever frustrated that his films were not more widely known. He seemed to get somewhat shy before looking away. "I believe," he said, "in what I call the secret mainstream. Kafka was there too. Today, yes, we know Kafka was the voice of an overwhelming bureaucracy with a deep evil inside of it. Often we see these figures in the secret mainstream. I am one of them."

With that, I told Herzog how much I admired him, and how thankful I was he had agreed to see me. Herzog seemed neither surprised nor pleased by my effulgence. Instead he looked at me for a disarmingly long time—so long, in fact, I began to feel like a character in a Werner Herzog film. Finally, he said: "There is a dormant brother inside of you, and I awaken him, I make him speak, and you are not alone anymore." We shook hands and he was gone. I walked outside, through a curtain of Los Angeles sunshine, to the street's edge, where I stood for some time, ecstatic and not quite alone.

—2006

KAPUSCINSKI'S
LAST JOURNEY

Ryszard Kapuscinski disappeared in the dead of winter, January 2007, half as well known as his influence would lead one to expect. He went into the beyond Nobel-less, like Joyce and Proust and Nabokov, but to many who read him he was as iconic: "deity" was used, more than once, in his assorted funeral songs. While desperate formulations such as "world literature" conjure up bongos, beads, and sitting Indian-style, the books Kapuscinski wrote may actually qualify, as evocative and singular in English as they are in their native (and what is said to be austerely fine) Polish. For many of us, the day of his death was a dark cold day.

Until 1983, most Western readers would have mistaken the man for Polish espresso. Thanks to the efforts of the husband-and-wife team of William R. Brand and Katarzyna Mroczkowska-Brand, Kapuscinski's first book to appear in English was *The Emperor* (originally published in Polish in 1978), a spell-casting oral history of Haile Selassie's rule over Ethiopia. *The Emperor* was followed in 1985 by what many believe to be his masterpiece, *Shah of Shahs* (originally published in 1982), a short, tense, fragmentary account of the 1979 Iranian revolution. It was followed in 1987 by *Another Day of Life* (originally published in 1976), his bizarre and shattering reportage from Angola as its former Portuguese overlords fled for their lives. These three books brought Kapuscinski Western acclaim as perhaps the world's leading literary journalist. The acclaim was rather tardy, seeing that for the past three decades Kapuscinski had been filing dispatches from the Indian subcontinent, Asia, Latin America, and, most often, Africa, initially in the service of a Polish youth journal as its first and only foreign correspondent and later for the Polish Press Agency. As his now famous about-the-author note from *The Shadow of the Sun* (2001) informs us, Kapuscinski "witnessed twenty-seven coups and revolutions" and "was sentenced to death four times." A biographical précis many nonfiction writers would do anything, short of earning it, to have.

Kapuscinski's African dispatches largely made his name. Like his countryman Joseph Conrad, to whom he is often compared and to whom he bears almost no resemblance, Kapuscinski has become embedded in the continent's literary firmament. Upon Kapuscinski's death, however, the young Kenyan writer Binyavanga Wainaina attacked "the racist writer Kapuscinski" as being the author of some "all-time classic lines about Africa," such as, "In Africa, the notion of abstract evil—evil in and of itself—does not exist." It is hard to blame those angered by some of Kapuscinski's more careless statements about Africa. His risky generalizations may suggest a seeming lack of recognition of Africa's varied and heterodox cultures, but that seems a minor sin in light of how deeply he attempted to understand it and how much of his life he spent there. Kapuscinski knew, of course, how complicated his subjects were. "The European in Africa," he wrote in *The Shadow of the Sun*, "sees only part of it," and can only fall short when attempting to describe "the immense realm" of African psychology. His subject matter was local but his tone was cosmic, dislocated, and sometimes surreal. His miner's light lingered deep in recesses of totalitarianism, mysticism, and revolution—places where truth begins to lose access to the photosynthesis of fact. A coloration not often noted by those in opposition to Kapuscinski is that his is the Africa of a man from a subject country who discovered it just as its nations were snapping the leashes of their colonial masters. In the end, great nonfiction writing does not necessarily require any accuracy greater than that of an honest and vividly rendered confusion. The limits of human perception cruelly bind us all.

Kapuscinski's final book, *Travels with Herodotus*, is about the Father of History, a man so bound by his fifth-century BCE perception and experience as to appear by modern standards almost intellectually comatose. "He had never heard of China," Kapuscinski writes, "or Japan, he did not know of Australia or Oceania, had no inkling of the existence, much less the great flowering, of the Americas. If truth be told, he knew little of note about western and northern Europe." He also believed that Ethiopian men ejaculated black semen. Yet, to Kapuscinski, Herodotus was "the first globalist," and "the first to argue that each culture requires acceptance and understanding." How much Herodotus actually traveled we cannot know, and a good deal of *Travels with Herodotus* is occupied with Kapuscinski's ceaseless wonderings about his early life ("Did he build sand castles at the edge of the sea?"), family history ("Might Herodotus's father have been a merchant himself?"), and personality ("Perhaps he had a naturally inquiring mind?"). The book's true nature, however, is that of an unabashed memoir, the author's first, and it opens with Ryszard, aged nineteen, studying Greek history at Warsaw University. Although a Polish translation of Herodotus was not available until 1955, shortly after Stalin's death, Kapuscinski became a lifelong pupil of Herodotus's time, "a world of sun and silver, warm and full of light, populated by slender heroes and dancing nymphs." It was also a world that seemed determined to destroy itself through internecine warfare.

Kapuscinski shortly graduated and became a journalist. After being censured, hounded, and then exonerated by the authorities for writing an exposé of a grisly Polish factory intended to be a Communist showcase—a story curiously unmentioned here—Kapuscinski was rewarded with his first foreign assignment. He had asked for Czechoslovakia, the strangest place he could then imagine. He was given India. His assigning editor presented the young journalist with a gift: "It was a thick book with a stiff cover. . . . On the front, stamped in gold letters, was Herodotus, THE HISTORIES."

Kapuscinski took the book with him everywhere—to India, to Afghanistan, to China, to Cambodia, to Rangoon. "Sometimes," he writes, "when the offices emptied in the evenings and the hallways grew quiet . . . I reached for *The Histories of Herodotus* lying in my drawer." We are thus intended to believe that Herodotus served as Kapuscinski's lifelong companion and was, in some ways, his intellectual hero. Yet one will search in vain for any mention at all of Herodotus in Kapuscinski's previously published books in English. Is it all a device? If so, similar slipperiness has earned Kapuscinski no small amount of criticism from the sheriffs of nonfiction, most recently *Slate*'s Jack Shafer, who plucked the press tag out of Kapuscinski's fedora in an early 2007 piece titled "The Lies of Ryszard Kapuscinski." But calling Kapuscinski a liar is akin to one of the Pharisees investigating Jesus's story of the prodigal son and proclaiming that the young man in question never left home at all. Obviously, one should not set out to consciously deceive in a piece of writing that purports to be true. From this understanding the gradations begin.

A nonfiction writer's style provides the first corresponding clue as to how we are to approach the facts at hand. The style of the plainspoken, rigorously invisible journalist semaphores one kind of approach, that of the poetical, allusive, and interactive journalist another. These are not competitive styles. One is contentedly earthbound while the other mingles in a Milky Way where morality is not a matter of proper dates and chronology but of representational accuracy, context, language. Its mode of communication is not discursive, or even necessarily informative, but visionary. It is called poetic license for a reason: one has to earn it. As Kapuscinski once said, the subtle tyranny of what happened "is exactly what I avoid." He continued, "If those are the questions you want answered, you can visit your local library."

There is distressingly little to argue over in *Travels with Herodotus*. The narrative floats about like an uncaptained trireme— in the Sudan, Kapuscinski meets some questionable individuals, smokes a joint with them, goes to a Louis Armstrong concert, and then ponders the Nile, which gets him thinking about Herodotus—and the pectorals of his language have lost some definition. "I burned the midnight oil studying up on guerrilla warfare in the jungles of Burma and Malaysia," he writes at one point. Whether the presumably comparable Polish phrase being translated here is as hoary can only be guessed. It may be unreasonable to expect a writer in his seventies to strive toward the same kind of originality as he did in his youth. But the writer in question is Ryszard Kapuscinski. There is a reason we do not allow our superheroes to grow old.

Those who know Kapuscinski's work have their favorite moments. The scene in *Shah of Shahs* wherein Kapuscinski imagines a moment in which a police officer threatens a man in a crowd, who for the first time in his life "doesn't budge . . . and this is precisely the beginning of the revolution." His description of how half of the Angolan city of Luanda was shipped away in crates during its siege, "as if a pirate fleet had sailed into the port, seized a priceless treasure, and escaped to sea with it." The sorcerer casts a few enchantments in *Travels with Herodotus*, but only one of them comes within range of either of the above. It occurs with Kapuscinski's account of the construction of the Great Wall of China, built over thousands of years with "dedication and devotion" and "exemplary discipline." And then the classic Kapuscinskian reversal: "This is how the world's energy is wasted."

A nameless energy gathers as one reads deeper into *Travels with Herodotus*, and one begins to realize that, in many ways, Kapuscinski's previous books, however brilliant, were somewhat impersonal. Here, finally, we experience the early tremors Kapuscinski underwent for the privilege to write them. Not all of it is painful; much of it, in fact, is delightful—especially the revelation that Kapuscinski learned English from Hemingway. And one finally sees that in writing about Herodotus Kapuscinski is actually writing about himself. Herodotus tried to get the best information available, Kapuscinski notes, "and, given the epoch, this speaks to a tremendous expenditure of effort and to great personal determination. . . . And if he knows something, how does he know it? Because he heard, he saw."

Kapuscinski saw more, and more clearly, if not always perfectly, than nearly any writer one can think to name. Few have written more beautifully of unspeakable things. Few have had his courage, almost none his talent. His books changed the way many of us think about nonfiction, and made many of us want to travel for ourselves, and see for ourselves. Herodotus, Kapuscinski reasonably imagines, interviewed many of his subjects by campfire.

"Later, these will be called legends and myths, but in the instant when they are first being related and heard, the tellers and the listeners believe in them as the holiest of truths, absolute reality," he writes. And so "the fire burns, someone adds more wood, the flames' renewed warmth quickens thought, awakens the imagination." How much smaller and colder the world now seems with Kapuscinski gone.

—2007

SYMBOLIC VALUE

On Martin Amis's *The Second Plane*

Martin Amis's *The Second Plane* is a collection of essays, short fiction, and book reviews arranged in order of composition. It thus functions, in some ways, as a walking tour of the motley post–September 11 mind—its fears, madnesses, misapprehensions, and insights. While the book's first essay, written in the immediate aftermath of the attacks, aches with the same "reflexive search for the morally intelligible" (as Amis elsewhere calls it) that animates the desperate relativism of the paleo-left, the end of the book finds him, having now enlightened himself on modern Islam's intellectual traffic jam, condemning the very same Left's "hemispherical abjection" to the "Thanatism" of radical Islam.

The author of several of the funniest novels ever written, and arguably the world's most entertaining writer of prose, Martin Amis has also periodically examined some colossal human bummers and published his findings in what are typically slim but rigorous volumes. Predictably, the Amis of this mode has his detractors. *Einstein's Monsters* (1987), with its forceful denunciation of nuclear weaponry, was slighted as little more than an empty declaration of seriousness. (It wasn't.) More recently, *Koba the Dread* (2002), a historical sleigh ride through the Left's collaborations with Stalinism, rolled many eyes with its supposedly needless revisitings. (They weren't.) Yet these books were, in some ways, vulnerable to belittling encapsulation. So is *The Second Plane*, which might be called a psychic survey of our terror-haunted terrain—the smoking fumaroles, flash-flood magma flows, and exploding horizons. Some of its sentiment ("the extreme incuriosity of Islamic culture has been much remarked") is coarsely put, and some of its broader arguments are undoubtedly wrong. Like its predecessors, then, it, too, will be ridiculed—but not by any reader who has attempted to read it or Amis carefully.

The centerpiece is a long essay here titled "Terror and Boredom: The Dependent Mind." (When it appeared in the *Guardian* in September 2006, the title was "The Age of Horrorism." During an Internet roundtable six months later, a cheeky youngster asked Amis if he had any more such "unintentionally hilarious" phrases. "Yes," he replied. "Fuck off.") This fiercely argued and frequently striking essay attempts to drop a rhetorical neutron bomb upon radical Islam and its soft-minded apologists. Reading Martin Amis inveigh against radical Islam is almost identical to reading Martin Amis on nuclear weapons: However much fun you (and he) are having, there's something inescapably imbalanced about the confrontation, as though one were watching Einstein fly through multiplication tables.

Along the way, Mr. Amis, leaning heavily upon other writers and scholars (and he remains a cribber of unparalleled gifts, which sounds like faint praise only to someone who's never had to do it), fashions an affecting portrait of Sayyid Qutb, the Jeremy

Bentham of Islamism, whose sojourn in the "pullulating hell-house" of Greeley, Colorado, in the late 1940s somehow radicalized him. (Noting the "drunken, semi-naked woman" Qutb claimed to have once run into on an America-bound ocean liner, Amis writes, "It seems probable that the liquored-up Mata Hari, the dipsomaniacal nudist, was simply a woman in a cocktail dress who, perhaps, had recently had a cocktail.") Amis's goal here is only partly ridicule. It's also an attempt to understand how a parochial Egyptian came to provide an entire movement with its philosophical rationale for mass murder. Amis's Qutb, in his sentimentality, unexamined contradictions, and cross-eyed rectitude, seems an almost familiar character—as if Keith Talent, antihero of *London Fields* (1989), had settled upon not darts and statutory rape but rather memorizing suras as his life's work.

Other portions of the essay are less compelling, as when Amis writes, "Like fundamentalist Judaism and medieval Christianity, Islam is totalist. That is to say, it makes a total claim on the individual." For a writer whose interest in Islam was discreet prior to the fall of 2001, Amis discusses its essences with surprising comfort, and it should be said that after the original version of "Terror and Boredom" appeared, the Amis effigies began to snap, crackle, and pop. The most devastating critique came from Pankaj Mishra, who noted that, despite his essay's length, Amis described only one direct personal experience with a Muslim. As for the attempt to link radical Islam to more familiar historical terrors ("the influence of Hitler and Stalin"), Mishra allowed that such cogitation satisfied "the nostalgic desire of some sedentary writers to see themselves in the avant-garde of a noble crusade against an evil 'ism,'" but did not at all "deepen our understanding of the diverse nature of Muslim societies or of the schisms and contradictions within those we call radical Islam."

Anyone who has used the phrase "Islamofascism" (I have)

knows the bluff Pankaj Mishra called, and any traveler who has been treated with kindness and respect by Muslims with alarming core beliefs (I have) recognizes that the totalist fanaticism Martin Amis describes does justice to precious few actual human beings.

Although Mishra obliterated the arch of Amis's argument, much of its foundation remains. His description of radical Islam as "a massive agglutination of stock response, of clichés, of inherited and unexamined formulations" is memorably put and indisputably correct, and his frustration that adherents of only one faith can be driven to violent fulmination by the cruelties of Scandinavian cartooning is difficult to counter.

Thankfully, no particular expertise is required to point out hypocrisy or mock papier-mâché pieties, and Amis does both as well as or better than anyone. (He has also written the single funniest observation ever made about Osama bin Laden: "I found myself frivolously wondering whether Osama was just the product . . . of his birth order. Seventeenth out of fifty-seven is a notoriously difficult slot to fill.")

"Geopolitics may not be my natural subject," Amis acknowledges, "but masculinity is." Here's where those in recent opposition to him have erred. They're right to question his belief (made clear in the imagined, and very nearly unforgivable, speech Amis provides the American *talib*, John Walker Lindh, on the eve of September 11, 2001) that the appeasement-prone leftists of the West can only collapse against the tides of Islam. The right-wing motives attributed to Amis, however, are wrong. He not only foresaw that the American response to September 11 was "almost sure to become elephantine"; he laments and condemns the "moral crash" of America's embrace of interrogatory torture and regards the Iraq War as a "fatal forfeiture of legitimacy." These are not the handholds of a man listing rightward.

"I'm a passionate multiracialist," Amis recently told *The*

New York Times, "and a very poor multiculturalist." Yet this self-assessment makes the same mistake his critics make. A very poor multiculturalist would never think to step behind Islamist eyes, yet Amis does this throughout *The Second Plane*, not only with Sayyid Qutb but also with some young Pakistanis he pauses to contemplate while they're preparing to assault his friend Christopher Hitchens. But it's in "The Last Days of Mohammed Atta," one of *The Second Plane*'s two short stories (the other being "In the Palace of the End," a fussy performance piece), that he attempts his most radical feat of transference.

Let us set aside whether "The Last Days of Mohammed Atta" is a successful piece of fiction, with the codicillary recognition that its title alone ensures its need to be something beyond well written. Let us instead soberly weigh the ramifications of what he has attempted. First, who is Martin Amis's Mohammed Atta? We learn that he "wasn't like the others," has no particular religiosity, and enjoys no human capacity for love. This Atta has "allied himself with the militants because jihad was, by many magnitudes, the most charismatic idea of his generation." A few of these biographical liberties fly in the face of *The 9/11 Commission Report*, but as the story unfolds one thing becomes clear: Despite Atta's vividly evoked constipation, he's no cartoon, no Arab remix of one of the joyless nihilists from Amis's early novel *Dead Babies*. The mind of this Mohammed Atta is at once empty and full, dull and terrifying, familiar and extraterrestrial. It is, in other words, convincingly human.

When Amis imagines an early meeting between those responsible for the "Planes Operation," Atta suggests attacking a nuclear power plant, thereby irradiating the American East Coast for seventy thousand years. But Atta's minder, Khalid Sheikh Mohammed, demurs. "The Sheikh gave his reasons (restricted airspace, no 'symbolic value'). But Mohammed Atta sensed a moral qualm, a silent suggestion that such a move could be considered exorbitant." A considerable expenditure of imagination is necessary to believably distinguish the probity of Mohammed Atta from that of Khalid Sheikh Mohammed, much less to provide a psychic window into Atta as he worries over how he will feel when he saws through the windpipe of a nearby flight attendant. When, in the story's final paragraphs, Amis writes of Atta bearing down on Queens and feeling "glad that he wouldn't have to plow down into the city, and he even felt love for it, all its strivings and couplings and sunderings," it's easy to forget, as the North Tower grows closer, that Amis has accomplished an act of audacious authorial empathy— one unimaginable to any self-respecting Islamophobe.

Beyond writing about it, Amis has no use for Islamism—and even less use, it occasionally seems, for those who live in anything short of apocalyptic fear of it. But consider the recent performance of the Islamists themselves. Give them a full-blown occupation and they're capable of the usual guerrilla brilliances. Provide them with the canvas of an open society and their operational élan grows less apparent, as do (in what is surely no coincidence) their grievances. The ballet of airborne horror on September 11, 2001, is the exception. The graceless imbecile Richard Reid trying to set his shoe on fire is closer to the rule. Meanwhile Osama bin Laden's chillingly tranquil smile is indicative of nothing more than his brain's comprehensive absence of interesting ideas. His lone contribution to his movement, as Amis points out, is image. There's nothing to sustain a movement built on the back of suicides *but* image, and the more global significance pumped into Islamism, the more besieged it appears, and the more notionally attractive to the disaffected it becomes.

We, of course, are vulnerable to the same perceptions: Hundreds of thousands of Americans volunteered for military service in the months following the WTC attacks; today virtually no branch can meet its recruiting goals. It's no fun, apparently, being the bully. Martin Amis is no bully, but how strange that the utterly unnecessary polarization of the past eight years has opened him up to such an accusation, and how sad that he can regard his position on Islamism as being either lonely or brave.

—2008

GREAT AND
TERRIBLE TRUTHS

David Foster Wallace

I n the autumn of 2005, an email with the unpromising subject
header of "Thought you'd like this!!!" landed in my inbox.
The sender, a family friend, was an incurable forwarder of
two-year-old John Kerry jokes, alerts for nonexistent computer
viruses, and poetry about strangers who turn out to be Jesus. This
latest offering contained not the expected link to a YouTube video
of yawning kittens but several dozen paragraphs of unsigned, cha-
otically formatted text. It bore this title: "Transcription of the
2005 Kenyon Commencement Address—May 21, 2005." Before
I had reached the end of the first paragraph I believed I could
identify the author. A quick search verified it: the commencement speaker for Kenyon College's graduating class of 2005 was,
indeed, David Foster Wallace.

The novelist Richard Ford spoke at my college graduation; thirteen years later, I can recall precisely nothing of what
he said. Which does not mean it was bad. The commencement

address—not quite an essay, more intimate than a speech—is a highly particular literary form. It is also a uniquely disposable one. Imagine you have written the greatest commencement address in history. What do you do with it, once it has been delivered? The answer: nothing. I wrote a rather nice one a few years ago for the graduating class of my hometown community college. Would anyone like to read it? I suspected as much. When the graduation caps are thrown into the air, the commencement address's only obvious utility is jettisoned along with them.

Wallace's address managed to avoid this fate not because it was great (though it was). The address was saved, rather, thanks to the enterprising soul who transcribed it from video and posted it on the Internet, where, somehow, it came to the attention of my family friend—a woman who would not have known David Foster Wallace if he fell on her. Thanks to the enthusiasm of people like her, and the magic of the cut-and-paste function, the address became a small sensation and must now rank high among the most widely read things Wallace ever wrote.

Wallace was often accused, even by his admirers, of having a fatal weakness for what Nabokov once referred to as "the doubtful splendors of virtuosity." Standing before the graduates of Kenyon College, Wallace opted for a tonal simplicity only occasionally evident in the hedge mazes of his fiction. He spoke about the difficulty of empathy ("Think about it: There is no experience you've had that you were not the absolute center of"), the importance of being well adjusted ("which I suggest to you is not an accidental term"), and the essential lonesomeness of adult life ("lords of our tiny skull-sized kingdoms, alone at the center of all creation"). Truthful, funny, and unflaggingly warm, the address was obviously the work of a wise and very kind man. At the edges, though, there was something else—the faint but unmistakable sense that Wallace had passed through considerable darkness, some of which still clung to him, but here he was, today, having beaten it, having made it through.

I knew Dave Wallace well enough to have responded to the news of his September 2008 suicide with overwhelming grief, though I did not know him nearly well enough to have had any knowledge of his decades of depression. In my shock I sought refuge in the only oasis I could find: his work. While I knew no answers would be found there, I hoped that rereading Wallace would provide some vague, analgesic insight into his (then) unfathomable decision. Many others were doing the same, and a number of commentators pointed to a passage in Wallace's Kenyon College commencement speech, where he discusses "the old tired cliché about the mind being 'an excellent servant and a terrible master.'" Wallace goes on to say, "It is not the least bit coincidental that adults who commit suicide with firearms almost always shoot themselves in the head. They shoot the terrible master."

"Transcription of the 2005 Kenyon Commencement Address— May 21, 2005" now has a proper title, *This Is Water,* and a colophon belonging to Little, Brown, Wallace's longtime publisher. In it, part of the above passage has been gently removed, and it is not difficult to understand why. Any mention of self-annihilation in Wallace's work (and there are many: the patriarch of *Infinite Jest* is a suicide; Wallace's story "Good Old Neon" is narrated by a suicide) now has a blast radius that obscures everything around it. These are craters that cannot be filled. The glory of the work and the tragedy of the life are relations but not friends, informants but not intimates. Exult in one; weep for the other.

Over the last six months, at least, this is what I have been telling myself. For all the obvious extraliterary reasons, *This Is Water* is often an extremely painful reading experience, and in this opinion

I cannot imagine I will be alone. When Wallace defines thinking as "learning how to exercise some control over how and *what* you think," when he describes his own mental "default setting" as one of selfishness and solipsism and despair and then explains that part of being an adult is developing the discipline "to care about other people and sacrifice for them, over and over," and when he suggests that the "capital-T Truth" of life "is about making it to thirty, or maybe even fifty, without wanting to shoot yourself in the head," his intended audience of college graduates floats away and the haunting, answerless questions crowd suffocatingly in. To whom, you wonder, was he really speaking?

While some may question the decision to publish Wallace's address as a book—and its interior design of one sentence per page is not much of a rebuttal to that question—it would take a small, charred heart to find any impure motives here. Future readers of *This Is Water* will have less trouble reconciling what it says with what its author ultimately did, and they, I think, are the audience this book is meant for.

The terrible master eventually defeated David Foster Wallace, which makes it easy to forget that none of the cloudlessly sane and true things he had to say about life in 2005 are any less sane or true today, however tragic the truth now seems. *This Is Water* does nothing to lessen the pain of Wallace's defeat. What it does is remind us of his strength and goodness and decency—the parts of him the terrible master could never defeat, and never will.

—2009

CINEMA CRUDITÉ

On a bathwater-warm night in Portland, Oregon, several hundred people waited outside Cinema 21 to see a six-year-old film that was widely available on DVD. Nearly everyone here had seen the film at least once, and some had seen it twenty times. It was around 10:00 p.m.; show time was not for another hour. I walked up and down the line, gravitating toward anyone who seemed particularly displaced or puzzled. One young woman was staring fixedly into space, her grinning boyfriend beside her. When I asked what brought her out, she thumbed toward the boyfriend. "It's *so* poorly made," he said, exultantly.

A large shaggy kid in a black leather jacket walked by with a handheld camera—an aspiring journalist, it turned out. He wanted to document tonight's premiere; he hoped that, as soon as tomorrow night, his movie would be up on YouTube, where it would join many other, similarly homegrown opening-night chronicles. "This is *amazing*!" the aspiring journalist said, as people recounted for him their favorite lines from the film: "Leave your stupid comments in your pocket!" "I feel like I'm sitting on an atomic bomb waiting for it to go off!" "You are tearing me apart, Lisa!"

A man wearing a tuxedo-print T-shirt and in the obvious employ of the theater began to work the line, dispensing rubber-banded bouquets of plastic spoons. Soon, all along the line, the spoons were clicking like castanets in the hands of the impatient crowd.

By 11:15 I was in my seat. The film itself, meanwhile, was in no danger of starting. After a while, the young man in the tuxedo-print T-shirt bounded to the front of the theater and climbed onto the stage. He introduced himself as Ian and told us that he "got on his hands and knees to get this movie here." He urged us to keep in mind while watching the film that its director, one Tommy Wiseau, submitted it for consideration to the Academy Awards in 2003. Ian reminded us of the spoons he had handed out and specified when we were supposed to throw them at the screen. "Don't blow your wad on spoons all at once," he said. "You'll have plenty of chances." Finally, he warned those who had not yet seen tonight's film that the first twenty minutes "are kind of . . . unusual. This movie doesn't work in the way other movies work. Or in the way reality works. You have to acclimate to it." With a carnival barker flourish, Ian raised his hands as the curtains behind him parted. The WISEAU FILMS logo appeared onscreen to a volley of spoons. The opening bars of the film's tasteful, insipid piano-and-bassoon soundtrack resulted in the first of several standing ovations. Following that, potted shots of San Francisco's Golden Gate, Alcatraz, the Bay, a trolley car—all filmed at defiantly diverse times of day. The equally unrecognizable names of the cast and crew cycled by to various levels of applause. The last name to appear was that of Tommy Wiseau. The first character to appear was played by Tommy Wiseau. His first line in the film ("Hi, babe!") is a tiny miracle of inorganic delivery, but no one that night could hear it: half of the audience was still chanting his name.

When *The Room* was released in 2003, it was marketed as a drama with the searing intensity of "Tennesee [*sic*] Williams." Independently produced movies that lack the garlands of film-festival approval are rarely marketed at all, but *The Room* came backed by a multidisciplinary campaign: television and print ads, a making-of companion book, and a gaudy Los Angeles premiere to which Tommy Wiseau—the film's director, writer, star, producer, executive producer, and distributor—pulled up in a rented limousine. At some of *The Room*'s first screenings, half of *The Room*'s first audience walked out after twenty minutes; the other half, according to one witness, was paralyzed by laughter. Its two-week take cashed out at a reported $1,900. At that rate, in order to earn a return on Wiseau's $6 million investment in the film, *The Room* would have had to play for another twelve decades.

The artist gambles, the art emerges, both withdraw in disgrace. A shapely, sad, familiar story—and it should have ended there. But among *The Room*'s costlier marketing ploys was a billboard, on which, looming over L.A.'s Highland Avenue, could be seen a one-story-tall reproduction of Wiseau's strikingly asymmetrical face, which resembled nothing so much as the mug shot of a man arrested for solicitation after a sixty-hour meth bender. Despite *The Room*'s disastrous first run, Wiseau paid to keep the billboard up for one year, then two, three, four. By the time it was taken down in 2008, the billboard had turned into one of those odd, Brown Derby-ish landmarks in which Los Angeles specializes. (Wiseau, who is known to bat away all questions regarding his personal life, has never revealed how much the billboard set him back, but he has said, "Let's put it this way: It cost a lot of money. You can buy a brand-new car. Maybe two." The average monthly rate for Hollywood-area billboard rental is around $5,000.)

Thanks to the billboard, and Wiseau's efforts to convince one Los Angeles theater to offer monthly viewings of *The Room*, word of the film, and its mysterio creator, slowly got around. By 2006, *The Room* was a cult hit in Los Angeles. Today the film is playing as a midnight movie in two dozen cities around the country; it recently opened in Toronto and London, and screenings are being planned in Scotland and New Zealand.

Wiseau, meanwhile, has been forced into a peculiar marketing position. The serious drama heralded by *The Room's* original campaign was now being called by its director a "quirky new black comedy." The marketing copy branded on the film's DVD case typifies this doublethink. "Can You Really Trust Anyone?" the first, sober tagline reads. Just below it: "It's a Riot!"

A disinterested plot summary of *The Room* might go as follows: A kindhearted San Francisco banker named Johnny is caught in a love triangle with his fiancée, Lisa, and his best friend, Mark. Among those pulled into the orbit of the affair are Denny, Johnny's quasi-adopted ward; Claudette, Lisa's stingily calculating mother; and Peter, Johnny's psychologist friend. Although *The Room* opens with Johnny arriving home to a tableau of seeming domestic bliss, we soon learn that, because Johnny is so "boring," Lisa no longer loves him. Shortly thereafter, Lisa seduces Mark, who at first cavils ("Johnny is my best friend") but quickly caves. The remainder of the story is a somewhat inert game of cat and mouse: Lisa gets Johnny drunk on a peculiar mixture of vodka and whiskey (which *Room* fans have christened the Scotchka) in order to accuse him of hitting her; Johnny overhears Lisa admit she is having an affair, after which he begins taping her phone calls; Lisa throws a disastrous surprise birthday party for Johnny in which her sundry deceptions are exposed, after which Johnny busts up their condo, somehow finds a gun, and exacts his revenge.

"So bad it's good" is the prevailing wisdom on why *The Room* has become such a phenomenon. In this view, *The Room* stands ineptly beside other modern paragons—*Showgirls*, *Roadhouse*—of the midnight movie. The first time you see *The Room*, there seems little in this position to quarrel with. Wiseau's osmium-dense, east-of-the-Carpathians accent, for example, which falls somewhere between early Schwarzenegger and Vlad Dracul, makes for an incomprehensible leading man. The dialogue, meanwhile, is interplanetarily bizarre. At one point, Lisa proclaims to Mark, "I'm gonna do what I wanna do, and that's it." Pause. "What do you think I should do?" At another point, Johnny walks out onto his apartment building's rooftop in a state of savage agitation, having just learned that Lisa has accused him of hitting her. "It's not true!" he says to himself, throwing aside his water bottle. "I did not hit her! It's bullshit! I did not hit her! I did *not!*" He then notices Mark sitting off screen. "Oh, hi, Mark," Johnny says pleasantly, having a seat beside him. "What's new with you?" Mark proceeds to tell Johnny a horrible story of a woman who was beaten and hospitalized by her cuckolded boyfriend. In response, Johnny laughs with ghoulish warmth. Later, when Mark presses Johnny for some business information, Johnny lectures him that such information is confidential and, without missing a beat, asks, "Anyway, how is your sex life?"

This is not a frivolous question: *The Room*'s characters enjoy hearty coital appetites. Altogether the film's quartet of sex scenes takes up almost 10 percent of its total running time. The first and longest such scene, between Johnny and Lisa, unforgettably occurs five minutes into the film. Much of it is shot through diaphanous white bed curtains and what appears to be a hotel-lobby water sculpture. Whereas the rose petals Johnny picks up and decoratively drops onto Lisa's breasts and the adult-contemporary R&B soundtrack both come straight from the *école du* Cinemax, the vision of Johnny's strangely mispositioned alabaster behind pistoning up and down upon what appears to be Lisa's navel has no cinematic precedent.

Technically speaking, *The Room* is a difficult film to extol. Wiseau takes pride in the fact that *The Room* was filmed simultaneously with two cameras, one a standard 35-mm and the other hi-def. Wiseau's most mystifying decision was to shoot *The Room*'s several rooftop vignettes against a panoramic green screen, against which a shimmering digital vista of the San Francisco skyline was later badly composited. Wiseau's unbudgeable insistence* on filming *The Room* with two cameras and preference for expensive technology that could have easily been done without are triple-play rarities in modern filmmaking: at once financially improvident, visually unsatisfying, and definitively unnecessary.

The Room's narrative strategies, meanwhile, amount to one kamikaze after another. In one scene, Lisa's mother, Claudette, offhandedly mentions that she has just received some upsetting medical-test results. "I definitely have breast cancer," she tells her daughter, with an annoyed little shudder. The dramatic impact of Claudette's cancer revelation, which is never mentioned again, is nicely captured by the scene's DVD chapter title: "Claudette and Lisa/Cancer." Late in the film, during Johnny's surprise party, Lisa is confronted by an agonized, furious man who has just caught her canoodling with Mark. This man expresses his disgust for

---

* In a victory-lap interview filmed for *The Room*'s DVD release, we find Wiseau's disarmingly frank explanation for why he chose to shoot his film with two cameras: "Because at the time I did not have sufficient information and was confused about these two formats."

Lisa's behavior and speaks of his fear that what she is doing to Johnny will destroy their friendship. We have never met this man. We have no idea who he is, why he is worried, how he knows Johnny or Lisa, or what he is doing at the party.

The centerpiece of *The Room* is a scene involving a character with the typographically striking name of Chris-R. A goateed thug and drug dealer, Chris-R finds Johnny's ward, Denny, dribbling a basketball on the green-screen-corseted rooftop. After a brief argument, Chris-R pulls a large silver handgun on Denny and holds it to his head. Johnny and Mark appear, intervene, and hustle Chris-R off camera. With that, Claudette and Lisa somehow materialize, and Lisa and Denny proceed to have this escalatingly hysterical exchange:

> Denny: I owe him some money.
> Lisa: What kind of money?
> Denny: I owe him some money.
> Lisa: What *kind* of money?
> Denny: I bought some drug off of him.
> Lisa: What *kind* of drugs, Denny?
> Denny: It doesn't matter! I don't have them
> anymore!
> Lisa: WHAT KIND OF DRUGS DO YOU TAKE?

Denny's explanation for this worrisome turn of events is a logic sinkhole. As he explains to Lisa, he needs to "pay off" some debts. Which suggests that he was buying the drugs to sell them. Why, then, if he has already bought the drugs, does he owe Chris-R money? Is Chris-R running some kind of drug layaway program? Why does Lisa appear to believe there are different kinds of money? None of these questions get answered, or even addressed, because the matter of Denny's drug buying or drug abuse (or whatever it is) immediately joins Claudette's breast cancer in the foggy narrative beyond.

I have not mentioned the fact that *The Room*'s male characters frequently play football while standing three feet apart from one another, sometimes while wearing tuxedoes; or that one character, for no detectable reason, collapses in pain in the middle of an otherwise procedurally sane scene; or that Johnny and Lisa have around their apartment several enigmatically framed portraits of spoons.*

By now I have seen *The Room* at least twenty times. I know I will watch it again soon. I am probably watching it right now. "Bad" and "good" are incapable of capturing how I feel about *The Room*. Sometimes I think about Wiseau's thespian-berserker charisma. Other times I think, Why football? Why a rooftop? Why a drug dealer? Mostly I think about how everything that captures Wiseau's directorial interest flies straight into the lessons-learned headwinds generated by a century of filmmaking.

A collaborative medium such as film is structurally designed to thwart people like Tommy Wiseau—and, indeed, during *The Room*'s production, Wiseau fired the entire crew four times over. Yet anyone with the know-how, perseverance, and fanaticism to not only conceive but write, cast, direct, produce, and distribute a film *should* be versed in the prevailing aesthetics of his time, if only to reject or subvert them. Wiseau tried to make a conventional film and wound up with something so inexplicable and casually surreal that no practicing surrealist could ever convincingly ape its form, except by exact imitation. It is the movie an alien who has never seen a movie might make after having had movies thoroughly explained to him.

As you watch and rewatch *The Room*, categories melt away: Is

---

* This has resulted in the film's central ritual of audience participation: whenever the framed spoons appear, anyone holding must throw their own plastic spoons at the screen.

this a drama? Comedy? Joke? None of them? All of them? Every filmmaking convention across which it stumbles is sundered. Take the convention of the exterior establishing shot. According to the grammar of film, such a shot is used to indicate the passage of time and a spatial relocation to another site within the film's world. That is not how things work in *The Room*. At one point, we are at Johnny's birthday party. Wiseau cuts away to an exterior establishing shot of what appears to be an office building. The viewer assumes—no, *believes*, given how thoroughly films have trained us—that the next shot will take us inside that office building. The next shot shows us that we are still at the party.

Wiseau understands the placement and required tone of certain conventions but not at all their underlying meaning. What makes him interesting is the degree to which his art becomes a funhouse-mirror version, an inadvertent exposé, of a traditional film. He shows, however accidentally, that the devices and conventions we have learned to respond to do not necessarily solve or even *do* anything. More than any artist I can think of, Wiseau proves Northrop Frye's belief that all conventions are, at heart, insane. Or, as I overheard someone say as I left Cinema 21, "Maybe this is what originality looks like now."

What does it say about contemporary American culture that the *Rocky Horror Picture Show* of our time is not a likable exercise in leering camp and butt-shaking grooviness but a brain-stabbingly earnest melodrama distinguished by what it is unable to provide? Why are so many people responding to this megalomaniacal feat of formal incompetence? Is it the satisfaction of seeing the auteur myth cruelly exploded, of watching an artist reach for the stars and wind up with his hand around a urinal cake? Some viewers clearly relish this aspect of *The Room*, but others come away from the film strangely exhilarated. In an entertainment culture in which everything from quiet domestic dramas to battling-robot fantasias is target-audienced with laserlike precision, *The Room* is as bereft of familiar taxonomy as a bat from Mars. In an entertainment culture in which bad and good movies alike have learned to wink knowingly at their audiences, *The Room* is rivetingly unaware of itself or its effect. In an entertainment culture in which "independent filmmaking" is more of a calculated stance than accurate accounting of means, *The Room* is a film of glorious, horrifying independence.

Tommy Wiseau is not, in any sense, an easy interview. I got in touch with him through his website, after which a man named John, the "administrator" of Wiseau Films, requested that I write up all the questions I intended to ask Wiseau during our interview. I emailed back a long and, I hoped, thoughtful email explaining why I did not work that way and why I preferred to meet and simply have a conversation. Unmoved, John, whose bludgeoned English ("Does your peace is for print or/and on line viewing?") bore a telling resemblance to that of one T. Wiseau, emailed back a request to submit my interview questions beforehand. I made another, equally thoughtful argument as to why I did not want to do that. John responded with another, identical request to submit my interview questions. So I did. A few days later I was apprised of the time and place where Wiseau and I would meet.

Although the address John gave me turned out to be wrong, I managed to find the appointed Beverly Hills delicatessen. Wiseau, riding shotgun and exactly on time, pulled up to the deli in a silver SUV, a THEROOMMOVIE.COM decal on the rear passenger-side window.

His flyaway hair looked as though it had been soaked in printer ink and I had not seen skin so pale outside of Edmonton, Alberta, in February. His lips were nearly colorless, his jaw as large and square as a shovel. He was wearing a heavy green jacket that looked too warm for Los Angeles in September, dun-colored cargo pants with a complicatedly studded belt, and combat boots. The overall effect was that of a vampire who had joined the Merchant Marine. Wiseau took off his jacket once we sat down, revealing a black tank top identical to one Johnny dons briefly in *The Room*. Wiseau had been in anatomy-model shape at the time of *The Room*'s filming; he remained so today.

One of my first questions concerned the mysterious John. I asked Wiseau if he was "a young Hollywood-assistant-type."

"You may say that," Wiseau said. "He's doing . . . freelance. He has limited hours." He laughed, all but admitting the ruse.

After some initial chitchat, I asked Wiseau if he had any friends he could put me in touch with. Someone, I said, who could help me fill out the personal side of Tommy Wiseau.

"I have dozens of friends," Wiseau said. "But this is your job. It's not my job to suggest."

"But I don't know your friends."

"I'm not here to say, 'Talk to this person about me.' That's nonsense."

This was, I told Wiseau, fairly standard procedure.

"I'm against that. You know, this is your . . . you're a journalist."

"But I'm not a private investigator."

"You don't need to be a private investigator. You can go to screening, you can talk to many people about *The Room*, about me, whatever." He shrugged. "You can go in so many different angles, if you ask me."

By this Wiseau meant one angle, as he refuses to answer any questions about his personal life. Nevertheless, I made a few anemic lunges. The intensity of the scorn the film heaps upon Lisa—and, it must be said, women in general—has led many to assume that *The Room* is Wiseau's revenge upon a former lover.

When I asked about this, Wiseau replied with the same answer he had given many journalists—that *The Room* is a perfect mirror of human experience and that in everyone's life there are many Lisas and Johnnys and Dennys, etc.—but he did claim that he used to be married and had once lived in San Francisco. That was as deep as he was willing to let me go.

"I speak French," he said. "I speak, you know, another language, and English, and I understand some other languages." This "another language" was, no doubt, that of his native country, which I pressed him to reveal. When he refused I began throwing out former Communist bloc states. Romania? Hungary? "Wrong, actually," he said, laughing once again. He did admit, or seem to admit, that his homeland was "a few countries," which led me to guess he was from the former Yugoslavia. "I'm an American," he said, "and I want to be treated as an American. Bottom line. You may say whatever you want. I think we are entitled to our privacy in America."

America is among Wiseau's major talking points: "We are Americans," he told me, "and we cherish our freedom." Americanness is also the central, and centrally unexamined, theme of *The Room*. Wiseau cast himself within the film as a hunk of Johnny Americana, with no corresponding recognition of how absurdly ill fitting this role actually is. Whenever the film's Johnny throws a football, you do not see Johnny. What you see is the ungainly shot put of an eastern European who did not grow up throwing footballs. This is the most longingly human aspect of *The Room* and, not at all coincidentally, the hardest thing to laugh at.*

The two most-asked questions about Wiseau concern his age and the origin of the personal fortune he used to fund *The*

---

* In one scene, Lisa orders Johnny a pizza with his favorite toppings: half Canadian bacon with pineapple, half artichoke with pesto, and "light on the cheese." As Wiseau later explained, there is a binary symbolism at work here: one, Wiseau likes pizza; two, the exotic toppings represent the freedoms all Americans enjoy.

Room. As to the first, his Wikipedia page lists his age as forty-one, though he looks as though he is in his early fifties. "I am thirty-something," Wiseau told me. As to the source of his money, one uncorroborated story has to do with Wiseau's vaguely sinister-sounding involvement in some sort of Asian-market clothing-import concern—Chinese jeans, possibly? According to Wiseau, his involvement in imported garments was straightforward and artisanal: "I used to design jackets, leather jackets, a long time ago. I've been designing, selling, whatever."

Whereas the precise truth about Wiseau's past is never going to be as interesting as the rumors (my second favorite: Wiseau is an erstwhile Serbian warlord; my favorite: Wiseau is a cyborg from the future), his evasiveness bizarrely extends into the most mundane matters, as when I asked him about whether he had made contact with any of his celebrity fans, which include Paul Rudd, David Wain, Jonah Hill, David Cross, and other members of the Hollywood humorati. Wiseau's answer: "If I say I met a big director, I'm not dropping any names—I've met everybody, for your information—so if I met, let's say, one of the big directors, who's from New York, just to give you a clue. He has a business in Santa Barbara. You see, you can assume who is the person, because there's only one."

I had no idea who or what he was talking about. But surely, I said, there were actors, directors, or writers he drew particular inspiration from?

"Again," he said, "I don't want to drop the names. Because you'll be blogging about it." All I eventually wrung from Wiseau was that he admired the work of Tennessee Williams, Orson Welles, Elizabeth Taylor, and James Dean, and that he had recently seen *Twilight* and was seeking investors in a vampire film he wanted to shoot in Austin, Texas. At this news, I confess, I restrained myself from writing a check payable to Wiseau Films then and there.

*   *   *

The critic Robert Hughes once said, "The greater the artist, the greater the doubt. Perfect confidence is granted to the less talented as a consolation prize." I thought about this maxim more than once during my lunch with Wiseau. When he talks about his work, the explanations range from more or less normal ("*The Room* was done to provoke the audience. That's the bottom line") to puzzling ("And you see, in entertainment, we have such a limited presentation. You have comedy, you have drama, you have melodrama, and that's about it, basically"), to incomprehensible ("You see, black comedy is related to melodrama, leans toward melodrama, but it's not melodrama. That's the difference. So it's realism, if you really think about it. Melodrama is not real"), but they are always Jesuitically certain. I tried, several times, to formulate a humane way of asking Wiseau how he felt to be locked out of all artistic time and space, but he could not answer because he, of course, fails to see it that way. The things I wanted to know about *The Room* could never be addressed by Wiseau, the Intentional Fallacy made flesh. *The Room*, as a work of art, must remain a mystery—at least to its creator, who not only views *The Room* as mainstream entertainment but himself as a potential diamond mine for future mainstream entertainment, constantly letting it be known that he is "open for any projects."*

Wiseau, who by his own admission is as demanding and finicky as Samuel Beckett, told me in one breath that he is prone to firing anyone who deviates from his vision ("I deal with it in a very simple way. I say, 'You see the door there? Go through the door and don't come back'"), and in the next said, "If the studio

---

* Wiseau has, in fact, made one non-bizarre film. This is *Homeless in America*, a somewhat naive but rather touching 30-minute-long documentary of which Wiseau is justifiably proud.

decided to hire me, for example, I will say, 'Sure, tell me what to do. I'm ready.'" When I said I imagined he would have a hard time working within traditional studio confinements, Wiseau disagreed. "I can make millions," he said. This hard-nosed and eccentric control freak is also a craven sellout. The contradictory tension between these selves would surely drive mad anyone who was aware of them. I believe that Wiseau could make a studio film. Or at least I believe that he believes he could, and I am probably not alone among Wiseau's fans when I say I would happily watch anything he commits to film—other than that.

When I asked Wiseau about his fan base, he said, "Talking to the fans is fun. I'm thrilled by it. I really enjoy it." Hundreds if not thousands of people around the country have worked to get *The Room* into theaters and promoted it on their own time. Did Wiseau have intense feelings of gratitude and connection to those people? "Oh, yeah," he said, leaning back. "Absolutely." He mulled over this for a moment. "That's a pretty interesting statement, what you're saying right now. That's correct. People want to be involved with promoting *The Room*, for some reason. For nothing, basically."

"And that's weird," I said. "Isn't it?"

"It is, but I'm very happy with that."

As to the discordant matter of negative reviews, Wiseau attributed all such reactions to *The Room* to "tripping" critics and reporters, none of whom "understand that, by design, any movie has to entertain people. . . . They think they hurt me because they say something negative. No, they hurt themselves because they're not true to the audience." For the first time during our talk, Wiseau became agitated. "This is what I'm furious about," he said. "The people writing, they don't know anything about acting. They don't understand the concept that entertainment is something that you take from yourself and give to people, and let people decide what they want to do. And there's nothing wrong when people say, 'Oh, yeah, I don't like your movie, but I like this little shot.' Or, 'Oh, you have a heavy accent.' But you have people who actually go the extra mile and say, 'I hate it.'" He shook his head. "Why do you write about it if you hate something? Why spend so much time? Because you're not honest with yourself. Because, no, you're not hating. It's because I, as a director, opened certain doors for you, and you don't want to be there. *That's* why."

Wiseau's contention that his critics do not want to be in the room to which *The Room* leads is correct, but, in a perfectly Wiseauian move, correct for reasons he does not and probably cannot recognize. We are all of us deeply alarmed by the Wiseauian parts of ourselves, the parts of us that are selfish and controlling, that crave attention at any cost, that imagine ourselves as superlatively gifted, that arrange all sources of light—whether literal or metaphysical—to be flattering. To watch *The Room* is to see that part of ourselves turned mesmerizingly loose. During lunch, he was heroically without shame as he described his plans to turn *The Room* into a Broadway show ("It will be musical. People say it's comedy, but I don't care what they want to say"), a cartoon ("based on the same characters—however, they will be approached for kids"), and a video game ("You can be Johnny, you can be Lisa, you can do whatever you want to do . . . like play football, for example"). He then startled me by saying, "My idea has always been that I want ninety percent of Americans to see *The Room*. That's the idea I have."

I looked at him. "Ninety percent?" I asked, if only to make sure he did not say "nine percent."

"Ninety percent. Absolutely."

At this I all but laughed in his face. "Good luck."

"Because ten percent, you see, it's the kids, and it's R-rated, and they're not supposed to see it."

"You want every adult to see it?"

"I think so, yes. That's the goal."

"I don't think everyone has even seen *Snow White*."

"I'm not concerned with other movies. I'm concerned only about *The Room* at this time. If that's your analogy, that's fine with me. But, yes, absolutely, we will eventually beat *Snow White*."

"Bigger than *Snow White*!"

He grew preposterously thoughtful. "It's not a question of bigger. Every American should see *The Room*."

"You realize," I said, "how ridiculous that sounds."

"No," he said, "it's not at all."

A month after our meeting, I attended a midnight Halloween screening of *The Room* in Los Angeles, to which Wiseau showed up in a state of inebriation somewhere between Richard Yates drunk and Keith Richards stoned. He delivered an impenetrable speech to the several hundred people waiting in line, attempted to return to the safe confines of the Laemmie Sunset 5 Theater, found that he had been locked out, made the best of it, threw off his jacket, and proceeded to play football with a few audience members. At one point he launched an impressively long bomb that hit a young woman in the face. (Several of her friends assured her that this was, in its way, an honor.) During the pre-screening Q&A, he seemed particularly angry and defensive about a recent *Los Angeles Times* profile of him, and lashed out at one audience member who asked him to recite one of Shakespeare's sonnets, which Wiseau has previously been happy to do. He abruptly ended the Q&A when he was asked for his views on health care reform. The whole ordeal was so crushingly sad that during the screening I barely laughed. At one point in the film, Johnny is sitting on the edge of his bed after Lisa has announced her intention to leave him. When Johnny says, in a childlike falsetto, "I haven't got a friend in the world," I confess to having felt a pre-lachrymal tickle in the back of my throat.

Whether Tommy Wiseau is evolved or stupid, brave or blind, his work makes me and thousands of others feel catastrophically alive. Whatever he tried to do, he clearly failed, and whatever he succeeded in doing has no obvious name. (Sincere surrealism? Sincerealism?) But The Room's last remaining ritual of audience participation might be for everyone to imagine seeing one's most deeply personal attempt at self-expression razed by a hurricane of laughter. Most of us, I think, would fare more poorly than Wiseau. That night in Los Angeles, he was as famous and well loved as he has ever been and nevertheless seemed like an unfortunate cultic animal we had all come together to stab at the stroke of midnight. We were laughing because we were not him, and because we were.

—2010

A SIMPLE MEDIUM

Chuck Lorre and the American Sitcom

S oundstage 24 on the Warner Bros. lot, in Burbank, California, is a sand-colored, pyramid-like hangar identical to the many stages that surround it, as though the pharaohs had developed an air force. Some time ago, Stage 24 was designated the "*Friends* Stage" in honor of the decade-long residency by Rachel, Phoebe, Joey, Chandler, Monica, and Ross, and their improbable Manhattan apartments. According to an engraved plaque near one of the entrances, *Blade Runner* was filmed there too, in 1981. So was the ABC sitcom *Full House*, which ran from 1987 to 1995. The ghosts of actors, directors, and audiences past linger in these curious structures, and, when a new show is assigned its stage, cast, crew, and visitors alike can sense them.

One afternoon in mid-August, the latest production to occupy the *Friends* Stage—*Mike and Molly*, a new CBS sitcom created by Mark Roberts and executive produced by Chuck Lorre—was having a network run-through. This is a weekly rehearsal attended by various studio and network executives and representatives from CBS's Standards and Practices department, and it takes place relatively early in the production process. The show's cast members were still carrying their scripts, which they had first seen three days earlier. The actors would finish a scene, hustle to the next set, finish a scene, hustle to the next set, all while being trailed by various supporting camera haulers and cable draggers. It looked a bit like speed-dating, but with a pit crew.

Watching the proceedings was Lorre, a fifty-eight-year-old man with a lean, bearded face and mussed, curly hair some stalemate shade between black and gray. He was wearing a soft-collared dark-green shirt, gray jeans, and blue-gray running shoes. On set, Lorre is unfailingly calm, but it is the intensely focused calm of, say, a model builder or a calligrapher. Lorre is the kind of person of whom one is always aware, even in a crowd, just as one is aware of the presence of fire, even if it is far away.

Mike and Molly is the sixth sitcom to go on the air that Lorre has produced, created, or cocreated. His two most recent shows, *Two and a Half Men* and *The Big Bang Theory*, are currently the number-one- and number-two-rated comedies in America, and have been for some time. Not since Norman Lear—who revolutionized the American sitcom in the seventies, with shows like *All in the Family*, and who, at one point, had seven hit shows on the air—has one man so dominated the genre. When *Big Bang* was picked up by CBS, in 2007, Lorre went to see Lear and asked the man whom he had long idolized, "How do you do more than one show at a time? How do you prioritize?" Lear warned Lorre he would probably not like what he was going to say. "His answer," Lorre told me, "was, basically, you run around like a madman."

Once a television show has become successful, most executive producers ascend to a cloudier level of day-to-day involvement. As Suzanne McCormack, Lorre's assistant, told me: "If his name is on it, he's involved." He runs the writing rooms of *Two and a Half Men* and *Big Bang* and is volubly present for every table read, network run-through, camera run-through, pre-shoot, live taping, and sound mixing for all three of his shows. The camera run-through, which takes place on the day an episode is filmed and serves as a final rehearsal, exemplifies Lorre's meticulousness. At this point in the process, Lorre sits in the soundstage section reserved for the live audience and watches the rehearsal through the studio monitors in order to ensure the quality of every shot. Many shows do not bother with a camera run-through; for someone in Lorre's position to take an active part in one is basically unheard of.

As one might expect, Lorre's daily agenda, which he refers to as "Chuck's Inferno," slots in five-minute pauses to pee, identifies potential nap opportunities, and issues a final, joking directive to GO HOME. Most shows, *Two and a Half Men* included, operate on a Monday-through-Friday schedule. The production schedules of *Big Bang* and *Mike and Molly*, however, are stacked and staggered through the week, which essentially creates a Lorre workweek made up of nothing but Mondays and Fridays. During the month of August he had only two days in which he was not tied up in some aspect of production.

When I asked Lorre how long he could expect to maintain such a pulverizing pace, he waved the question away. "There were a couple moments last week where I thought I was going to cry," he said, "but it's all going all right." Later in the day he would tell me, "Come back in six weeks and I might be on a catheter."

All of Lorre's shows are multi-camera sitcoms (also known as four-camera sitcoms). The genre is distinguished by a few core features, such as the obviousness with which they are staged, how heavily they favor the written over the improvisational, and the fact that most are taped before a live studio audience. This is in contrast to audience-less, location-shot, "one-camera" shows like *Arrested Development* or *30 Rock*. If single-camera sitcoms are effectively short films, the multi-camera sitcom is more like a short play, and it is the baseball of network television: old-fashioned, American, rule-bound, and deeply resistant to change. (*I Love Lucy* and *Everybody Loves Raymond* are, formally, about as different as their titles suggest.) The critically acclaimed sitcoms of the past half decade have tended to be single-camera shows with niche audiences (such as *Curb Your Enthusiasm* and *The Office*), and many television critics regard the multi-camera sitcom as a retrograde, even defunct, form. At the same time, mass audiences have been deserting comedy altogether for shows like *C.S.I.* and *American Idol*. Twenty years ago, eight of the ten top-rated television shows in America were multi-camera sitcoms. By 2006, only one was even in the top twenty: Lorre's *Two and a Half Men*.

The apparently unstoppable success of Lorre's multi-camera sitcoms in an inhospitable television climate seems mysterious, but Lorre's belief in the format is boundless. "It's a very intimate genre," he told me. "There's no music. There's no camera magic. There are no editing tricks. It's not a visual medium. It's about people and words."

Mike and Molly is about a police officer and grade school teacher who meet in the pilot and, in subsequent episodes, fall in love. The show's sets are familiar variations on the Midwest Proletariat *décor* of *Roseanne*: charmless diner, dreary bowling alley, knick-knack-infested living room. Less familiar was Roberts and Lorre's decision to cast as the show's leads Billy Gardell and Melissa McCarthy, two relatively unknown actors of a size rarely seen on television in leading roles. (It was Lorre's idea to have their first encounter take place in an Overeater's Anonymous meeting.) Soon after *Mike and Molly* was commissioned, people began calling it "that show about fat people." An excellent way to make Lorre mad is to mention this.

The network run-through had come to a crucial, mid-episode scene in which Mike takes Molly to a bowling alley, where he hopes to impress her with his skill. Mike's plan does not go well, and he ends up humiliated. Roberts had originally written the scene as taking place in a movie theater, where Molly displays a knowledge of film that intimidates Mike. Upon reading Roberts's script, Lorre said, "What if it's bowling?"

In Roberts's revised script, Molly rolls two strikes in a row, after which a now nervous Mike steps up to the lane, begins his elaborate pre-roll ritual, swings his arm back, and loses hold of his ball. Even though Mike's bowling ball was a squishy prop bowling ball and the sound effect used to simulate its crash landing was a shattering-glass cliché, Roberts, Lorre, and the episode's director, James Burrows, all burst out laughing. These men had seen thousands of sitcom rehearsals between them. Hearing them laugh at such easy slapstick felt like encountering Henry Ford, near the end of his career, whistling in awe as another Model T rolled off his assembly line. Lorre's laughter was the most distinctive: high-pitched, desperate, I-may-be-dying laughter. It had chord changes and movements, sometimes turning into a coughing fit, other times terminating with a foot stomp.

Lorre laughs like this all the time, during every run-through and rehearsal and filming, take after take, joke after joke, even when it is a joke he heard just moments before, in a previous take. Because Lorre's shows are taped before a live audience, his laughter frequently winds up somewhere in the final broadcast audio mix. My first thought was that Lorre was laughing for the benefit of the network people who were there to watch a new, untested show. When I asked him about this later, he maintained that his laughter is completely sincere. At the same time, he said, it "serves a double purpose. It's a timing mechanism to get [the actors] to imagine the audience. But it's got to be genuine. If you laugh and there's no laugh there, you're preparing them for disaster."

It was somewhat surprising, then, that the moment Lorre finished laughing, he began to question whether the bowling-ball moment needed to be included at all. The point of the scene was not to stress Mike's oafishness but establish his feeling of unanticipated inferiority to Molly, and he's defeated, dramatically speaking, the moment Molly rolls her strikes. "What is it gonna get us," Lorre asked, "to see him bowl?" No one had a good answer, and the sequence was cut.

After the run-through, the network people approached Lorre with their notes, or rather their note. ("One of the biggest things you notice," Dave Goetsch, a writer and co-executive producer on *Big Bang*, told me, "is that Chuck doesn't get notes from the network and the studio.") The network's note was a suggestion that Molly seem "more flirty" with Mike during the bowling scene. Lorre agreed that this was a good idea. Next, a representative from Standards and Practices approached him. In the middle of the episode, Molly calls Mike a "dick" in a moment of anger. Before the Standards and Practices representative could even speak, Lorre asked her, "We gonna get the 'dick' or are you gonna turn on us at the last minute?"

The Standards and Practices representative shook her head. "You're not gonna get it."

Lorre seemed genuinely surprised. "Why? It's really funny." It had, in fact, elicited from Lorre the rare triple-play combo—laugh, coughing fit, *and* foot stomp—that was most cherished by his actors. But the Standards and Practices representative did not budge.

* * *

Lorre claims to have learned how to work hard from his father, who ran what Lorre describes as "an eight-seat luncheonette" in Bethpage, on Long Island, that fortified commuters with pre-work scrambles and post-work burgers, and he does not remember his father ever taking a day off. Lorre was born Charles Michael Levine in Brooklyn, in 1952, and by the time he was twelve, he was working in the luncheonette as a short order cook and soda jerk. At night, he and his father watched television together, usually comedians like Jackie Gleason, Jack Benny, and Bob Hope. One of Lorre's "most formative" television moments occurred while watching *The Ed Sullivan Show*. "Henny Youngman came on and said, 'I went to the doctor and said, "Doctor, it hurts when I do this." And the doctor said, "Don't do that."' It was the funniest thing I ever heard in my life. *Don't do that.* The logic of it was astonishing." Despite their mutual love of television and comedy, Lorre's relationship with his father was often strained. He especially regrets that his father, who died in 1976, did not live to see what he calls the "ongoing miracle" of his television career.

After high school, Lorre enrolled at SUNY Potsdam, but dropped out to play the guitar professionally. Photographs of Lorre around this time show a young man with the smeary mustache of a 1970s porn stallion and stupendous head of black curls more cowl than hair. At the age of twenty-eight, he changed his name to Chuck Lorre. "My mother hated my father's family," Lorre explained. "'You're no good; you're a Levine,' was routinely thrown my way."

Lorre admits to having lived hard and unwisely during the seventeen years he spent playing cruise ships, bat mitzvahs, weddings, and "Big Daddy's Lounge in Long Beach from nine p.m. to four a.m." He did manage to write a pair of songs that stuck to the sneaker sole of American pop culture: the theme song for the *Teenage Mutant Ninja Turtles* animated series, which he cowrote;

and "French Kissin,'" Deborah Harry's biggest non-Blondie hit, which Bill Prady, who cocreated *The Big Bang Theory* with Lorre, has described—accurately—as "remarkably average."

Lorre turned to television writing in the mid 1980s. Although he claims that his only ambition was to get health insurance for his family, it was, in some ways, a natural outgrowth of his music career. Many of the songs Lorre wrote were dark-edged, purposefully comic "story" songs. "I was enamored of Randy Newman," Lorre told me, especially the persona songs in which Newman sang in the voice of an ugly, unlikable person, but with empathy rather than anger. In Lorre's mind, television had something else going for it: it appeared to be easy. In music, Lorre said, "the bar seemed much higher. I mean, McCartney and Lennon and Springsteen and Stevie Wonder and the Rolling Stones—just in pop music!" He now admits his confidence "was arrogance fueled by stupidity. I had no idea what I was doing when I started."

Lorre's first steady television jobs were in animation. At Marvel Comics, he wrote fifteen drafts of *Muppet Babies* scripts ("I didn't write that many drafts of the *Two and a Half Men* pilot!") and was fired from *My Little Pony* ("I didn't have that *Pony* voice"). At night, he wrote spec scripts for prime-time comedies and used what few connections he had to get them read. Lorre managed to get a *Golden Girls* script into the hands of Betty White, for instance, whose neighbor he knew. White told Lorre she liked the script, which prominently featured her character ("I'm not an idiot. If you know Betty's neighbor, write for Betty"), and also that she would take it to the show's producers. Looking back, he does not care to imagine the looks on the producers' faces when White presented them with a spec script written by her neighbor's associate. "It couldn't have gone well," he said. The script was returned with a form letter but led to freelancing work for lesser sitcoms such as *Charles in Charge* and *My Two Dads*.

Lorre's first prime-time break came with *Roseanne*, on which he worked from 1990 to 1992. The first time Lorre set foot on the *Roseanne* set, he experienced a sudden, confidence-building epiphany. "Roseanne was doing a scene with Laurie Metcalf and John Goodman," he told me, "and I turned to one of the writers and I said, 'They're saying what we wrote!' I was stunned. They were big stars."

Lorre's work on *Roseanne* impressed the show's prolific and influential producers, Marcy Carsey and Tom Werner, who offered him the chance to create a show about, in Lorre's words, "a fifty-year-old middle-class woman coming into her own." Why you? I asked him. "I was the perfect choice," he told me, deadpan. *Franny's Turn* premiered in 1992 and was canceled after five weeks.

Nevertheless, *Franny's Turn* inaugurated Lorre's long, incongruous stint developing sitcoms about women of a certain age. His next project, *Grace Under Fire,* also for Carsey and Werner, brought Lorre to Elgin, Illinois, in order to gather research for a show Carsey and Werner envisioned as revolving around a struggling single mother. In Elgin, Lorre met with nurses, factory workers, and women living in the local YWCA—one of whom he asked if she would even *want* to watch a show about a single mom working in a factory. The woman needed to know one thing: What time was it on? Her job, you see, left her too wiped out to stay up very late. Lorre returned from Elgin thinking that the show, which became *Grace Under Fire*, was about "the hero's journey." He was particularly pleased with the pilot, which, he said, "managed to bring in some elements that I don't think had ever been in a sitcom before," including domestic violence. Much of that material was drawn from the stand-up act of show's star, Brett Butler, with whom Lorre often battled. "She was dissatisfied with almost every line of every script," he told me. "It was an impossible situation. I began writing defensively, which isn't writing. It's predicting the future." He left the show after one season.

In 1995, Lorre created a vehicle for Cybil Shepherd that explored an erstwhile ingénue's identity crisis when she learns of her impending grandmotherhood. *Cybil* had a hugely successful first season—Christine Baranski won an Emmy for her role as Shepherd's rich, alcoholic friend—but, once again, Lorre found himself struggling with a show's star. One legend holds that Shepherd had Lorre fired because he clapped too enthusiastically for Baranski at the Emmys. Lorre says this is not accurate, and characterizes his removal as being more about Shepherd's displeasure with "how the humor was being apportioned out" in the second season. (Shepherd demurs: "Chuck knows why he was fired.") Whatever the case, Shepherd's power play took Lorre "a long time to wrap my head around," he told me. And now, he knew, the soot of several burned bridges had darkened his reputation.

A television show provides hundreds of people with steady employment in an industry not celebrated for its stability, and successful shows are defined by their longevity. Television is thus a more or less congenial industry. A brooding artiste or tantrum champion may thrive within a short-lived film production, but television rewards those who are able to meet deadlines while also getting along with their coworkers. In 2007, an *Entertainment Weekly* profile that emphasized Lorre's combative history described him as "the angriest man in television."

The characterization still irritates him, and yet, to hear Lorre tell it, anger drove him through much of his early career. The success of *Dharma and Greg*, his sitcom about a mismatched couple that ran from 1997 to 2002, helped him learn to relax. For the first time, Lorre's distinctive sitcom voice was not forced through the mediating comic funnel of a headlining star. But it was not until *Two and a Half Men*, a show about a womanizing ruin of a man and his fussbudget brother, that Lorre found comic focus: men behaving like idiots.

When I first met Lorre, he told me what he had been "slowly learning" during these last eight years: "If I'm not frightened and angry and obsessed with anything other than doing good work, then maybe an environment gets created where people can do good work." But Lorre has fun with his hammerhead reputation. Visitors to his office building on the Warner Bros. lot, for instance, will encounter the heraldic crest of Chuck Lorre Productions. The crest's motto, *Humilitas Ficta*, or "feigned humility," is wreathed by the following sub-mottos: NEUROTIC ANXIETY, UNFOCUSED RAGE, SELF-OBSESSION.

Lorre remains annoyed about one thing, though—his shows' lack of critical recognition, especially where *Two and a Half Men* is concerned. He once said of television critics, "They hate our success and believe that if they martyr themselves they'll wake up in show business with real jobs." He does not say such things anymore, at least not publicly, and prefers not to talk about television at all, if he has the choice.

Lorre's standing among critics is not helped by his staunchly traditional approach to the sitcom. He is well aware of the shifts that have taken place in sitcom writing during the past twenty years, but he does not care all that much about them. *The Office* and *Modern Family*, two of the most formally adventurous contemporary sitcoms, use a mockumentary framing device that, increasingly, seems as mannered as the three-walled rooms of a traditional, proscenium-style sitcom—a word that Lorre resists using to describe his shows. "The comedies we really love," he said, "they're not situational at all. *The Honeymooners* was just a man struggling to get respect in the world. Archie Bunker was a man out of touch with the culture." In place of *sitcom*, Lorre uses "character-com" or "half-hour comedy."

By whatever name, the sitcom is an oddly purgatorial form of entertainment. The same characters appear week after week, displaying the same tics, and having the same arguments, in the same rooms, hallways, stairwells, and offices. Within the traditional sitcom, there are complications but rarely solutions; challenges but rarely triumphs. Indeed, when sitcoms attempt to do more dramatic stories, a show can come unmoored, as Lorre learned on *Dharma and Greg*. Faced with pressure from ABC to feature "promotable" story lines, Lorre eventually capitulated, which he regards as "one of the more regrettable actions in my career." At one point Dharma toyed with an extramarital relationship; at another, an accident consigned her to a wheelchair for several episodes. "I couldn't have been dumber," Lorre said. By listening to ABC, he told me, he undermined "the very nature of what's great about a four-camera, audience show, which is an opportunity to get to know these people." Lorre believes that the "magic trick" of the traditional sitcom is that the characters "make very small, incremental progress without ever really changing."

Bill Prady, who has worked with Lorre since *Dharma and Greg*, told me that Lorre hates stories of unnecessary—or any—narrative intricacy. What Lorre loves are stories in which the driving force is one character buying a birthday present for another. "And he's right," Prady said, "because a sitcom is now down to about twenty-one minutes. If you're going to fill [a show] with plot, with events that *must* occur, there's no room for people to talk."

"I was sitting in a club recently," Lorre told me, "in Hollywood, listening to different people get up and play. I thought to myself, 'They're all playing the same song.' It's a fundamentally very simple medium, the blues." He was, I guessed, making a point about the sitcom. "Yeah," he said, "and I fought against that for a long time, until I realized: it's like a haiku. It's very simple and very structured."

Visiting the set of a sitcom you enjoy is like witnessing the exposure of a large and organizationally complex lie. The familiar and comfortable sets, once you are standing within them, seem cramped and flimsy. Touch a door and the wall shakes. Carpets turn raggedy wherever the cameras do not reach. Behind every wall is a world of chicken-coop fencing stapled in place and dark, narrow passageways somehow redolent of asbestos. Someone says, for the purposes of lining up a shot, "Lose the wall," and suddenly half the set is folded away upon undetectable hinges. The area between the sets and the audience seating area is called "the floor," but it is more like an alley. What little floor there happens to be is marked with inscrutable pieces of tape.

During tapings of *The Big Bang Theory*, the audience sits at an angle from several of the sets, which means that it watches a good deal of the live proceedings on television monitors. Meanwhile, Lorre and his battery of writers and producers—hidden from the audience by long black curtains—sit crammed within one of the sets, watching their own monitors, holding scripts and wearing earpieces whose tightly coiled cords looked like black fusilli. Everything that is not part of the set, not bipedal, and not a chair, has wheels, because throughout the night it is continually being moved to whichever of the sets is not being used.

The Big Bang Theory is Lorre's best show to date. (*Two and a Half Men*, though funnier than its detractors admit, too often allows its characters to stand there and trade unrealistic sitcom barbs that in just about any other imaginably fictional context would get someone punched.) If sitcoms at the top of their game can feel like verbal ballet, sitcoms working the middle register are often insult rodeo. Lorre calls this phenomenon "selling out characters for a joke," and even very good sitcom writers resort to it, especially when, in his words, "you're tired and exhausted and you're trying to make something arrive at a level of comedy."

Big Bang's main characters, Leonard and Sheldon, are physicists, and not in the way that Ross, from *Friends*, was a paleontologist, a subject with which he seemed as conversant as a randomly selected eleven-year-old boy. Leonard and Sheldon drop references to Richard Feynman and Asimov's three laws of robotics; explain how Schrödinger's cat is applicable to dating; and open episodes with lines like, "Here's the problem with teleportation," before going on to reveal what, from a physicist's perspective, the problem actually is.

Lorre and Prady's first attempt at a *Big Bang* pilot was rejected by CBS (the network, unusually, encouraged them to have another go), and it was not an immediate hit. I happened to catch the pilot the night it aired, in September 2007, and heard, in the first three minutes, references to Papa Doc Duvalier and Vladimir Nabokov. Its prospects appeared to me valiantly doomed, like those of a dog walking a tightrope. When the 2007 writers' strike crippled production, CBS wound up running *Big Bang*'s first batch of episodes several times, which played to the show's gabby strengths. Before long, it had earned a huge and devoted following.

In the show, Leonard and Sheldon live across the hall from a beautiful aspiring actress named Penny, for whom Leonard pines. Leonard wants more from life, which is his tragedy. Sheldon does not, which is his tragedy. A man of unfeelingly Vulcan arrogance and deeply hidden vulnerabilities, Sheldon discusses his childhood by saying he did not have imaginary friends; he had "imaginary colleagues." Not many sitcoms would permit Sheldon's unpleasantness to be so emphatic, but CBS maintains a relatively hands-off approach to Lorre and his shows. Dave Goetsch told me that the "edges that get sanded over in other network sitcoms" become, in *Big Bang*, the "cornerstones of comedy."

Although *Big Bang* is unquestionably a traditional, multi-camera sitcom, it does not always feel like one. One explanation for this is that its writers love to violate core sitcom rules, such as resorting to what Prady calls "the 'Are you my mother?' structure, like the children's book," in which a similar scene is done two or even three times in a row. It is most useful when "Sheldon's bothering everybody," Prady said, because it is fun to explore how different characters react. Plot, in other words, is never a concern. "We say the number of things that occur within a *Big Bang Theory* scene is one or zero," he said.

A typical episode of *Big Bang* takes around four hours to film, with lulls that can last twenty minutes or more. The many things that slow the process down include the frequency with which Lorre and his writers send the actors revised or new jokes; the banter among the actors between takes; the announcement of a guest star like Mayim Bialik (tonight playing Sheldon's girlfriend, Amy), whose appearance was applauded by the audience for two dozen seconds while she stood there and waved back at them uncomfortably; the patter delivered by a stand-up comedian ("Which side of the room is having a better time? This one or... *this* one?") thanklessly tasked with keeping the audience's energy up; the number of times what is called "the bell" rings out, even though it sounds like a buzzer and nothing like a bell; and, finally, how long it takes to move the production's four cameras, which look less like cameras and more like precision-laser, deep-earth-mining devices.

At the taping I attended, lines that the actors had grown visibly sick of during the camera run-through, lines that even Lorre had stopped laughing at, were getting huge laughs. Everyone seemed lightly narcoticized by the audience's presence, the audience included. Lorre's shows are sometimes condemned for using a laugh track, a charge that infuriates him. His shows, Lorre insists to anyone who will listen, never use laugh tracks. When, later, I sat in on a sound edit for *Two and a Half Men*, I witnessed several occasions in which Lorre requested that the laugh be brought *down* from its recorded level. When one laugh wound up swallowing a joke's payoff line, Lorre, visibly frustrated, asked the sound engineer why on earth the audience was laughing at the joke's least funny part. The sound engineer shrugged. "That's what they did," he said, to which Lorre responded with a sigh.

For much of the night the rewriting tasks were mild. Sheldon, for instance, had a brief tangent on the relative merits of the Empire from the *Star Wars* films, telling Leonard, "Despite their tendency to build Death Stars, I've always been an Empire man." The line did not get a huge laugh, and the writers began throwing out new spins on it: "Despite their tendencies to build Death Stars that blow up at the drop of a hat . . . " "Despite their rather shoddy human rights record . . . " Later, a Tinman reference—used to describe Sheldon's lack of emotion—was discarded for a more audience-appropriate *Star Trek: The Next Generation* reference.

I asked Lorre whether I was seeing a lot or a little rewriting tonight. I was seeing the usual amount. "You keep tweaking until you run out of time," Lorre explained, adding that he found working this way nerve-racking. "I like to write in a room, privately, not in here with two hundred people waiting for us to finish. The danger is you might come up with a new line that gets a big laugh not because it's better, but because it's new."

We came to the episode's central scene. Sheldon and his girlfriend, Amy, a neurobiologist, sit down with Leonard and two other friends in the physics department cafeteria. Sheldon explains that he has brought Amy to see his work, which Amy concedes is "very impressive," before adding, "for theoretical work." Sheldon asks Amy if she's being condescending. Amy responds, "Compared to the real-world applications of neurobiology, theoretical physics is . . . what's the word I'm looking for? Cute." What follows is an argument that Prady, who worked on it, described to me as "very technical" and "jargony." He first showed it to Lorre to see if it needed to be shortened. "No," Lorre told Prady. "This is great. In what other comedy do you see this?"

Sheldon asks Amy how a neurobiologist like Joseph Babinski could ever "rise to the significance of a physicist like James Clerk Maxwell or Paul Dirac." Amy's scripted response:

> Oh, Sheldon. My colleagues and I are mapping the neurological substrates that subserve global information processing, which is required for all cognitive reasoning, including scientific inquiry, making my research ipso facto prior in the ordo cognoscendi. [TO THE OTHER GUYS] That means it's better than his research, and by extension of course, yours.

In the script, Leonard responds to this Latinate avalanche with a curt, startled, "Sure, I got that." The audience's response, meanwhile, was a restive and uncertain chuckle. And so the writers went to work. First came the dead spot of Amy's opening "Oh, Sheldon." Steven Molaro quickly came up with a line for Amy that had Lorre quite literally slapping his knee: "I'm stating it outright. Babinski eats Dirac for breakfast and defecates Clerk Maxwell." Next came Leonard's "Sure, I got that," a line of which Lorre said, "There's nothing *there*." Every writer's head lowered, and a few moments later the rewritten line—Molaro's, once again—was sent out to the floor. Now, when Amy finished her rant, and turned to Leonard, his line became, "I'm still try-ing to work on defecating Clerk Maxwell." It got the biggest laugh of the evening. I asked Molaro how it felt to experience something like that. He said that changing jokes on the fly, work-ing under all the lights, and before a live audience, had a defi-nite "athletic" component. He then added, "It's the *only* athletic component."

As we moved to another set, I asked Lorre whether single-camera sitcoms suffered from not having this audience-writer feedback loop. Lorre was hesitant to say yes, but pointed out the biggest danger for sitcom writers whose material was not vetted by an audience: "You never find out if you're wrong."

Lorre's house is one of his neighborhood's more modest and his car one of its least obviously Viagral. Most of the homes nearby stand behind walls. Lorre's home can be seen from the street.

"Welcome to the sitcom house," he said, opening his front door. While he made us tea in his kitchen, he asked me to look at some text on the screen of his laptop. I instantly recognized what I was reading as one of Lorre's vanity cards. Vanity cards are the production-company logos that TV producers flash up onscreen just after the credits have rolled. On the first episode of *Dharma and Greg,* Lorre pushed the name of his company, Chuck Lorre Productions, up to the top of the screen to make room for a mes-sage far too long to be read in its brief moment of screen time: "Thank you for videotaping *Dharma and Greg* and freeze-framing on my vanity card. I'd like to take this opportunity to share with you some of my personal beliefs." An eclectic set of convictions followed—"I believe that Larry was a vastly underrated stooge"; "I believe that my kids are secretly proud of me"—and continued on the card for the next episode, and the next, and the next. Soon, a vanity card announced that Lorre had run out of beliefs, and the texts started to range more widely.

In the twelve years since, they have included elliptical fictions, rueful musings about his life and the state of the country, and jeremiads against CBS censorship. (Sometimes he relays obscene jokes that he was prevented from using in an episode, and sometimes CBS ends up censoring the card too, in which case he posts the unexpurgated version on his website.) If any single mode predominates among the more than three hundred cards Lorre has written, it is probably the rant, and it is hard not to see these compressed, intense utterances as rebellion against the constraints of TV writing—moments of id, on the run from the superego of network programming.

The vanity card that I read on Lorre's laptop was directed at television critics: "You have absolutely no power to affect ratings and the likely success or failure of a TV show. In that arena you are laughably impotent. You are not unlike a flaccid penis flailing miserably at a welcoming vagina." Lorre had just decided not to use this vanity card for the first broadcast episode of *Mike and Molly*. I told him that I thought he had made an extremely wise decision. He wound up using it, minus a few genital references, on *Two and a Half Men*.

We went out onto Lorre's redbrick back patio, its small pool surrounded by a dozen deck chairs. When he was married, Lorre told me, there had been rose gardens outside and the house was much more elaborately decorated. He has been married twice, a topic about which he has sensibly little to say, and has two children from his first marriage. His daughter works with him on *Big Bang*, and his son in a nurse.

We talked about what I had found surprising when I watched him at work. I mentioned having seen Kaley Cuoco, who plays Penny on *Big Bang*, sitting on the couch in Leonard and Sheldon's apartment during a rehearsal, apparently checking her email on an iPad. The sight of Cuoco engaged in nonfictional behavior within fictional surroundings, I told Lorre, was strangely distressing.

"After all these years," Lorre said, "when I watch the actors on one of my shows go on Leno or Letterman and talk about the funny thing that happened to them while they were building a sauna in their Beverly Hills home or whatever, it just breaks my heart. I want to protect the fiction. I don't want to know what goes on behind the screen."

I asked if this accounted for his inability or unwillingness to delegate more of the responsibility for his shows. "I've had such a volatile career," he said. "I quit *Grace Under Fire*. I got fired from *Cybil*. I left *Dharma and Greg* too soon. I made some tragic mistakes both in the writing of the show and leaving it before it had run its course. I don't want to make those mistakes again." He went on to say, "It's a body of work. Whether you like the body of work or not, it's a body of work that I have accumulated and I want to stay close to it and protect it."

Later, he expanded on the point: "This is the shot I've been given to communicate as a writer. This is my shot. This was the door that opened, and if I take it for granted then it's ridiculous." He went on, "When I started out writing in the late eighties, I heard guys say, 'Aw, screw it. It's just a sitcom,' or, 'It's just TV. We'll add laughs to it in post, and it'll be fine. No one will know.' I heard guys talk that way and it was really offensive. It was *really* offensive."

Films, perhaps, show us who we want to be, and literature shows us who we actually are. Sitcoms, if they show us anything, show us people we might like to know. Because of this, the sitcom is a medium designed to reassure. The more reassuring the sitcom, the better its chances become at winding up in the financial promised land of syndication, where multi-camera sitcoms fare far better than their single-camera brethren. Most sitcoms are about families, and for the millions who watch them, a sitcom becomes a kind of mental family. Week after week, your couch faces the couch of characters you feel you know, characters whose problems can never quite get solved.

Look at the characters of *Cheers*, Lorre said. "Society would judge them to be losers, but they created a family with each other. That was the hope of the series." A lot of sitcoms are, in fact, darker than you realize. At its core, *Two and a Half Men* is about loneliness. *The Big Bang Theory* is about alienation. *Mike and Molly* is about self-hatred. You would never know it from the shows themselves, but you do, sometimes, feel it while watching them. To laugh at these things with our mental families may allow us to cope with our own loneliness and alienation and self-hatred. It may be that the sitcom's consistent avoidance of any final, dramatic catharsis is its accidental strength. If so, that would make this least lifelike form of entertainment the most comfortingly similar to real life.

I arrived at the *Mike and Molly* taping, a few days after the network run-through, to learn from a smiling Lorre that the live audience had loved the show's pilot. There was always a risk, Lorre said, in showing something new to an audience. "These are brand-new faces, and they really responded."

Early in the taping the audience laughed hard at things that were not even intended to be funny. I wondered what might have happened if the bowling-ball gag had survived into the live shooting and asked Lorre if an audience can ever be wrong. "Sure, they can be wrong," he said. "We need to ask if the experience will translate to a person sitting alone on their couch. And that's a judgment call."

Lorre's attention was soon consumed by another editorial legacy of the run-through, when a Standards and Practices representative from CBS refused to allow Molly to call Mike a "dick." Molly's line had now become: "You big knob!" It got a laugh from Lorre during the camera run-through earlier in the day, but, hearing it now, he seemed frustrated. Nothing about it worked, he decided, because Molly's motivation did not line up with her reaction. "She's been charming," Lorre said of Molly. "It's his problem; he's an asshole. But CBS won't let us call him an asshole."

"Or a dick," one of the writers said.

After several minutes of fretting, Lorre looked up. Why doesn't Molly insult Mike's bowling ability? That, he said, was a convincingly nasty thing for her to zero in on. Mike hurt her; she is now going to hurt Mike. A line, Lorre's, was rushed out to Melissa McCarthy: "You bowl like a girl!" What made the line so funny came from the explosively vicious way McCarthy delivered it. She seemed surprised by her anger, which was exactly what Lorre had intended.

The evening's most interesting dilemma surfaced when Mike retreats to his friend Carl's house after his date with Molly. While Mike and Carl chat, Carl's grandmother, played as an aging sexpot by Cleo King, comes downstairs, has a seat, tells Mike that he was threatened by Molly's intelligence, and advises him to go back to her, since there is "nothing sexier" than a man being honest. At the end of this lesson, a male voice calls Granny back upstairs. She smiles and crosses the set. "That man is as honest as the day is long," the script has her say of her upstairs lover. "And vice versa."

The joke utterly died in performance, which stunned Lorre and his writers. "I would have bet the mortgage on that one working," Lorre said. "But it's a thinker. There's too many steps." I suggested that the joke's problem was internal: the payoff laugh after the audience's initial, instinctive laugh never came because the implicit comparisons between "day," "long," "honest," and "man" did not find each other in the mentally swimmy period during which the joke was processed. The *real* joke was about an old lady going upstairs for a shafting. My cogitation on this matter was of approximately no interest to the writers, who all stared blankly at the floor.

Suddenly, one of them, Don Foster, began nodding. He had something. This was what he had: "That man is as honest as the day is long, and if he wasn't honest I never would have found out he was long."

It was, I thought, a terrible line: clunky, wordy, and marred by a rhythmically meretricious repetition of "long." About the only thing going for it was its grammatically correct failure to use the subjunctive. But when King delivered the line, with a slight backward look and little kick to her rump on that second "long," the audience exploded. It was a good line, after all. Lorre stared contentedly at his monitor. For once, he did not laugh.

—2010

INVISIBLE GIRL

Jennifer Hale, the Queen of Video-game Voiceover

If you are waiting for an actor to arrive at Technicolor Digital Productions in Burbank, California, there is a strong possibility that you will not hear him or her coming. In the past few years, the voice work for hundreds of video games and animated features has been recorded within Technicolor's mix rooms, and the first thing any voice-over performer learns is not to wear noisy clothing. On a recent morning, actors signed in at the Technicolor reception desk and silently flitted away toward their assigned mix rooms while I sat in the lobby anticipating the arrival of Jennifer Hale, whose performances in more than a hundred and twenty video games have led her colleagues and many ordinary gamers to regard her as a kind of Meryl Streep of the form. Hale turned up wearing a long-sleeved cotton shirt and black jeans. "If you're wearing nylon, forget it," she told me. "You're naked in five minutes."

To actors, accustomed to the vagaries of a fundamentally insecure profession, the burgeoning and profitable world of video games represents a welcome growth area. But the peculiarities of the work extend well beyond the need for silent attire. Most acting, from Ibsen to the thirty-second skin-cream ad, is linear. Video games—in which the variable fortunes of any given player tend to necessitate a script that is a maze of branching possibilities—often aren't. Most actors are happiest when they understand their character's "motivation" and "arc." Video-game actors become skilled at working with little or no context, and at providing varying inflections for any line on demand—a practice discouraged by many standard acting texts. (Stanford Meisner's classic, *On Acting*, insists that "the foundation of acting is the reality of doing," and that "making readings in order to create variety" is fraudulent.) Strangest of all, perhaps, for a profession in which one's face is an important source of one's fortune, video-game actors work in conditions of near anonymity. Hale told me that when she drives around Los Angeles and sees billboards for games she has worked on, she sometimes feels like "the invisible girl," but she understands that this is a necessary corollary of voice-over work. "My job," she said, "is to not exist."

Hale is in her late thirties, with long, thick dark-brown hair that has faint almond highlights. In Technicolor's corporate Day-Glo precincts, she cuts an incongruous figure, projecting a pleasant, outdoorsy effect that stopped just short of hippie. She loves hiking, rock climbing, and riding horses. She openly deplored my consumption of diet soda, and eventually persuaded me to quit for a month and to report my findings. I soon found that Hale had never played any video games herself. "I have so little free time," she said with a shrug, explaining that she preferred to spend what free time she did have outdoors, in the "dirt."

Hale was at Technicolor to record dialogue for BioWare's *Mass Effect 3*, a sprawling science-fiction game whose first two installments sold more than five million copies. In the new game, which will be released in the spring of 2012, Hale reprises the role of Commander Shepard. Shepard is the character the player controls, and quite a bit of dialogue is assigned to her. This was Hale's second recording session for *Mass Effect 3*, and it was to last four hours and cover several sections of the game. During the next few months, she had at least twenty further *Mass Effect 3* sessions to look forward to.

The *Mass Effect* games are, by and large, written before they are animated—an unusual sequence in game development but the norm at BioWare. The script's emphasis on dialogue and decision gives the game experience an unusual narrative richness; writing for the *New Yorker*, Nicholson Baker praised *Mass Effect 2* for its "novelistic" quality. The script for the first *Mass Effect* ran to 300,000 words; the second to 370,000. (By comparison, a typical English translation of *War and Peace* has around half a million words.)

We walked past the doors of several mix rooms. In one, an audio engineer was sitting at a brightly lit soundboard while an actor performed on the other side of a large window, urgently gesticulating but inaudible. In another, Hale introduced me to Caroline Livingston, *Mass Effect 3*'s voice-over producer and director; Mac Walters, its lead writer; and David Walsh, a Technicolor audio engineer. Livingston asked Hale if she wanted anything to drink. Hale requested a glass of water—if possible, not in a plastic glass. "I'm nursing," she said. "I may not have a clean system, but I'd like to give one to my son."

Talk quickly turned to the earthquake-spawned tsunami that had, the day before, devastated northern Japan. "I'll be surprised if L.A. doesn't have a quake in the next two months," Hale said, and proceeded to speak knowledgeably about the tectonic interrelatedness of New Zealand, Japan, and California. She then described coming home one night some years ago in Los Angeles, and how "the smell of skunk was so pervasive it actually burned my nose going into my house." Once inside, she said, "I just got the willies; I couldn't get comfortable." A few hours later, the 1994 earthquake hit. She had been able to sense the quake, she believed, because she had been in "a place of stillness. I think animals feel earthquakes because they're so quiet. They're connected to the earth and not bombarded by the Internet." Hearing a prominent video-game actor share these thoughts moments before a recording session was rather like watching the College of Cardinals debate the merits of atheism while electing a new pope.

Walters told Hale that he wanted to show her a recently completed cinematic from *Mass Effect 3*, the dialogue for which Hale had recorded only a few weeks before. Also known as "cut scenes," cinematics are potted narrative segments that contain little, if any, gameplay. In the cinematic, Shepard was shown speaking to the representatives of some interstellar admiralty. The music that would underlay the scene was not yet in place and the game's lightning system was still not functioning, one result of which was a pronounced dramatic sterility. Hale's performance as Shepard, however, was taut and forceful. "Is this a big, pivotal moment?" Hale asked, concerned by the seeming disconnect.

Walters explained to her what she was not seeing. "It's rough," he admitted, "but it's good to see it."

"It's *great* to see it," Hale said. "It really helps."

Hale left for the recording booth, a ten-by-ten room, with gray carpet and gray ceiling and gray sound-absorbent padding on the walls. BioWare records its game dialogue in Los Angeles, Edmonton, and London, but every word of dialogue used in its games is recorded in the same conditions and with the same peerlessly sensitive equipment. When Hale drank from her ceramic cup of water, her front tooth struck the cup's rim with a resonant *ching*. Hale readied herself, the booth's track lighting lending her face a glossy ivory glow. A microphone anchored in a shock mount was arranged to hang just below her eye level. The two most important technical considerations when working with such a microphone are to maintain one's "mike distance" and try to keep from "popping" one's consonants. Shielding the mike was a circular and darkly translucent windscreen, which minimized any plosive miscalculations.

A few minutes into the session, Hale was asked to vocalize the noises the player would hear when he or she pressed a button to make Shepard sprint. While making these noises, Hale had to avoid moving and keep her mike distance. I had heard versions of this sound probably hundreds of times while playing *Mass Effect*. Hale, standing perfectly still, softly huffed and puffed into the microphone. When I closed my eyes, I could see Shepard running.

At the beginning of *Mass Effect*, the player must choose a gender for Shepard. If one opts for a female Shepard (FemShep, to the game's fans), Hale performs her. If one opts for a male Shepard (BroShep), Mark Meer, a Canadian actor, performs him. According to BioWare, 80 percent of players select BroShep, a statistic that is regarded as something of a tragedy by the gaming intelligentsia. Kirk Hamilton, the games editor for the magazine *Paste*, told me, "It's always been hard for me to communicate to people just how much Hale's performance improves the experience of *Mass Effect*. She works at a slow burn; each pause and inflection accumulates over time until you can't help but care for the character she's playing."

"It's certainly very frustrating to hear Shepard spoken of primarily as a man," Hale told me. She attributed the situation to how society perceives women in leadership positions. It probably hasn't helped that all the *Mass Effect* promotional material thus far, including the game box, has featured images of a male Shepard—a thoroughly generic space-marine lunkhead. At one point in *Mass Effect 2*, BioWare hints at an admission that FemShep has been grossly shortchanged: a teammate mentions that Shepard was used as a poster girl for military recruitment, but she did not test well among focus groups and was replaced with a composite figure.

As the game progresses, players make further decisions about Shepard. Shepard can react to other characters with relative kindness (the "Paragon" option), behave with hard-charging recklessness ("Renegade"), or take a nameless, middle-of-the-road approach. How the player decides what to say and do is governed by what BioWare calls the "paraphrase system," a clever (and patented) in-game user interface system that presents the player with an array of paraphrastic summaries ("I'm honored," "This is unexpected," "This is a terrible idea"). Once the player picks a paraphrase, Shepard speaks accordingly ("I'll do everything in my power to help you," "It would have been helpful to know about this earlier," "I'm not a lawyer!"), and the conversation continues. In most cases, when the player selects a paraphrase, one or more avenues of discussion are closed off in order to maintain conversational consistency. This means that even someone playing as FemShep will require several playthroughs to hear all of Hale's recorded performance.

If one of the secrets of successful stage and film acting is seeming to be unwatched—also known, absurdly, as "looking natural"—the secret to Hale's video-game acting may be disguising the fact that she is reading lines first seen only minutes beforehand and for which she has been given comparatively little context. A film or television actor knows where her character begins and where her character ends up, which allows her to create the illusion of dramatic momentum even if something is filmed out of sequence. Hale works off a much narrower store of available information. Frequently, all she has to go on is the copy in front of her and the scene-setting description provided by writers and producers. She works not from *a* text but from text.

As she prepared to record one scene, Hale wanted to know whether she could insert into her performance sighs and other off-script inflections. "We can't do that," Walters said, "because there's two of you." FemShep's and BroShep's lines, though separate, have to match because both Shepards share the same interlocutors. Going off script, even slightly, can alter the intended tone of an exchange.

"I always forget that!" Hale said. "There should only be one!" She laughed, and apologized, and laughed again. She asked how much ambient noise would be added to the scene.

"Lots," Livingstone said. "There's a sandstorm."

To manage *Mass Effect 3*'s script, BioWare was using a new system, called VADA, or Voice and Dialogue Editor and Recorder. ("The acronym doesn't match for reasons I can't even begin to get into," Livingstone told me. My guess: a more easily harvested acronym that VADA would be VADER, a trademark registered by LucasFilm.) The system is paperless and allows for scenes to be called up instantly, by file name. On the master VADA screen, which Hale could not see, all the game's scenes were listed as file names. Walsh used a trackball to navigate through the scene list, controlling the recording process via his computer keyboard. As Hale spoke, Walsh's fingers moved as though he were playing a tiny, silent piano. Meanwhile, in the booth, Hale was reading off a wireless iPad-like tablet. Her lines—attributed to PLAYER: MALE & FEMALE—appeared in clusters, with the line she was supposed to perform enlarged into bold, thirty-point type. There were stage directions, too, or "cinematic comment," in VADA speak: "This is NOT casual conversation"; "This is a fairly intimate conversation. Normal intensity." The cinematic comment was there to provide Hale with additional bits of context. Hale later confessed to missing the paper-based dialogue system used during *Mass Effect 1* and *2*, which allowed her more freedom to "flip ahead and read as much as I can."

Livingstone told me that Hale's "secret" was to do three or four and sometimes five highly variant takes of a single line reading in a row. "Jennifer could do seventeen thousand readings and they'll all be completely different," Livingstone said. "And we can use them all. They all *could* work." Hale finished and Livingstone gave her verdict: Take Two was an "alt" and Four was a "keeper." Every alt and keeper was made part of the VADA scene library and could be summoned with a keystroke for playback.

Michael Abbott, a professor of theater at Wabash College and proprietor of the influential gaming blog brainygamer.com, told me, "You'd expect players to be tired of hearing Jennifer Hale's voice after dozens of games, but she's made herself untraceable. She's played everything from a love-struck English schoolgirl to a stoic battle-tested soldier. She's a chameleon. It helps that she has a knack for making exposition and technical language sound like dinner conversation."

I noticed that when Hale performed as Shepard, her lush, dulcet speaking voice hardened, somehow, as though edged in concrete. "Shepard's a military person," Hale told me later. "Military people do not get what they want by being emotional." Indeed, during the session Hale stopped herself a few times because she knew she had gone "too emotional." It was not merely Shepard's martial bearing that constrained Hale. Because of the non-linearity of the dialogue, she had to be vigilant about letting feeling from one line spill over into another. Hale performed with an intensity that she could, apparently, summon at will. She seemed to immerse herself, often looking around maniacally, her teeth bared in primate agitation. Then as the context of a new line was explained to her, she would pace, picking at a cuticle or rubbing her arms or looking intently at her screen.

The loneliness of acting in a booth, with no one to respond to, can be difficult. "It has to be all in my head," Hale told me. "Environment, ambient noise, history with this person, what I need from this person, what I want from this person—all these decisions have to be made on the fly, in the moment, as quickly as possible."

Quite often, before Hale would do her takes, Livingstone would say something like, "Okay, you've just finished a big fight." Other contextual phrases Hale was fed to color her takes included "professional," "romantic," "combat," "intimate, not romantic," "not romantic," "distance," "before combat," "walking" (also known as "walk-and-talk"), "exertion," and "after combat." Sometimes Hale was not always able to recall the space-opera particulars of the *Mass Effect* universe. When the criminal organization Cerberus was mentioned in one exchange, Hale paused to ask, "Is this the first time I've heard of Cerberus?" Walters, without missing a beat, reminded Hale that Shepard spent the entirety of the previous *Mass Effect* in Cerberus's employ. Hale later maintained that she was asking if this was the first time Shepard had heard of Cerberus in *Mass Effect 3*, but I wasn't so sure. Either way, it was like hearing Tom Hanks ask, "Which one is Woody again?" in a *Toy Story 3* outtake.

Hale was born in Labrador in 1972, and holds dual Canadian-American citizenship. She grew up mostly in the American South. Her mother, who died four years ago, was what Hale called "a wandering master's degree pursuer" who eventually settled on a career in epidemiology. Hale's biological father is an outdoorsman and intellectual ("He'd be really pissed if he heard me call him an intellectual") who still lives in Labrador. The man who Hale says "has been my dad most of my life," and who was married to Hale's mother for five years, is a semi-retired microbiologist and researcher for the Gates Foundation. Based on this, one might imagine Hale's childhood as a procession of bookish family dinners, cheerily contested Trivial Pursuit games, and bedtime stories starring friendly prokaryotes. In reality, Hale told me, "I had, probably, a more challenging experience growing up than most middle-class chicks."

She got on well with her stepfather but did not get to know her biological father until she was in her twenties, and her relationship with her mother was a difficult one. "She was in a lot of emotional pain," Hale told me. "When you're a kid, you don't know that. You just know someone's screaming at you, and flailing at you and kicking you around mentally and emotionally." Hale's mother told young Jennifer that she was half Native American; that she was born so premature that she nearly died; that she was descended from the Pilgrims at Plymouth. None of this was true, but it may have helped prepare Hale for a lifetime of pretending to be other people. Hale now thinks that her mother's prevarications must have been a way to assuage her crippling sense of inferiority.

One of Hale's first acting roles was when, as a teenager in Birmingham, Alabama, she was asked to perform voice-over on the radio and paid thirty-five dollars for her trouble. "For talking," she said. "For talking! I was out of my mind." Hale believes that one of the reasons she was hired for the job was that her mother had discouraged her from speaking with a Southern accent. She went on to study acting at the Alabama School of Fine Arts and Birmingham Southern College, but found that the latter's program did not suit her. "The style was broader than what I was interested in doing," she told me. "I wanted something more filmic." Hale eventually got a degree in business. Her explanation: "You gotta eat."

Amazingly, when she auditioned for her first film—an NBC movie of the week—she booked the part. After other roles, she was selected, out of six thousand aspirants, during a nationwide search conducted by the soap opera *Santa Barbara*. "At the time I wore giant T-shirts and baggy pants and there were some seriously hot girls in this line. I was like, 'How did this happen?'" Hale did a couple episodes of *Santa Barbara*. After that, she worked steadily as a regional actor, but in search of "a bigger game to play" made the inevitable move to Los Angeles.

In the nineties, Hale made the rounds on shows that reliably cycled through young actors—*Melrose Place*, *ER*, *Charmed*—but after two years of this she was desperate for more stable and lucrative work. She told me, "I thought, Well, I'll just take voice-over and see if I can make some money there." A month later, she had landed her first cartoon series, *Where on Earth Is Carmen Sandiego?* To the best of Hale's recollection, she had, at that point, never seen a cartoon in her life. She struggled, initially, with the unfamiliar demands of cartoon voice-over and enrolled in a cartoon acting class, where she learned how to "bring a tiny being to life" and travel "so far away from my physical self and stretch my voice to a different place."

It was through *Carmen Sandiego* that Hale first discovered video-game acting. The cartoon spawned a video-game spinoff, and Hale was brought in to record for it. She was startled by the disassociated, scattershot approach of the process, as when she was asked to record dozens of geographical factoids. "We're doing how many flags?" she remembers thinking. "I have to say the name of how many countries? How is this going to be used?" She shrugged. "I didn't get it."

From there, Hale moved comfortably into commercial voice-over—a field that, when she was starting out, was dominated by men. She begged her agent to give scripts specifically written for male actors and, to her agent's surprise, began booking those roles, too. Nowadays, Hale noted happily, "it's mostly women you hear narrating commercials." When I asked Hale if she felt similarly proud of having broken into action video games, probably the most male-oriented voice-over field of all, she smiled. "I like to take the boys' jobs," she said.

For years, many of the "actors" corralled for video-game voice-over were game developers themselves, and the results were predictably indifferent. One of the first game franchises to pioneer the use of high-profile film and television actors in video games was Rockstar's *Grand Theft Auto*, though in the last few years Rockstar has moved in the opposite direction, hiring relatively unknown talent for prominent roles. Michael Hollick's Niko Bellic in *Grand Theft Auto IV* and Rob Wiethoff's John Marston in *Red Dead Redemption* are generally ranked among the finest video-game performances to date, and the performances are extraordinary, in part, due to the unfamiliarity of the actors' voices. Overexposure is thus a pressing concern for video-game actors, and Hale spoke several times of her worries that, one day, her voice might be thought too recognizable.

The voice-over community is, by acting standards, an unusually cordial one. Hale's friend Nolan North, who portrays Nathan Drake in the *Uncharted* franchise and is possibly the most recognizable male voice in video games today, enthused about the nature of the community. "It's not filled with jealousy," he said, "and we go head-to-head for jobs. We're never mad at each other for getting something." North believes that this collegiality is a by-product of the invisibility of video-game actors in the culture at large. "If you're talented and a handful, there's no place for you," he said. "The people who do well in voice-over are the people who are genuine. Everybody makes the same amount of money, too. There's not the disparity of income you see in other areas of acting."

"We're paid a flat fee," Hale told me. "We get no percentage of any kind. That fee is based on union scale. If you're very lucky you can get over scale." A few years ago, she said, she was paid 1,200 dollars for a game that made 270 million. I asked if that was at all galling, but she deflected my question, pointing out that game developers "do all the front-end work, and they do all the back-end work."

David Hayter, a friend of Hale's who portrays Solid Snake in the *Metal Gear Solid* franchise, is rumored to have been paid more for the role than the industry average, though he would not comment on that. A successful screenwriter whose credits include *X-Men* and *Watchmen*, Hayter is so deeply associated with Snake that it has become, effectively, his only role. Apart from those projects that his "twelve-year-old self couldn't say no to"—he recently agreed to play a Jedi in a LucasArts game, for instance—Hayter has more or less given up video-game acting, which makes him slightly more willing to discuss the ways in which game actors are paid and, arguably, underpaid. "The video-game industry is actively trying *not* to go the ways of movies, with residuals and things like that," Hayter told me. "If you starred in a movie that made $250 million," he said, "you'd get more for your next movie. That doesn't happen in games. You get, maybe, double scale." But then, video-game actors lease out a smaller portion of their essence than film actors: voices, after all, are more interchangeable than faces.

Toward the end of her day at the studio, Hale came to a scene with a character referred to as A/K. It was the most emotional scene of the day, and also one of the most technically tricky, because of the way that player's choices in *Mass Effect 1* and *2* carry over into the new sequel. A/K refers to two characters, Ashley and Kaiden, both of whom are Shepard's teammates in *Mass Effect 1* (and, depending on Shepard's gender, potential love interests). Near the end of that game, however, the player is forced to save one character and sacrifice the other, and, in *Mass Effect 2*, whichever of the two was saved reappears to remonstrate with him or her. The result of that conversation, which can go a few ways, determines how the script-merged but game-distinct character of A/K will interact with Shepard in *Mass Effect 3*.

The scene Hale was about to perform involved Shepard's reaction to A/K being harmed. The first line of the scene was simple enough: "Let her/him go." But Hale had to say it multiple times, with different emphases, in order to communicate every possible state of alarm with which Shepard would regard the sight of A/K in peril. Hale did her customary four takes of "Let her go," which she followed with four takes of "Let him go." Two were growly, hateful takes, and two were hard, urgent takes. When she finished, Hale flexed to indicate her deepening transformation into Shepard. She was then told that her lines had to be recorded as though she were running.

"I have a question," Hale said. "It's pretty emotional for Shepard here. How big do you want it?"

Walters explained that he wanted Shepard to seem like more of "a real character" in this game, a character who showed "his frailty." At Walters's use of the masculine pronoun for Shepard, Hale smiled. "I want Shepard's vulnerability to come out," Walters went on, "even though not every player will choose to experience it."

"Is Shepard sick of fighting?" Hale asked.

Walters winced in slight equivocation. When recording with Mark Meer, they had tried to communicate a war-weary

Shepard, Walters said. "But we got feedback that the male Shepard sounded whiny."

Hale went through the "Let her/him go" process again, recording five takes this time.

"I'll take Five as the keeper," Livingstone said, "and Four as a back up."

Hale's next line was "No!" Livingstone turned to Walters and asked, "Is this a panicked 'No,' or an angry 'No'?"

"It's a"—Walters hesitated—"futile 'No.'"

Hale nodded. "No!" she said, stirringly, a moment later.

"More compassion," Livingstone said. "Less heightened."

Hale tried again, and her "No!" seemed to emerge from some alarmed, half-strangled place in her throat.

By the end of the session, Hale had completed twenty-seven scenes and run through 220 lines of dialogue. When I asked Livingstone how many scenes the game contained in total, she answered, "Hundreds." Livingstone would sit through most recording sessions. How much time would that amount to? I asked, suddenly concerned for her. "I don't know," she said, looking away. "Eight hours a day for three months. How long is that?" Over 1,200 hours. Hale would get off easier, but by the time *Mass Effect 3*'s voice production wraps, she will have spent more than three hundred hours portraying Shepard.

Before Hale could stop for the day, she had to perform one last virtuoso task: Shepard's grunts and pain noises. She was given direction for a pain noise to indicate she had been shot once, a pain noise to indicate she had been hit with a burst of energy, a pain noise to indicate she had been shot while moving, a pain noise to indicate she had been punched, a pain noise to indicate she was nearing death, and a pain noise to indicate she had died.

* * *

I decided that I couldn't leave Los Angeles without playing *Mass Effect 2* with Commander Shepard herself. Hale, after some hedging, agreed to try and came to the house where I was staying. A screen came up asking us to select the male or female Shepard. "Are you kidding me?" Hale said, choosing the latter. A load screen came up, and Hale passed the time by excitedly tapping her feet against the hardwood floor. She looked over at me. "Is my head going to explode?"

During her interactions with other characters, I asked Hale whether she would play as the Paragon Shepard or Renegade Shepard. "I'm going to go with the middle-of-the-road Shepard," she said. "I want to hear my middle responses, because they're the hardest to land. Filling them with energy and emotion takes a lot of focus."

Upon hearing her first spoken words in the game—"The distress beacon is ready for launch"—Hale groaned. "Drives me nuts," she said. "I could have made that better." When the opening cinematic gave way to actual gameplay, Hale looked helplessly at her controller. She tried, vainly, to move Shepard forward. "Wait," she said. "What am I missing? The right *what* moves me?"

"The right stick moves the camera," I said. "The left stick moves you."

She had somehow positioned the in-game camera in its least obliging position. "I'm looking at my own tush," Hale said. Soon she had Shepard running through the hallways of her spaceship as it came under devastating attack. Hale leaned forward to turn up the volume, so as to better hear Shepard's breathing. Something in her eyes changed, and she began to nod. "This," she said, "is actually really informative."

We watched the eerie scene in which Shepard is sucked out of an airlock and into the soundlessness of space, the only sound her increasingly labored breathing as her frantic, thrashing limbs gradually relax into death. Hale sat back. "I remember recording this vividly. It's really fun to die specifically."

In the game, of course, Shepard is swiftly resurrected. Soon, Hale had her first taste of combat. She struggled with learning how to take cover, shoot, move while shooting, climb over cover, reload, and find ammunition, all the while keeping the camera centered in front of her. But when the game required Hale to find a grenade launcher and dispatch a platoon of hapless robots, she did so quickly and efficiently. "Handled it!" she said, in a tight, confident voice. It was, I realized, Shepard's voice. The game soon brought Hale into contact with a character called Jacob, yet another of Shepard's potential love interests. During Shepard and Jacob's conversation, Hale mined the paraphrase system to get as much information—and hear as much of her performance—as she could. At one point in the conversation, Hale cringed. "There's a segue error there," she said. "The energy in the transition was wrong." I pointed out that she could hardly control that. This was true, Hale said, but "I need to have that information somewhere."

After an hour so, she indicated that she was ready to stop playing. But I realized that the next sequence would bring Shepard into her first contact with a character known as the Illusive Man, who is played by Martin Sheen—an actor she had never met. "We should really keep going until you have your conversation with Martin Sheen," I said.

Hale perked up. "I should *always* have my conversation with Martin Sheen. He's my favorite president."

During the interaction with the Illusive Man, Hale pursued every available line of conversation possible. When the Illusive Man, at last, dismissed Shepard, Hale put the controller down and stared at it. It seemed unlikely that she would be picking up another controller anytime soon.

"So how did that feel?" I asked.

It was helpful, she said, but beyond gaining a basic understanding of what playing games is like, she felt surprisingly unaltered. Or maybe that was not so surprising. "I'm used to living in a disassociated universe," she said.

—2011

THE THEORY AND PRACTICE OF NOT GIVING A SHIT

On a Visit with Jim Harrison

I grew up in the Upper Peninsula of Michigan, which is, essentially, a New England–sized forest with the population density of Siberia. As of this writing, the U.P. has coughed up a major league pitcher, a couple world-class coaches, and exactly no movie stars, film directors, celebrity chefs, giants of finance, reality television geeks, or (as far as I know) porno queens. Its sons and daughters, by and large, dream feasible dreams. For the U.P.'s young writers, though, it is a little different. This difference is largely due to Jim Harrison, who has been publishing fiction and poetry about the U.P. for the last forty years, a good deal of which was written in a cabin up near Grand Marais, a two-hour drive from Escanaba, the U.P. ore town in which I grew up.

My father and Harrison, who is now seventy-three, are old friends. They met through the writer Philip Caputo, with whom my father served in Vietnam. My father, like Caputo and Harrison, is a keen bird hunter, and during the autumns of my childhood the three of them would head up to Grand Marais and hunt pheasant and grouse. A few times, while passing through Escanaba, Harrison came by our house for dinner, seeming less like a man to me than a force of nature with a Pancho Villa mustache.

"Jim Harrison is a writer with immortality in him." Or so the *London Sunday Times* once said—a high-mileage blurb Harrison's publishers have understandably splashed across several of his books. Once I developed an interest in writing, I would sometimes stop and ponder my father's Harrison collection, which comprised almost all of the fiction and none of the poetry. (It is not actually clear that my father knows Harrison writes poetry.) I noted the paperback jackets' comparisons of Harrison to Melville, Hemingway, and Faulkner, but I was also aware of the Harrison Legend, which in the meantime has only grown: the films made from his work, the friendship with Jack Nicholson, the immense foreign readership, the incomprehensible appetite (he once ate a thirty-seven-course lunch and lived to write about it). There was also the way he wrestled with nature in his work. For Harrison, the natural world was not something to be cherished because it was pretty; rather, it was something to be howled at, gloriously, in the night.

Imagine my puzzlement. The man who occasionally sat at our dining room table wrote stories set in the U.P., and critics in New York, London, and Paris regarded these stories as literature. Until that point in my life, I had heeded the inadvertent lessons of my English classes: literature was something written by the dead for the bored. Literature was decisively *not* about the towns I knew.

One day I pulled Harrison's first novel, *Wolf*, from my father's shelf. Subtitled "A False Memoir," *Wolf* is about a Harrison stand-in named Swanson who retreats to Upper Michigan after youthful city living in an attempt to spot a wolf in the wild. I stopped at the line where Swanson says something about "the low pelvic mysteries of swamps." I was fifteen years old and for the first time in my reading life I underlined a phrase not to retain its information but to acknowledge its mystery.

I followed *Wolf* with *Just Before Dark*, a collection of Harrison's nonfiction. I latched onto its first essay, which moves from an opening account of Harrison ice fishing on the bay in front of my father's house to an anecdote involving Harrison's dinner with Orson Welles. How was it possible, in life or in writing, to go from ice fishing in front of our house to dinner with Orson Welles?

The simple fact of Harrison's existence demonstrated that you could slip from one world to the other, Escanaba to Orson Welles, smuggling literature both ways. Maybe it was time to thank him.

Harrison no longer lives in Michigan. Nine years ago, he and Linda, his wife of forty-one years, sold their cabin in the Upper Peninsula and their farm in the Lower Peninsula and relocated to the environs of Livingston, Montana, for the summer and Patagonia, Arizona, for the winter. It was the early summer, so off to Montana I went.

States do not get prettier than Montana. Driving across its landscape is like being trapped in a beer commercial wrapped in the National Anthem. The only place I have visited that rivals its rough, mountainous beauty is Kyrgyzstan. I kept this to myself. MONTANA: AMERICA'S KYRGYZSTAN was a motto unlikely to appeal to locals. I was supposed to meet Harrison and Linda at the 2nd Street Bistro, Livingston's best restaurant, at (for some reason) 6:07 p.m. I arrived at 6:00 and was promptly seated at a table that had been set with a hefty cheese and salami plate around the edge of which WELCOME HOME JIM & LINDA had been written in drizzled milk-chocolate script.

Harrison and Linda arrived at 6:07. "My son!" Harrison said in greeting. It was the first time I had seen him since 2006, at a party in New York City. At the time he had been so afflicted with gout that he needed a cane to walk. Now Harrison's cane was gone; his gout was mostly under control, as was his diabetes. His shingles, however, were dreadful, and he moved as deliberately as a cold-slowed bumblebee. This was not easily reconciled with the humon-gously vigorous Harrison of my youth. I suspected that Harrison's current condition was rather more difficult for him to accept.

If you are describing Jim Harrison physically, you are pretty much forced to start with his eye. When he was seven, a young girl, her motives unknown, pushed a broken glass bottle into his face, permanently blinding his left eye. When Harrison looks at you straight on, his left eye appears almost cartoonishly miscen-tered, as if he had taken a blow to the head and needs another, corrective blow to fix the problem. After six decades of double work, Harrison's right eye has weakened, as evidenced by a milky blue rim around its iris. (These days, Harrison told me, he could read no more than twenty-five pages of prose before the headache became unbearable.) But it is an amazing face, an iconic face, and Harrison's goofy left eye was like the bump in Anna Akhmatova's nose: an essential, defining imperfection.

Everything else about Harrison seems big. His round, substan-tive head looks as though it belonged on the end of something a Viking would use to knock down a medieval Danish gate. His body is big, too, but not really fat. Rather, it seemed *full*—the body of a skinny person that had been forcibly stuffed with food. Harrison's face and hands are an identically bright blood-pressure red.

It was something of a relief when we finally took our seats. Linda, whom Harrison has described as "the least defenseless woman I've ever known," was seated beside me. She and Harrison have known each other since they were teenagers. One day Harrison spotted her climbing stairs in her riding pants and thought, I must have her. She was fifteen, he seventeen.

When I told Linda that I had last seen her when I was twelve, she laughed, lightly, as though this were the most absurd thing she had ever heard. The Bistro's head chef, Brian, brought a basket of fries to our table. Harrison greeted him, too, with "My son!" Brian's fries were maybe the tastiest I had eaten outside of Paris, so I asked him, one Harrison boy to another, for his secret. Here it was: salt, fresh garlic, skillful frying.

Harrison was studying the wine list. "Do you like wine?" he asked me. Harrison is a wine hound of international note, so this was a bit like being asked by Popeye if you like spinach. The first bottle came and, suddenly, another. I do not recall much of the night after the second bottle's splendid arrival, and by the end of the evening I felt as though I had been beaten up by our meal. Harrison was in comparable shape. Outside, he hugged me—an act of affection nearly triggered emesis. Harrison asked if I was familiar with Chief Joseph's famous dictum of dignified defeat. I nodded. "'I will fight no more forever,'" I said grandly. Harrison smiled and said, with identical grandiosity, "I will eat no more forever." Somehow I doubted that.

This fall Harrison will publish *The Great Leader*, his seventeenth work of fiction, and *Songs of Unreason*, his fourteenth book of poetry. A large number of these books were written in the last fifteen years, an unusual burst of late-career fecundity. When I asked about this, Harrison explained that after a high-impact life of travel and sport and carousing, all he really did anymore was write and fish. "I'm trying to make my life smaller," he said. "I'm tired of living a bigger life."

Harrison was born in Grayling, Michigan, in 1937, to intensely practical but literary parents. His mother was a homemaker and his father was a government agriculturalist who worked with local farmers. He grew up in a close, warm family in what he "was slow to learn . . . was poverty," as he writes in his memoir, *Off to the Side*. After his blinding, Harrison became a "berserk waif" whom Michigan could not hold. After lying about his age, he found work as a bellhop at a series of resorts in the American West's quadrilateral mountain states. These first, wondrous travels ended when a cop spotted Harrison putting a blackjack in his boot. The sixteen-year-old was unceremoniously shuttled back to Michigan.

He was just getting started. The following year he hitchhiked to the "threadbare nirvana" of New York City, where he lost his virginity to a sex worker. In Massachusetts, at nineteen, he met one of his early literary heroes, Jack Kerouac, who was impressively tanked. Eventually Harrison returned home and completed a bachelor's degree long-delayed by hoboing at Michigan State, where his classmates included the novelists Thomas McGuane and Richard Ford. (McGuane remains Harrison's close friend: they have exchanged weekly letters for the last forty-five years.)

In 1962, when Harrison was twenty-two, he delayed the start of his father and sister's hunting trip by debating whether he should accompany them. In the end, he decided not to. Judith, Harrison's sister, was the only member of his family who shared his obsession with art and literature; the day Harrison waved goodbye to her was the last time he saw her alive. A few hours later, a drunk driver plowed into his father's car; there were no survivors. Soon after the funeral, he wrote the first poem he was able to consider finished. When I asked Harrison about these events, he said that his father and sister's deaths "cut the last cord holding me down."

A few months later, Harrison was sent to Boston to stay with his brother, John, who was working at Harvard's Widener

Library. Through a chance connection Harrison managed to get some of his poems to the poetry consultant for the great independent publisher W. W. Norton, which offered him a contract. Until this point, virtually no one but Linda had seen Harrison's poetry.

One can discern how utterly everything has changed—culturally, commercially, even *tonally*—when one reads the flap copy of *Plain Song*, Harrison's first book: "In his late twenties, Jim Harrison is a mature person and a poet who has found his own voice." (When I read this aloud in Harrison's presence, he disputed the factual basis of both statements.) "After graduating from Michigan State University, Mr. Harrison became a teaching assistant while he worked for a while on his MA, but he abandoned the academic life because it was in conflict (for him) with the life of poetry." (This was more accurate.)

The publication of *Plain Song* landed Harrison at SUNY-Stony Brook on Long Island, where his colleagues included the literary critic Alfred Kazin (who argued for Harrison's promotion to assistant professor) and the young writer Philip Roth. "I wasn't very long at Stony Brook," he admits in *Off to the Side*, "when it occurred to me that the English department had all the charm of a streetfight where no one actually landed a punch."

He returned to Michigan after being awarded an NEA grant in 1967 and a Guggenheim the following year, at which point he realized the woods meant too much to him; he could not go back to teaching or Stony Brook. During Harrison's otherwise liberating Guggenheim year, however, he fell off a cliff—literally. The spill left him miserably bedridden for months. At the urging of McGuane, he used this time to write *Wolf*. When he finished, Harrison, who did not have an agent, sent the only copy of his manuscript to Simon and Schuster, but a postal strike stranded the manuscript somewhere between Michigan and New York City; Harrison assumed it would be lost forever. When the book, at long last, made it to New York, Harrison was offered another contract.

Manuscripts of which a single copy exists? Postal strikes potentially derailing careers? Young novelists without agents being published by major American houses? Such are the antique emblems of a vanished world; we might as well be talking about illuminated manuscripts. Harrison is aware of this, and refers to his jobless, institutionally unattached literary ascendancy as "the old way."

At the beginning of my writing career, a decade ago, the "old way" still seemed an available, even noble, path for the young writer to try to follow. The literary world in which Harrison came up, and of which I caught the very tail end, has now been tectonically ripped apart. How to navigate the adrift plates of this new literary world is not yet apparent—not to me, and not to most of the thirty- and forty-something writers of my acquaintance. In this respect, visiting Harrison was not unlike climbing to the top of a mountain in search of a wise man. You want him to say the old way is still there because he is still there.

One Jim Harrison aperçu or another is usually floating around in my mind. Here is what bobbed to the surface while I drove to his house the morning after our dinner: "No matter how acute, the pain of hangovers can't rise above farce." My farcical hangover was not helped by the rental-wreckingly potholed dirt road along which the Harrisons lived. At least the view was spectacular. To my left: the Yellowstone River, swollen with snowmelt, and the snow-topped Gallatin Mountains, which looked like what a child might come up with if asked to draw mountains.

As I pulled into the Harrisons' driveway, the man himself emerged from the small cabin he uses as a writing studio, which is adjacent to the main house. "Look around!" he called over. "What don't you see?"

"What?" I called back.

"Any other houses," he said. I met him halfway between the cabin and the house. He was wearing a fleece vest, unbelted pants, and rubber boots. With his cowlicky hair and potbelly, he looked a bit like a friendly garden gnome. When I complimented his view of the mountains, he nodded and said, "They're full of grizzly bears that will *kill* you."

His dogs came running up: Mary, an elderly black English setter; and Zil, a squat-legged Scottish retriever with a stick clamped between her teeth. "Don't throw her stick," Harrison told me. "Under *any* circumstances. It will never end." Harrison looked at Zil—wet and filthy from a recent dip in the Harrisons' pond—and shook his head. "She's such a fuckhead," he said. "But she's a free woman. I adore her."

Linda came out after the dogs and regarded the long-sleeve thermal Patagonia shirt Harrison was wearing beneath his fleece vest, which looked as though it had been recently used as a barmaid's rag. "That shirt is filthy," she said.

"I know," Harrison said. "It *must* be washed. Eventually."

Here the Harrisons started telling me about the rattlesnakes. At the dawn of creation, apparently, Montana received a generous helping of rattlesnakes. Until recently an ungodly amount of the fell serpents considered the Harrisons' property home turf. Linda admitted that she had long been terrified of snakes, but no more; she stabbed one to death last summer. "It's amazing what you learn to live with," she said. In 2003, one rattler, startled from its indented glide by Harrison's beloved English setter Rose, reared up and nailed the dog. Rose lived but was so neurologically damaged Harrison had no choice but to put her down. This was war. On one legendarily sanguine afternoon he shot twenty rattlers variously nestled around his property. The creatures kept turning up until he hired a local snake guy to find their den, which turned out to be about five hundred yards from where we now stood. The den was gassed, after which Harrison's snake guy filled two barrels with dead rattlers. The thing with rattlers, Harrison said, is this: You have to kill the alpha male. If the alpha male leaves the den and does not return, he will not be followed. Harrison smiled, as though this had all sorts of other implications.

He took me inside the main house and showed me his "business" desk (upon which were five differently diminished bottles of aspirin) where he pays his bills and answers his mail and signs his contracts and daily faxes his handwritten pages to his assistant, Joyce Behle, in Michigan, who types up the pages and faxes them back. "I can't revise except in the type form," Harrison told me. "I don't get a sense of it, the language, without it being typed."

On his desk I noticed a letter from Harrison's French publisher. "Those people saved me financially," Harrison said bluntly. Indeed, Harrison's books sell in the hundreds of thousands in France, where he is known as "the Mozart of the Plains." Over the years, he told me, he has met four or five dozen little French girls named Dalva, the titular heroine of what many regard as Harrison's best novel. A French critic once told Harrison that his countrymen so adore Harrison's books because most American fiction is about either the "life of the mind" or the "life of action"; Harrison's books were about both.

Harrison handed me a small steel mess kit, which, he said, a Frenchman had given him at a reading a few years ago before hurrying away. Harrison opened it for me. Inside were a hundred beautifully tied handmade fishing flies. "This is weeks of work," Harrison said. "I'm trying to figure out how to find him and thank him." He paused. "They don't have very good fishing in France."

By now Harrison was smoking. Harrison smokes so much that even when he is not smoking it still seems like he is smoking. While he lit up, he diverted my attention to a lovely framed photo of some autumnal Michigan woods. Did he miss Michigan? I asked. "Terribly," he said. "I've thought about it every day for nine years. I don't miss the Lower Peninsula at all. The cabin I owned in the U.P. for twenty-three years saved my life."

When I asked why he loved the Upper Peninsula, he said, "Because it's isolated and there's all these millions of acres of what I call 'undifferentiated wilderness.' It's empty because, other than pulping, you can't really make any more money off of it. It's been utterly and totally plundered by logging, mining, and everything. All the areas I love in the U.P., nothing more can be done with them." I thought of how Harrison had once described his own career as "an independent contractor in a non-extractive industry. I drilled and mined my head, as it were." The natural world and the human mind had that much in common, at least: Strip them of resources and, sometimes, a terrible beauty was born.

As we headed out to his writing studio, Harrison talked. He talks unceasingly, about everything, his endearingly permanent Midwestern accent a cross between Blackbeard the Pirate, *Fargo*'s Marge Gunderson, and Harvey Fierstein, and his mind wonderfully crammed with both experience ("I ate a gross of oysters once, to see if I could. I could. I got gout the next morning") and knowledge ("Certain bears eat eighty pounds of moths *a day*. Can you imagine?").

"I hope I'm not disrupting your writing day too much," I said, as we sat down inside his studio. Not to worry, Harrison said. "I just finished a second section of a Brown Dog." Brown Dog, who has featured in five novellas thus far, is one of Harrison's more singular creations: a lusty and maleducated Upper Michigan Indian whose adventures include finding a frozen body at the bottom of Lake Superior and working as the errand boy of a craven Los Angeles screenwriter. Harrison described the section he just finished, in which Brown Dog overhears two well-heeled women in a restaurant discuss the importance of having a clean colon. Brown Dog wants to know: How do you know if your colon's clean anyway?

This seemed as good a time as any to ask Harrison about his health, which I had heard was not great. He was feeling okay lately, he said, but he had not been the same since a book tour five years ago, in which, at sixty-seven years of age, he did nineteen cities in twenty-four days. It "ruined" him, he said.

The shades in Harrison's cabin were all pulled and the wall above his desk was bare; he does not like distractions while he writes. Arranged with still-life exactitude upon his desk were some shotgun shells; a few feathers; a copy of Nabokov's *Ada* ("a completely deranged book," Harrison said approvingly); two Ziploc bags, one filled with bark from a Michigan birch tree and the other filled with sand from the shores of Lake Superior; three separate pairs of eyeglasses; and a Pompeiian amount of cigarette ash.

Pinned to the big bulletin board next to his desk were photos of Anne Frank, Arthur Rimbaud, a woodcock, a polar bear, several of Harrison's Indian friends, his deceased Zen teacher, the poet Gary Snyder, and his grandchildren. Behind him, on the far side of the room, were shelves piled with animal skulls and turtle carapaces and various Native American artifacts, including a tenth-century soapstone pipe, something called a peyote rattle, and a rather formidable tomahawk. Also here was a self-portrait of a bare-breasted fan of Harrison's, who had sent him the photo with a letter indicating that she was a lesbian.

I was most surprised to find a photo of Ernest Hemingway, the writer to whom Harrison has been most frequently compared. The *New Yorker*, for instance, once called Harrison "one of the more talented students of the école du Hemingway." But this is not a school the student ever willingly attended: Harrison once nastily described Hemingway's work as a "woodstove that didn't give off much heat." Harrison still resents the comparison, he told me, "because there's no connection whatsoever" between his and Hemingway's work. For what it is worth, I agree with Harrison, whose large, ecstatic voice is more indebted to Joyce, Faulkner, Nabokov, and García Márquez. But Harrison writes of hunting and fishing and Michigan, as did Hemingway: for critics who neither hunt nor fish nor know Michigan from Minnesota, these are literary doppels that gänger. "In my lifetime," Harrison told me, "the country has gone from being 25 percent urban and 75 percent rural to 75 percent urban and 25 percent rural." He writes, in other words, of a world and type of people increasingly unimaginable to the cultural elite. A critic from a major American magazine once asked Harrison if he had ever personally known a Native American.

Harrison has outlasted those critics who initially wrote him off as a Hemingway-derived regionalist, and at times he has been as successful as a modern American writer can possibly be. For the first half of the 1970s, however, Harrison was trapped in the odd half-success of acclaim that had no commensurate financial recompense. From 1970 to 1976, he made around $10,000 a year. Things got so bad for him and Linda that several people came to the Harrisons' aid. The novelist (and eventual suicide) Richard Brautigan, for instance, loaned Harrison the money he needed to write *Farmer*, which a few Harrison fans, myself included, regard as his most perfect novel. Jack Nicholson, whom Harrison had met through McGuane, kept him afloat through another difficult period. Harrison's financial troubles were considerably worsened by the fact that he did not file tax returns for half a decade.

Harrison's unlikely solution to his penury was to write *Legends of the Fall*, a book of novellas—a genre considered so defunct in 1977 that several publishers claimed not to know what a novella was. Harrison thus helped to resuscitate a venerable literary form, and few American writers have written more great novellas than Harrison. (Short stories, alas, are another matter: "I think I've written two short stories in my life," Harrison told me. "I just can't do it. I've tried.") He wrote the title novella of *Legends* in nine days, basing large parts of the story on the journals of Linda's grandfather. "Legends," which is written in prose with the angry density of cooled lava, concerns a father and three sons whose fortunes wrathfully diverge around a woman. In 1977, *Esquire* published "Legends" in its 15,000-word entirety—an impossible thing to imagine today, assuming James Franco does not try his hand at novellas—and the movie rights for *Legends*'s trio of novellas were quickly purchased. David Lean originally wanted to direct the title novella, while John Huston expressed desire to direct its companion work "Revenge." Neither project came to fruition, but two pretty good movies resulted farther down the line, with Edward Zwick directing *Legends* and Tony Scott directing *Revenge*. In 1978, Harrison was stunned to realize that he made more money in the previous year than the president of General Motors.

This led to several years of what Harrison has described as a "long screenplay binge." He is admirably clear-sighted on what drove him into screenwriting (greed) and what kept him from succeeding more (he was not very good at it). As a producer said to him: "I didn't hire you because you were a good screenwriter but because you can make up interesting people." (Later, while working for Warner Bros., Harrison had the chance to read some of William Faulkner's screenplays and "was appalled and amused by how terrible they were.") Harrison's Hollywood years had him lunching with a young Michael Ovitz and palling around with Warren Beatty. Sean Connery and Jack Nicholson had their first meeting at a lunch with Harrison. He did coke with George Harrison and was planning to write the screenplay for John Kennedy Toole's *Confederacy of Dunces* for John Belushi before the comedian overdosed. He wrote an unproduced western for Harrison Ford, who later made Harrison the godfather of his daughter. Werner Herzog was so determined to convince Harrison to write the script for *Fitzcarraldo* that during a hotel-room negotiation he followed Harrison into the shower.

This period strained his family life. Harrison has never shied away from discussing the years he spent chasing "actresses, waitresses," as he recently admitted to the *New York Times*. Still, he and Linda have remained married for fifty-one years.

Harrison and Hollywood had a less perfect union "I'm an arrogant person," he told me, "and I just couldn't deal with them. Once, in a meeting with a producer, I said, 'If your script girl uses the word *agenda* again, I'm walking out.' Because she'd say, 'What's your character's agenda?' That was the word they'd use for a while in Hollywood; I think they've stopped." He attributes some of his irascibility to "the problems everybody had at the time. Cocaine, you know?"

His literary friends, meanwhile, were as full of misbehavior as the loosest starlet. In Key West, Florida, of the early 1980s, McGuane, Caputo, Harrison, and several other writers and artists often gathered to fish and destroy themselves. McGuane, whose appetite for destruction had earned him the nickname Captain Berserko, designated this Key West demimonde Club Mandible. Harrison described for me one notably druggy Club Mandible convocation, during which he was sticking a straw in "a big Bufferin bottle of great coke. We didn't even bother doing lines." He shrugged. "Well, how are you gonna survive that?" When he returned home to Michigan from Key West he could not remember his cat's name.

"How many of your Key West friends didn't make it?" I asked him.

"Quite a few," he said. "I was thinking, though." And here he paused. "That writer who hung himself—"

And here I had to pause, for I knew Harrison was thinking of David Foster Wallace. Ten years ago, I published an essay about my efforts to quit dipping tobacco. The story was greatly influenced by a couple marathon telephone conversations with Wallace, who shared the habit. When the essay was published, I was delighted to find that I shared the issue in question with an essay by Harrison called "How Men Pray." Wallace wrote to me about my essay, but also made time to compliment "Harrison's prayer thing," which he "*really* liked." Wallace went on to say how "highly seducible" he was by Harrison's voice. I knew the feeling. For a young writer just starting out, this was indescribable. Two of my literary heroes were talking to each other, as it were, through me. It was one of the first times I felt that my work as a writer was greater than my computer, my bedroom, my mind.

Shortly after Dave killed himself I reread "How Men Pray" and remember wondering whether, in the midst of Dave's torment, he might have found consoling Harrison's belief that a writer is someone who "consciously or unconsciously takes a vow of obedience to awareness," and perhaps even smiled at Harrison's belief that the writer's gift is one of "excessive consciousness." Harrison could have finally reminded Dave of this: "There is no self-destructiveness without the destruction of others."

Harrison, who I now learned had corresponded with Wallace "just a little bit" about poetry, brought up Jonathan Franzen's much discussed *New Yorker* piece about Wallace, in which Franzen revealed that he could never get Wallace interested in his great passion of bird watching. "This is interesting," Harrison said. "Of the twelve or thirteen suicides I've known, none of them had any interest in nature. In other words, they had no interest in what Rimbaud called 'the other.' The otherness, say, of nature." They could not make, Harrison said, "that jump out of themselves."

I told Harrison how much I wished he and Dave could have met.

Harrison sighed. "Well, it's funny, because I know he liked my religion piece. Which was completely daffy." We were silent for a while. "You know," Harrison said finally, "he loved his dogs for that last year, but he should've been having dogs for thirty years. Every day of the year, the first thing I do after breakfast is take the dogs for a walk. They absolutely depend on it. But also it's what's best for me."

That afternoon we went for a drive in Harrison's truck, lingering at a crossing above the swollen banks of the Yellowstone River, its water all gray, churning turbulence. Harrison asked how my hangover was doing. Not great, I said. Harrison confessed to having grown weary of hangovers. "Moderation is no fun," he said, "except it feels better."

Harrison surprised me by asking if I wanted to check out his property's gassed rattlesnake den. "Do *you* want to?" I asked. That depends, he said. "If you want to spend an hour being incredibly careful and alert, we can go." Before I could answer, he told me that rattlers were locally evolving to lose their rattles. Loud-rattling snakes, after all, have a tendency to be eaten by wild pigs and shot by humans. This left more Darwinian room for quieter rattlers to breed. I decided there would be no visit to the rattlesnake den.

We talked of writers whose reputations had dimmed, of our mutual love for Norman Mailer's nonfiction, and of a young writer whose work Harrison had recently discovered and greatly admired. This was Elif Batuman, with whom I had a small, pointless public feud after she wrote something dismissive about my work. Pettily, I told Harrison about Batuman's and my contretemps. Harrison looked over at me queerly, as though to say, *Why are you telling me this?*

Then, possibly to make me feel better, Harrison confessed that he was unable to enjoy the work of Cormac McCarthy. When I told Harrison that the galley copy for *The Great Leader* compared his novel to McCarthy's *No Country for Old Men*, Harrison laughed, as I knew he would, given my strong suspicion that he did not bother reading his own promotional galley copy. But he laughed, I think, for another reason. *No Country* tries to sneak into what is ostensibly a thriller all manner of soul-squeezing metaphysics. Harrison's one attempt at something similar, the early "rural noir" novel *Warlock*, is the only book of Harrison's that he claims to loathe. McCarthy's novels are cold and coiled and nervous—rattlesnake novels. Harrison's novels are warm-blooded snake-trained setters that go instantly on point in the presence of such theatrics.

The hero of Harrison's forthcoming novel is Simon Sunderson, a retired U.P. detective poking around the American Southwest in search of a cult leader with a penchant for underage girls. Other than Sunderson's mid-book stoning by some fanatics, very little actually happens. It is a chase novel in which the chase never gets started, a mystery novel whose mystery-novel motor has been removed. While it is hugely enjoyable—Harrison is probably incapable of writing a novel that is not enjoyable—it is also slightly shambolic. Several of Harrison's later novels have a similarly loose-limbed quality: gone is the piano-wire tautness of his earlier books. The language, though, remains stunning, such as when Harrison describes U.P. winters as a "vast, dormant god" and describes some men "as a new kind of tooth decay in the mouth of the room."

What *The Great Leader* is really about is divorce (Sunder-son's wife has recently left him), napping (a pastime in which Sunderson—like his creator—frequently engages), the appro-priation of Native American religion (which is common among cults), and the curse of sexual persistence. Sunderson, Harrison told me, was "sort of in his last push, sexually. And it drives people a little bit crazy, that sense of waning sexuality. We don't get so much work on what it's like to be getting older."

The singular pleasure of age, Harrison said, was "really not giving a shit." Critics, for instance. Earlier in his career, he resented what he calls "the west of the Mississippi problem," whereby Western and Midwestern writers are marginalized by coastal arbi-ters. Today, though, he no longer cared. "I don't trust anybody that doesn't do good work. I don't give them any credibility at all. If they can't write, why should I believe anything they have to say?" Quite a few writers I know claim not to read their reviews; Harrison is the only one I believe.

When I was first reading his work, I told Harrison, the thing I responded to was the anger. "Your work gets better when you let go of your anger," Harrison said. "Because anger is always didactic, and the didactic is of no value for a novelist." He looked at me. "You gotta let a lot of people *into* your novels. Not people you made up, but people you allow to make up *themselves*, you know?"

If Jim Harrison did not exist, Jim Harrison would have had to invent him.

I drove out to Harrison's again the next morning, and again he offered to take me to the rattlesnake den. This time I said yes. We drove up into pale green hills, which soon became barren pastureland. When Harrison's truck ran out of gas we got out and walked. As we neared the den, Harrison pulled on my arm, and I realized we were standing amid forty, seventy, a thousand rattle-snakes, their tongues evilly forking from squat, ugly faces. I woke up. It was four in the morning and my hotel sheets were damp with night sweat.

A few hours later I pulled into the Harrisons' driveway and saw a tall and beautifully redheaded bird high-stepping around in the gravel. Inside I told Linda I was pretty sure I just saw a turkey. Linda was surprised and asked me to describe it. I did. "That was a pheasant," she said. "You're from Escanaba. Shouldn't you know what a pheasant looks like?"

"Don't tell Jim," I said, adding, a moment later, "I'm joking." She knew I was not joking. I had already humiliatingly confused a crow with a raven in Harrison's presence. (Harrison: "Most writers know only four birds—hawk, gull, crow, robin." I could not even fulfill this pathetic mandate!) While Linda smiled at me, I thought of one of my best writer friends, who once opened a magazine piece by making note of the "sugar pines" along a hill. I asked my friend how he knew what those trees were; such sensitivity to flora seemed unlike him. My friend told me he had no idea what a sugar pine was. He simply asked someone what kind of trees grew in the area. We both laughed.

The assumption of false authority was a useful writing trick, one I had used again and again, but maybe it's also insidious. After all, it actually means something to know what things are called. If you begin to assume false authority here, you will be tempted to assume it there, and then everywhere. You cannot share anything worth knowing unless you make it clear what you do not know. Harrison, for instance, has a wonderfully guileless way of refusing to hide his research. If Harrison reads a book to learn about something, the characters in his novels will invariably read the same book. It makes the stuff Harrison does know that much more striking.

Nature is slow, Harrison told me. "That's how I saw so much—because I was out there all the time. When it's slow you don't, of course, always see something. You just see what's there that day, and sometimes it's quite extraordinary."

It's this patience that has allowed Harrison to write lines so lovely as this: "A creek is more powerful than despair."

On the conservative talk radio station I was listening to on the way to the Harrisons, the host had said, "Unfortunately, Americans are not getting up in the morning thinking about the Constitution." When Harrison appeared from his writing studio I asked him if he believed Americans should be waking up thinking about the Constitution. He asked me what the fuck I was talking about. I told him about the radio lunatic. Harrison's face turned grave. "It's a dark day in America," he said.

"Why?" I asked.

"I just made that up."

We sat down for the last time in Harrison's writing studio. On his desk was a letter he had begun writing to McGuane; he had gotten as far as "Dear Tom." Harrison usually wrote McGuane on Sunday, and was planning to finish the letter before I arrived, but had fallen asleep. He showed me the most recent letter McGuane had written him. McGuane thanked Harrison for recommending Elif Batuman to him and ended with a postscript that maybe they should start thinking about publishing their forty-five-year-long correspondence.

When he woke up from his nap, he realized he wanted to tell me something, which was his dislike of "nifty gear" out-doormanship, such as the kind he imagined was favored by the readers of *Outside*. He wanted to make sure I got that into the piece. He quickly had second thoughts, though. "Take that out," he said, waving his hand. A moment later he said, "No, put it in; they need to hear it."

Sometimes when you are talking to Harrison he gets incredibly still. He looks away and starts breathing wheezily from his chest, and his eyes fade, and you begin to worry that he is in the middle of some kind of cardiac event. Other times, when he is talking about drinking or writing or his wife or his daughters or grandchildren, he becomes boyish, all the wrinkles ironed out of his face and his eyes slits of joy. Other times, when he is losing his patience, he resembles some kind of Indian werebear with a face wrecked by pit fighting. With Harrison it was impossible to feel something so simple as friendship. He suddenly seemed to me like the closest thing we have to a tribal elder. If writers ever needed permission to raid another tribe and steal its corn, we would need to ask Harrison. He would listen carefully and judge prudently. We would never doubt his judgment, even when we saw him playing in the stream an hour later.

Harrison lives close to his mind. You sense this more and more the longer you stay with him, especially if, like me, you sometimes have to swim across an electro-plastic sea of junk to reach your own mind. You want to know or touch that unmediated part of Harrison, to tell him things. I was not the only one. At one point in Livingston, during our drive-around, we ran into a young friend of his, who immediately launched into a story about how he and his now-ex-girlfriend had recently decided to abort their child. But the younger man danced around mentioning this explicitly, forcing Harrison to say, "You mean you killed it?" His younger friend swallowed with a big-eyed blanch, and so did I. Later still, we met an aspiring screenwriter, who asked Harrison if he would have a look at one of his screenplays. "I couldn't read a screenplay without puking," Harrison said. Sometimes politeness was just a way to escape what needed to be said.

Before I left him, Harrison wanted to take me for a quick, gorgeous drive down the road, toward the foothills of the Rockies.

There was a question I had been wanting to ask but was slightly afraid to. Since we only had an hour or so left together, I let it fly: "What did you think when you heard that one of John Bissell's sons had become a writer?"

He looked on toward the road. "I thought, boy, isn't this odd? I'd heard rumors, right along. And the main thing that always gets to me is just worry. I'm capable of worrying about anything and anyone. And I thought, oh God, what will happen to him? Why has he chosen this bloody voyage? That's McGuane's term for being a writer: a bloody voyage. But I was so pleased with your early successes."

"What are these hills here?" I asked, motioning out the window.

"What do you mean?"

"What are they called?"

"They don't call 'em anything."

How about those bushes? "Juniper," he said, and pointed up along the hills' escarpment. "See those rock formations? Full of rodentia. And rattlers." We circled back to his house and saw, in quick succession, a western tanager and a yellow-rumped warbler, Harrison's first of the season. A deer ran alongside the truck, and I asked Harrison why the deer in Montana looked different from the deer in Michigan. Montana deer are mule deer, he said. Dumber, slower, mangier, grayer than Michigan's whitetails. We passed the big pink tree that grew next to his driveway's entrance. What's that called? "Ornamental crab apple," he said.

We came back to the house and Harrison wanted to know if I was going to continue teaching, which, I had told him the day before, was increasingly cannibalizing my writing time. Over the years, Harrison said, he had been offered several "really cushy jobs" by various creative writing departments. "And I said, 'Why me?' And they said, 'We need some kind of name.' However minimal."

He always said no. "I turned one down for $75,000 in a year that we made $9,000."

"How were you able to do that?"

Harrison told me what he told them: "'Somebody's got to stay outside,'" he said. "And I still think that's true. Somebody's got to stay outside."

Before leaving Montana, I decided to drive through Yellowstone Park. Once more I was listening to conservative talk radio, and the voices were shrill and formless in my little rental, beneath the mountain cathedrals. While Sean Hannity spent an hour rhetorically decapitating President Obama, I looked at the landscape, feeling the pressure between Americans and America, between body and being, between reality and aspiration. I wound up at Old Faithful, which Harrison said had been weakened in recent years; it might not even blow, he warned me. I wanted to see it blow. Maybe it would relieve the pressure. After an hour, it had not blown, and I had to catch a plane home. I knew by then I would be quitting my teaching job. It felt too good to be outside.

—2011

GODDESSES AND DREAMS

Inside the Mind of William T. Vollmann

One morning, in 2000, while I was working as an editor for Henry Holt, a manuscript contained on several compact disks was delivered to my office. Back at the dawn of the twenty-first century, it was still relatively unusual for submissions to arrive in any form other than a stack of paper, so the occasion was memorable for that reason alone. More memorable yet was the manuscript's author, William T. Vollmann, who had been churning out thick, conceptually audacious books faster than New York publishing could keep pace. From 1987 through 1993, for instance, Vollmann published eight books through five different houses.

This new Vollmann manuscript, *Rising Up and Rising Down*, was sent on compact disk mainly due to its length: 3,800 pages. "Let me get back to you," I told his agent. I'd heard vague stirrings about Vollmann's gargantuan undertaking, in the same way I imagine London studio engineers were hearing about

Sgt. Pepper's in the winter of 1967. The book was said to be an attempt to define a philosophically coherent set of moral coordinates for when violence was acceptable. Many houses had already rejected it, which was why its fate had fallen to a twenty-six-year-old greenhorn such as myself. And now here I was, marshaling the entire assistantariot of Henry Holt to help me print the thing out.

A week later, I went to my boss and told him I thought we should do it. He'd read enough to agree, provided we could get Vollmann down to 1,500 manuscript pages, which was, given Vollmann's chosen font (I had taken to calling it American Minuscule) actually more like 2,000 manuscript pages. I knew enough about Vollmann to guess at his thoughts concerning the general barbarity of editors and believed my best shot was to convince him how much I loved the book and how sincerely I believed it would benefit from compression. One Monday afternoon, he heard me out over the phone. Our conversation ended with him saying, "This subject is too important for truncated treatment." Only while riding the subway back to Brooklyn that night did it occur to me to laugh.

In 2003 McSweeney's published a handsomely slipcased, seven-volume edition of *RURD* (as it's known to Vollmann fans), which was a finalist for the National Book Critics Circle Award. Two years later, Vollmann finally consented to publish a "truncated" one-volume *RURD*, through HarperCollins, though he did so, by his own admission, for the money alone. Today, copies of the McSweeney's edition can go for close to $1,000 on Amazon.

Fourteen years after our phone conversation, Vollmann and I walked down a quiet street in Sacramento, California, on our way to pick up shelving wood from Burnett & Sons, a lumber mill close to Vollmann's studio. As we moved through sawdust-spiced air, the man I was now calling Bill smiled to remember his and my long-ago talk. I wanted to know: Did I ever have a shot at convincing him to shorten the book? "Nah," he said.

Although Vollmann these days sports the punctilious mustache of a maître d', he still resembles the baby-faced boy wonder readers first encountered in his shocking late '80s author photo, in which he affectlessly held a pistol to his own head. Vollmann is a man of forbidding reputation, to say the least, which is why his speaking voice—as polite, deep, and expressive as someone selling you a vacation over the phone—so surprised me. He takes obvious pleasure in speaking, especially when he can add some mischievous wrinkle to whatever is being discussed: "Well, *Tom*, you *see*, the thing with *that* is *this*." You get the feeling he might have been a wonderful grade-school teacher in another, much weirder dimension.

Vollmann has often been linked to Jonathan Franzen, Richard Powers, and David Foster Wallace, which makes a good amount of literary and cultural sense. Not only are or were they all friendly; they also share Midwestern roots and began publishing at the same time, in the mid- to late-'80s. They were initially hailed as heirs to Thomas Pynchon and John Barth, writing fiction perceived as formally or intellectually challenging. In the intervening decades, Franzen has become one of America's best-selling and most critically acclaimed novelists; Powers stands as our go-to seismologist on the fault line between literature and science; and Wallace, following his 2008 suicide, is now widely regarded (especially by those who've never read him) as a literary saint. For his part, Vollmann began as an uncompromising visionary drawn to equally uncompromising material, and though he has mellowed as a man, his subject matter has, if anything, grown even more confrontational.

This month, Vollmann's twenty-second book, *Last Stories and Other Stories*, will be published by Viking. Not many writers could convince a large multinational publisher to go forth with a 680-page short-story collection about death, putrefaction, ghosts, and cancer, but Vollmann's career has never really cohered to any pre-existing template. This is to say nothing of his attendant identities: war correspondent, traveler, accomplished visual artist, parking-lot owner, gun lover ("I believe that the Second Amendment is really wonderful," he once told an interviewer), privacy advocate, and champion of homeless rights. We passed numerous homeless people while walking to his studio, including a legless man in a wheelchair with a milky, unwell eye, to whom Vollmann bid a hale "Hello! Good morning!"

I'd been in Sacramento a day and already noticed the perva-siveness of its homeless problem. The city seemed like California without the masks or pretense: a place where dreams were occa-sionally made but mostly torn apart. When I asked Vollmann why he'd chosen to live in Sacramento, he said, "Well, Joan Didion used to live here." Then he laughed. The truth was more banal: His wife, an oncologist, got a job in Sacramento about twenty years ago. "Space was cheap," he said. "So I made the best of it." Vollmann told me one benefit of Sacramento was not being part of any literary hothouse. (Vollmann's closest literary friend is Franzen, though, as he was sad to admit, they hadn't been in touch in some time. Franzen tells a hilarious story of being a young writer in New York, meeting Vollmann, becoming fast friends, and inaugu-rating a draft swap. A while later, they exchanged work. Franzen gave Vollmann a dozen chiseled pages. Vollmann gave Franzen an entire novel.) In Sacramento, Vollmann said, he was merely "a guy named Bill who writes books."

Vollmann's studio, which he has owned for the last ten years, was once a corner-occupying Mexican restaurant called Ortega's. Its windows are barred and curtained; its back door is fenced off, festooned with PRIVATE PROPERTY signs, and crowned with razor wire, which, he said, made him "feel like the Omega Man trying to keep the vampires out."Vollmann cheerfully described the surrounding neighborhood as "bad," and robbery remains a worry. Even so, he loves it here. Over the last few years he has had several offers to buy the studio. "I hear out their offers," he said. "Then I ask for two million dollars." What if some buyer went ahead and offered him $2 million? "I'd ask for five million dollars."

It has been said thatVollmann works sixteen hours a day, every day.To my relief, he refused either to confirm or to deny this. "I'm going to be fifty-five in July," he said with a sigh. "I'm a little less productive, a little less focused." His studio, in which he both paints and writes, is a de facto home, complete with a bedroom, shower, men's and women's bathrooms (this, and the fact that his bedroom closet is an old meat locker, are the most obvious artifacts of the space's previous identity), and a kitchen stocked with food and good whiskey. Most significant for Vollmann's productivity, and peace of mind, was his studio's lack of an Internet connection. In fact,Vollmann never uses the Internet. "I tried ordering from Amazon once," he told me. "I was almost all the way through and then they wanted my email. I couldn't do it." Along with the Internet and email,Vollmann also forgoes cell phones, credit-card use, checking accounts, and driving.

Half of Vollmann's studio felt like a proper gallery, with finished pieces handsomely framed and displayed. The other half was split into what looked like a used bookstore on one side and a struggling industrial arts business on the other. I imagined Vollmann had a gallery somewhere that showed his stuff, yes? Actually, no. "I've had a couple of photographer friends who have shows,"Vollmann said. "Every time, they always end up impoverished." He employs "a couple dealers" who sell his work to various institutions, but he considers his studio a "perpetual gallery." Vollmann gets additional income from Ohio State, which has been buying Vollmann's work and manuscripts for several years. Vollmann has no idea why Ohio State has shown such interest in his work, but he's grateful to the institution, which has been paying the mortgage on his studio for the last decade.

He began our tour proper while a dinging train from the city's light-rail line rumbled by, just feet from his curtained windows. Woodcuts, watercolors, ink sketches, silver-gelatin black-and-white photographs, portraits. "Gum-printing is a nineteenth-century technique," he told me. "It's the most permanent coloring process. But it's slow, and toxic. . . . I also have this device here, which is based in dental technology. . . . It's like a non-vibrating, very high-speed Dremel tool. . . . This was originally drawn with pen and ink, and then I had a magnesium block made with a photo resist." Some of the pieces he showed me were complete; most were not. He estimated that he has "dozens and dozens" of pieces going at any one time.

Vollmann's most important artistic influences are Gauguin and what he described as the "power colors" of Native American art. His other inescapable influence is the female body. The majority of Vollmann's visual art centers upon women generally and geishas, sex workers, and those he calls "goddesses" specifically. Usually they are nude. From where I was standing I counted at least two dozen vaginas, their fleshy machinery painstakingly drawn and then painted over with a delicate red slash. Vollmann uses live models, so every vagina within sight is currently out there right now, wandering the world.

We walked over to a shelf lined with paintbrushes in old moonshine jars and little acrylic tubes of paint as hard as toothpaste fossilized. Vollmann held out blocks of Norwegian wood into which he'd carved Norse runes and which he'd translated himself: "It took me a ridiculous amount of time, hours and hours . . . but I had a blast." The wood was given to him in exchange for his attendance at a Norwegian literary festival, along with his sole other request: Norwegian women willing to pose nude for him. One of the women who volunteered was an archaeologist in charge of excavating a site related to the worship of Freya, the Norse goddess of love, beauty, and war. "I wanted a Freya," Vollmann said, "so that's who we got."

Finally, Vollmann removed some sketchbooks from their protective plastic covers and set them down on a table for me to look at. Vollmann's sketchbooks, naturally, were about three feet by two feet across; turning a page was like opening a door. His Arctic sketchbook had page after page of beautifully hand-drawn and water-colored portraits of Inuit people, northern landscapes, and walrus hunts. They were exquisite, which I told him. "Oh, thanks!" he said. "I had fun." A sketchbook from Southeast Asia was thumped down before me. These were less colorful, and many were simple pen-and-ink portraits. The subjects were all sex workers. Vollmann explained that to fill up the back pages he'd encouraged the women to draw pictures of him. Some of the women, I observed, were quite skilled. "Yeah," he said. "They had fun!" The last sketchbook he showed me was titled *The Best Way to Smoke Crack*. (Once, when asked by an interviewer if he had ever smoked crack, Vollmann memorably responded, "I guess that I would say that I have.") I paged through a run of despairing watercolors depicting crack-addicted San Francisco sex workers. Vollmann stopped me when I came to a portrait of a woman languid on a hotel-room bed, a crack pipe beside her. The subject of the portrait, Vollmann told me, loved to steal his red paint and use it as lipstick, even though Vollmann warned her the paint was carcinogenic. According to Vollmann, she laughed off his warning, saying that something else was bound to get her. "And she was right," Vollmann said. "I heard she got strangled."

When I asked about his infamous fascination with sex workers,

Vollmann said, simply, "I love and admire them." In another interview, he'd gone so far as to describe sex workers as "almost like saints." Here, even the most liberal-minded will have their qualms. But Vollmann believes that, once one sheds any crypto-Christian assumption that sex must have a context deeper than pleasure, it becomes difficult to regard paying a consenting sex worker as all that different from paying a masseuse or psychotherapist. In the end, it's intimate labor, professionally applied. "I'd say there are almost as many different kinds of sex workers as there are different kinds of women," Vollmann told me. "I think, 'Well, how different is that from what I do—just running around worrying about how to finish paying off my mortgage?' I've never really answered that."

By his own account, Vollmann started hanging around sex workers as a way to get to know and better understand women. He first wrote about the subject in *The Rainbow Stories*, which is the kind of book Mark Twain might have written after smoking crank and hanging out with skinheads for six months. Like Twain's travel writing, or Isaac Babel's *Red Cavalry* stories, *Rainbow* is an amalgam of unlabeled fiction and nonfiction. It has several running threads, one of which is its narrator's pith-helmeted investigation into the lives of street prostitutes. After many harrowing passages, a footnote will summon one's attention down to the bottom of the page: "This paragraph cost me seven dollars," or "This revelation cost me twenty dollars." One story, subchaptered "While Trying Unsuccessfully to Make Ginger's Cunt Wet," features a narrator who self-identifies as Bill and appears to be Vollmann himself. Bill calls an escort service, finds himself with Ginger, and is doing as advertised. A supremely unmoved Ginger suddenly asks him, "Do you like camping?"

Butterfly Stories was Vollmann's first book-length plunge into the world of prostitution. Vollmann has described it as "strictly a novel ... based on documentary research with prostitutes," a phrase (as he knows) that can be interpreted any number of ways. The novel began as a nonfiction piece for *Esquire* about the Khmer Rouge's killing fields, but appended to that piece was a long, bonkers travelogue starring two journalists whore-mongering their away across Southeast Asia. Guess which part *Esquire* chose to publish? Shortly after the magazine hit the stands, Vollmann told me, "I was visiting my grandfather, and my mother and sisters were crying. My father took me down to the basement and said, 'Bill, do you have AIDS? Have you been sleeping with prostitutes?'" When I asked whether *Esquire* had published the piece as fiction or nonfiction—in *Butterfly Stories*, the main character, called "the journalist," eventually contracts HIV from an illiterate Thai prostitute—Vollmann shrugged and said, "I don't know what it was published as." *Butterfly Stories* reads like Henry Miller de-romanticized and poxed with STDs, with the added looming specter of Cambodian genocide. Its appalling central character ponders, at length, his predatory nature with illiterate, impoverished prostitutes and wallows in sexual crapulence. Despite or possibly because of that, the book ranks high among the most riveting things Vollmann has written.

Vollmann's most serious artistic statement on sex workers, and their clients, is *The Royal Family*, a gargantuan novel about a private investigator chasing the so-called Queen of San Francisco's prostitutes. Running at eight hundred generously text-crammed pages, and containing 593 chapters, the book lingers at a hypnotic remove from its nightmarish narrative material. It's also a moving and humane book, not only in how it handles its fucked-up characters but also in how it presents itself to readers, for it eschews many of Vollmann's formal pyrotechnics. There are, however, several sections that make it quintessentially Vollmann: an astonishing "Essay on Bail" (a piece of nonfiction originally commissioned, and then rejected, by *San Francisco Magazine*), a marvelous prose poem called "Geary Street," and the unendurably vivid confessions of a pedophile named Dan Smooth. One astute reader of the book imagined, probably correctly, that had it been shorter, less gruesome, and better emphasized its private-eye elements, it might have become a "blowaway detective best-seller." As it happens, Vollmann took a lower royalty on the book in exchange for not having it edited.

Standing with Vollmann amid his many portraits and paintings of sex workers, I asked him how his wife and teenage daughter felt about his subject matter. "Oh, they're used to it," Vollmann said. His daughter was particularly gleeful when Vollmann went public with his "thought experiment" inhabitation of "Dolores," a transgender woman, whom Vollmann discusses exclusively in the third person. There were quite a few photos and portraits of him as Dolores around his studio. And his wife? How did she feel about Dolores? Vollmann was silent for a moment. "She was not impressed," he said. "When I started doing the Dolores stuff, it was really fun because I thought, 'Now I can exploit the hell out of this person. I don't have to worry about ethics. I can show this woman as she is or whatever she is, in all her ugliness and vulnerability and vanity, and she has nothing to say about it.'" Like his earlier artistic excavation of sex workers' lives, Dolores was Vollmann's gambit to place himself in closer psychic orbit to women. As he put it, "Until I started doing the cross-dressing, I had no idea of what it was like to go out into the night and be afraid. That is what a huge portion of the human race has to go through, and I really get it now."

Vollmann admitted that, after he went public with Dolores, some of his friends "were really disgusted." This only underlined his point about what becoming Dolores meant. After a career of hanging out with neo-Nazis, pursuing sex workers, doing drugs, dropping thousand-page books the way Updike dropped short stories, and being suspected of being the Unabomber, Vollmann, without even meaning to, had managed to cross the last line of decorum. He had dared to abdicate his masculinity.

As for being suspected of being the Unabomber, William T. Vollmann was suspected of being the Unabomber. He discovered this accidentally, after he requested his FBI file, for a piece he was writing for *Harper's* about privacy. His FBI file is 785 pages long; only 294 were released to him. When Vollmann first discovered he was a Unabomber suspect, he thought: "'Wow, this is really fun!' I bustled about telling all of my friends. Then I started reading more of it." He's still angry that the content of his fiction was marshaled against him. His novel *Fathers and Crows*, for instance, is about the clash between the Iroquois and the first French missionaries to what was then called Kebec. An FBI operative rather ambitiously deduced that its title had something to do with the "FC" the Unabomber was known to scrawl on his bombs. "*Fathers and Crows*," Vollmann said incredulously, "which took place in seventeenth-century Canada. It was outside what's now the U.S. in a time before there *was* the U.S. It was evenhanded, I thought, about Iroquois and Jesuits. [But] they were saying, since he supports the Iroquois torture of the missionaries, he's clearly in favor of terrorism." (Not everything the FBI said about him was unkind, or not exactly unkind: "By all accounts, VOLLMANN is exceedingly intelligent and possessed with an enormous ego.")

Vollmann's politics, which are both coherent and somewhat bananas, run toward big-hearted Libertarianism—except when it comes to the environment. "The more I see of unregulated coal and nuclear companies," he told me, "the more I think, 'Boy, do we have to watch those people.'" At the same time, he believes we are living in a growing consolidated police state that will only get worse. The Internet, he told me, "is partly about government surveillance, and I have to reject that, given my hatred of authority. It's partly about helping these corporate types make money from me, which involves surveillance and targeted ads, and I have to reject that also."

These are not the fulminations of a department-chair radical. Vollmann is one of very few American writers who can claim to have fallen under concerted government surveillance based on nothing more than what he thought and wrote. Today, he's fairly certain his calls are still monitored; on one occasion, his studio's security system was remotely hacked into, possibly, he says, by Homeland Security. As a private investigator told him, "Once you're a suspect and in the system, that ain't never going away." Indeed, after the arrest of Ted Kaczynski, the actual Unabomber, Vollmann was upgraded to a suspect in a different case involving mailed anthrax.

"What's discouraging," he said, "is that I don't get a lot of mail. My poor Japanese translator has practically given up writing to me. One year, she sent me so many postcards. I never got one." Perhaps the strangest thing about all this is Vollmann's estimation that he's made tens of thousands of dollars writing and lecturing on privacy around the world since he went public with his FBI case file. It amounted to a rather ambiguous endorsement of the American Way: *We'll investigate you, we'll put you under secret surveillance, and we'll steal your mail, but we'll also make you rich when you accidentally find out about it, provided you're famous.*

Vollmann tried to be characteristically charitable when imagining the FBI's interest in him: "One reason that the FBI thought I might be the Unabomber is that I believe probably the thing most likely to save us, and save the planet, would be a massive epidemic. Because we can't regulate ourselves. If fifty percent or ninety percent of the humans died, maybe the rest would be better off. Would I push the button to release the virus? Probably not."

I listened for the off-white silence of the FBI bug planted somewhere around us, possibly behind one of Vollmann's effulgent paintings of a vagina. Then, smiling, I pointed out that Vollmann said "probably not," not "absolutely not."

Vollmann held up his hands. "I'd have to think about it."

In *On Becoming a Novelist*, the classic primer on fiction writing and writers, John Gardner argues, "A psychological wound is helpful, if it can be kept in partial control, to keep the novelist driven." If true, Vollmann was well prepared for the writing life. Like Gardner, who accidentally ran over and killed his younger brother, Gilbert, with a tractor, Vollmann lost his six-year-old sister, Julie, to drowning when she was left in his youthful care. This has understandably gripped Vollmann's imagination ever since, and he has written several books and stories in which pursuing and rescuing a woman is the central driving impulse. In the mid-'90s, a reviewer brought up Vollmann's compulsive attraction to human conflict—he has covered war as a journalist, but also ran off to fight the Soviets with the mujahideen in Afghanistan when he was in his early twenties—and wondered if it all wasn't some veiled suicide mission to join his sister. That could not have been an easy judgment to read, much less ponder.

Vollmann was born in Santa Monica in 1959. He moved to New Hampshire as a child and later to Bloomington, Indiana, where he went to high school. By all accounts, Vollmann did not have a happy childhood, at least when it came to other children. He describes the authorial stand-in of one book passing the time during his childhood "by reading and dreaming alone or by watching others, wishing that they liked him," and in the afterword to Dalkey Archive's reissue of the Yugoslavian writer Danilo Kiš's trim masterpiece, *A Tomb for Boris Davidovich*, Vollmann mentions being "beaten up on the school bus two or three times by big, tall, stinking boys," who were outraged by his book-reading.

Vollmann credits his father, a business professor, with giving him the encouragement he needed to pursue the life he wanted for himself: "He would always say, 'Bill, if it's not easy, lucrative, or fun, don't do it.'" Even so, Vollmann's career as a writer very nearly didn't happen. His first book, *Welcome to the Memoirs*, an account of his failed effort in Afghanistan, went unpublished (the version Farrar, Straus and Giroux published years later as *An Afghanistan Picture Show* was a much-revised version of the unsold manuscript), and for years he got nothing but "rejection upon rejection" by American editors and agents. "I think it was such a fluke that I got published at all," Vollmann told me.

Anyone who's taken a lot of creative-writing classes, or taught creative writing, has learned to dread a certain kind of manuscript. It's long, for one thing; it has irritatingly small type; it's grammatically meticulous when it comes to everything but punctuation, for which it has developed its own system of Tolkienic elaboration. An unagented manuscript of roughly this description landed on the desk of Esther Whitby, an editor at the British house André Deutsch, in 1985. Rather than do the sensible thing and reject it, Whitby went ahead and published *You Bright and Risen Angels*, Vollmann's bizarre fantasia of insect war. It reviewed well and finally garnered Vollmann an American publisher. He published his next six books acting as his own representation and sought the eventual help of his agent, Susan Golomb, only because dealing with foreign rights became unmanageable. The early critical success did nothing to dissuade Vollmann's view that his personal vision for his books trumped all other considerations. As he has often said, the money you're paid for your writing is never enough. Therefore, why compromise?

A number of Vollmann's books, I believe, would be better

if they were shorter, sometimes much shorter. At the same time, the unaccommodating nature of Vollmann's books is what many of his readers respond to. His books are too long in the way the Petronas Towers are too tall, the way foie gras is too rich: the manner of their excess is central to their essence. Vollmann is neither a readers' writer nor a writers' writer but a writer's writer, which is to say William T. Vollmann's writer. The point he comes back to in conversation, again and again, is how fortunate he has been to maintain his independence in a literary culture that can be hostile to such independence. "The reader that I write for will be open to beautiful sentences and will try to see why I'm doing what I'm doing," he told me. "That's the reader that I love and the reader who loves me." I've read a great number of Vollmann's books, but I've skipped around in many of them, too. *Fathers and Crows* is one of my favorites, yet I've read less than half of it. His best novel, the National Book Award–winning *Europe Central*, is one of the few that feels exactly the right length. Yet you don't go to Vollmann for structure or old-fashioned storytelling; you go to Vollmann for the sentences, the mood, the experience. You go to Vollmann for the same reason certain people chase storms.

Vollmann's public stature as a writer expanded following two events in the early '90s. The first was the publication of the opening volume of Vollmann's proposed mega-novel, *Seven Dreams: A Book of North American Landscapes*, which had its genesis, naturally enough, in Vollmann's fascination with sex workers. While researching *The Rainbow Stories*, he found himself standing outside numerous convenience stores and gas stations, "where the whores were doing their business. I thought to myself, 'What was the country like before all the parking lots were here?'"

Every book in the *Dreams* cycle dramatizes a particular epoch in the ongoing cultural collision between North America's native peoples and its European colonizers. The books are rich with

Norse, Huron, Iroquois, and Inuit myth; are filled with excursions into Catholic theology and European history; and contain beautifully observed descriptions of landscape, clothing, and weapons. In 1991, Vollmann predicted it would take him "at least ten years" to finish *Seven Dreams*. Twenty-three years later, he still has three books to deliver. He has written, and published, the cycle out of order, admitting that his work on the project has often been "so sickeningly depressing" that he has "deliberately interrupted the work" by writing other—often longer and equally depressing—books. On top of that, his devotion to on-site research has forced him to expensively travel to and inhabit the varied landscapes of his fictional dreams, sometimes at great personal peril. While researching *The Rifles*, his sixth *Dream*, which concerns John Franklin's doomed quest to find the Northwest Passage, Vollmann almost froze to death in the Arctic.

Not all of Vollmann's *Dreams* are successful. *Argall*, the fourth and most recently published *Dream*, about Pocahontas and John Smith, is written in an exhausting parody of Elizabethan language. At their worst, Vollmann's *Dreams* read like the 4:00 a.m. ravings of an insomniac associate professor of history in the middle of Nebraska. At their more frequent best, the *Dreams* have an unstoppably mad Melvillean energy—and even, yes, genius. While Vollmann's earliest books were spastic and quick-cutting—more like textual slide shows than proper stories—the *Dreams* are finely crafted watchmaker novels. Every volume has a narrative of daunting complication, corrals unimaginable amounts of historical research, and contains a present-day travelogue narrated by William the Blind, aka Captain Subzero, aka Vollmann himself, who considers his *Dreams* "simultaneously fiction and nonfiction."

Vollmann told me that Viking, which has been publishing his *Dreams* for decades, was currently "sadly contemplating" the publication of *The Dying Grass*, volume five, about the Plains

Indian wars of the late nineteenth century. For the first time in Vollmann's career, Viking had begun to impose page limits in his contracts. For *The Dying Grass*, the page limit was 700. "I gave them 2,100 and they weren't super happy," he said, "so I corrected it to 2,300." According to Vollmann, the book is composed mostly of dialogue. "It looks like a concrete poem," he said, "because I treat the printed page as a stage. Since we read from left to right, there might be dialogue which is occurring, say, on the left-hand side of the page, and then maybe in the middle part of the page people are thinking what they actually think as they talk to each other." It sounded a bit like William Gaddis, except more insane. I asked what would happen if Viking rejected it, which Vollmann knew was a possibility. He shrugged. "If they want to reject it, they can. Of course, I will be quite sad and worried about making a living."

The other defining event of his early career happened while he was covering the Bosnian War for *Spin* magazine in 1994. Vollmann was traveling in a rental car, near the city of Mostar, with his interpreter and a childhood friend who, like Vollmann, was a freelance journalist, when their car either hit a land mine or came under sniper fire.

Vollmann's memory of the incident is clouded by trauma, but he remembers "two sharp reports and small holes in the windshield." One of the bullets, Vollmann believes, struck one friend in the heart, while the other struck his remaining friend in the head. Afterward, he said, Muslim snipers came running down the road, laughing and waving their rifles. Vollmann sat in the backseat, convinced he would be next. When the snipers realized Vollmann was an American, and that the men they had just shot were not Croatian saboteurs but journalists, the mood very rapidly changed, and the Muslims began to suggest to the still-dazed Vollmann that his friends had hit a land mine. When the

American ambassador and Vollmann returned to the site the next day, "the authorities there had prepared some kind of a diagram saying it was a mine trap, there were these two mines. The car looked much worse than I remembered it." He suspects all this happened to avoid an embarrassing international incident, as the Muslims of Bosnia were greatly hoping for American protection. "They just made a mistake," Vollmann told me. "It was no one's fault." *Rising Up and Rising Down* is dedicated to the memory of Vollmann's friends, and his account of the incident in that book is as elegantly horrifying as Orwell's account of being shot in the throat in *Homage to Catalonia*.

The best piece in *Last Stories,* his new book, is "The Leader," a lightly fictionalized third-person account of Vollmann's return to Mostar twenty years after the incident that claimed his friends' lives. It's often harsh and unsparing: in it, the brother of Vollmann's childhood friend, here called Ivan, attacks Vollmann's stand-in for having had the misfortune to survive. "And now you'll cash in," the grieving brother predicts. "You'll have your dramatic story." Vollmann declined to discuss much of this with me, due to the poor relations he continues to have with the families of his dead friends (to which he seems forlornly resigned), but he did say he was pleased with the note of hopefulness that creeps into the last few lines of "The Leader," which provide a rare glimmer in a book whose skies are otherwise gray and unbroken.

That he'd write such a crepuscular book isn't a wild surprise. In 2004, he had a serious bike accident, and later that year suffered the first of several strokes, which left him unable to read, write, or speak properly for months. (Vollmann believes they may have been brought on by work- and finance-related stress.) It took three years for Vollmann to feel normal again, after which his beloved father died. In the aftermath of all this, Vollmann found himself staring into what he describes in *Last Stories* as his "lovely wall of ill."

The Vollmann of the early books was a bomb-throwing polymath determined to bring the novel, with its many formalities, to its knees. *Last Stories* is something else. There are ghost and horror stories here, parables, tales, and tender, more memoiristic stories, all enriched by Vollmann's travels to the Balkans, Scandinavia, Japan, Trieste, Bohemia, Buenos Aires, Mexico. It's less a story collection than a dozen interrelated mini-novels wrapped around various continents. Many of the stories have an antiquated, vaguely Middle-European feel to them. Back in the early '90s, one would have hardly imagined the author of *You Bright and Risen Angels* or *The Rainbow Stories* to one day seem so continental, so old-fashioned, but then Vollmann describes something fantastical, such as the Madonna descending into Hell, and he reminds his readers how capable he remains at launching the champagne cork of his imagination clear across the room:

> Through those depths Our Lady now flew, her alabaster face downcast, her lips parted as if she might even breathe, and amidst shiny ebony snails and pale green night-leaves she found both Lilith, who had been stalking a child's nine-hundred-year-old beetle-sized ghost, and Giulia, who was cowering in a temporarily vacant vampire hole. Gathering them both up into her arms, so that they nearly warmed the still Christ child she also carried, the Madonna ascended three hundred and thirty-two flights of stairs, each step paler and less nitrous than the last.

Vollmann has never been one to make the grotesque lyrical. When one of his characters in *Last Stories* makes love to a skeleton, he imagines his way through the procedure, painful abrasions and all. While there are numerous resurrections in *Last Stories*, what happens after the moment of death remains a mystery even to his dead. As one of Vollmann's resurrected characters complains of the living: "It upsets me that everyone up here mentions the future so unemotionally. Why don't they scream *death, death, death*?"

Vollmann stressed that in writing *Last Stories*, he really wanted to face up to death's psychological challenges. Death, he said, "is nothing, and therefore the only way we can engage with nothing is to personify it . . . to invent." For Vollmann, facing up to the inevitability of death involves remembering the orange he ate in his Bosnian rental car while his friends sat dead in the front seats. "It was a hot day," he said. "I was really thirsty. I ducked down and I was peeling one of these oranges and thought, 'This is probably the last thing I'm ever going to eat.'" Twenty years later, when he gets upset about something, he wills himself to remember that orange and the strange reassurance it offered. Any type of permanent consciousness in the afterlife would, he believes, inevitably devolve into torture, and there would be no parting orange to leaven it. Consciousness is to our mortality what beer is to Homer Simpson: the cause of, and solution to, all our problems.

"Where does consciousness come from?" Vollmann asked, and it took me a moment to recognize he really was asking. I told him I didn't have the faintest idea. Neither did Vollmann. "It makes no sense to me. None of it makes sense. It's all preposterous, no matter how I look at it." I reminded him that his first novel, *You Bright and Risen Angels*, seems to suggest that the collectivist social intelligence of insects might be preferable to the disquieting solitude of human intelligence—and it was possible that Vollmann spent more time alone in his head than any other living American writer. "Maybe," he said, "it's not so bad to be a social insect."

The next morning, Vollmann's model, Lindsay, arrived by bus from San Francisco for her session. "Hey, Goddess," Vollmann said warmly. "Did you bring a robe?"

Lindsay, a former exotic dancer in her mid-thirties, had not brought a robe. Vollmann suggested that she wear one of Dolores's robes. "Dolores doesn't mind," Vollmann assured her. "She likes it." While Lindsay went off and changed, Vollmann asked me if I wanted to pick out the music for today's session. That meant digging through the twin towers of Vollmann's compact-disc collection. Vollmann's tastes ran to classical and '70s-era thought rock: Bowie, Randy Newman, Jethro Tull. After looking through his discs for a while, I said Lindsay should probably pick the music. Once she came back out, barefoot in a thin black and white dress ("You look much prettier in that than Dolores does," Vollmann said, "but how could you not?"), she popped Lou Reed into Vollmann's Silurian disc-playing boombox.

He arranged before him the three paintings of Lindsay he was currently working on. One was a portrait, one was a nude, and another was a more impressionistic rendering of her as a gold-sequin-clad angel. All would receive "another layer" today. He'd been at work on these pieces for several months; he'd seen Lindsay at least six or seven times in the last year. Lindsay was a professional sitting model these days; when I asked how many people she sat for, she laughed and said, "Quite a few!"

Then Vollmann began painting. Once again, he told Lindsay she looked beautiful. How salacious—how Terry Richardson— this must sound: an artist repeatedly telling a younger model how beautiful she looks while he paints her in his studio. But it didn't feel that way to me, and Lindsay pretty clearly adored Vollmann. The afternoon before, at lunch, Vollmann told our waitress he had a question: "How did you get so darn beautiful?" Our waitress, an utterly normal-looking person, laughed and thanked Vollmann for noticing. It felt like a dorky, sweet encounter, but, again, I have no idea how it felt from her end. A man who constantly compliments women could be seen as wielding power over them, especially in social situations shaped by payment or gratuity, which I think is true whether we as men are aware of it or not. "I've never seen a woman who isn't beautiful," Vollmann said, as he painted. "When I talk to guys who say they had to dump their wives when she turned forty, I always think, 'Why?'" Vollmann would keep on living in his world of clumsy, sword-bent gallantry.

Vollmann's attitude about how he's perceived by others is simple. He doesn't care. Here he is, painting a naked woman in front of a journalist. Whatever you think that indicates is of no concern to Vollmann. I will admit to finding this calculated diffidence seductive. The morning before I visited Sacramento, I habit-checked my Amazon ranking on a book that came out seven months before and helped a friend fretting over the precise wording of a tweet he wanted to send to his four hundred followers. Twitter, Amazon, Facebook: so many writers have turned to these platforms and opportunities, if only out of grim self-promotional necessity. They allow us the illusion of tracking the fortunes of our careers in something close to real time. It would be interesting to find and interrogate the first American writer who thought this would be a good idea. When I told Vollmann how impressed I was by his determination to write exactly what he wanted, with no fear of reprisal, he shrugged and said, "I'm sure it helps that I'm not on the Internet and I don't know what they say." Writing is as much a struggle to control what gets into one's head as it is to transform what comes out.

Now Vollmann was mixing up the acrylic paint—mostly blues, whites, and yellows—he'd use to touch up Lindsay's hair. During their last session, he said, "I didn't worry at all about color. Just tone." Vollmann peeked around his canvas at Lindsay. "Goddess, what do you think is your most beautiful feature?"

Lindsay thought for a moment. "I think my nose."

Vollmann was using a thin brush to add some blue shadow along his Lindsay's jawline. "And why is that?"

"Because I used to hate it, but then I figured I'd better like it, because it's in the middle of my face."

Vollmann laughed. "That's a good reason."

She asked him what his favorite part of his body was.

"I think my hands," Vollmann said.

"You have nice hands."

"I know!"

Now Vollmann was working with yellow and blue to capture the light on his Lindsay's face. "What's the worst thing that ever happened to you as a stripper?"

Lindsay sighed. "I'd have to sit down and make a list."

I asked if either of them had seen George W. Bush's recent self-portraits and dog paintings. To my surprise, neither of them was aware that Bush had been painting. To my even greater surprise, both voiced their unwavering support for George W. Bush, Watercolorist. "Good for him!" Vollmann said. "I try to separate the art from the artist," Lindsay said. Suddenly Vollmann was urging me to set up an easel next to him and paint Lindsay, who was now naked, for myself. I thought: Why *shouldn't* Bush paint? Why *shouldn't* I try?

With a fine brush, Vollmann was lining the underside of his Lindsay's breasts with blue paint. "You look at someone's skin," he said, "and you realize, 'Oh, there are way more colors here than I thought.'" He took a break, and when I looked at the paintings again, ten minutes later, I noticed they seemed different. Vollmann was across the room, in his kitchen. "The tones changed," he called over. "It's the most fascinating part of this. As things become less liquid, everything—all the colors—shift around." He uncorked a bottle of Ardbeg whiskey. "Well, Tom—what could be better than this? Kicking back in an air-conditioned room and looking at a beautiful woman?" He poured us both a dram and walked back over. "Now, Goddess," he said to Lindsay, "how about stretching out your beautiful arms?"

—2014

EVERYTHING ABOUT EVERYTHING

Infinite Jest, Twenty Years Later

Something happens to a novel as it ages, but what? It doesn't ripen or deepen in the manner of cheese and wine, and it doesn't fall apart, at least not figuratively. Fiction has no half-life. We age alongside the novels we've read, and only one of us is actively deteriorating. Which is to say that a novel is perishable only by virtue of being stored in such a leaky cask: our heads. With just a few years' passage, a novel can thus seem "dated," or "irrelevant," or (God help us) "problematic." When a novel survives this strange process, and gets reissued in a handsome twentieth-anniversary edition, it's tempting to hold it up and say, "It withstood the test of time." Most would intend such a statement as praise, but is a twenty-year-old novel successful merely because it seems cleverly predictive or contains scenarios that feel "relevant" to later audiences? If that were the mark of enduring fiction, Philip K. Dick would be the greatest novelist of all time.

David Foster Wallace understood the paradox of attempting to write fiction that spoke to posterity and a contemporary audience simultaneously, with equal force. In an essay written while he was at work on *Infinite Jest,* Wallace referred to the "oracular foresight" of a writer he idolized, Don DeLillo, whose best novels—*White Noise, Libra, Underworld*—address their contemporary audience like a shouting desert prophet while laying out for posterity the coldly amused analysis of some long-dead professor emeritus. Wallace felt that the "mimetic deployment of pop-culture icons" by writers who lacked DeLillo's observational powers "compromises fiction's seriousness by dating it out of the Platonic Always where it ought to reside." Yet *Infinite Jest* rarely seems as though it resides within this Platonic Always, which Wallace rejected in any event. (As with many of Wallace's more manifesto-ish proclamations, he was not planting a flag so much as secretly burning one.) We are now half a decade beyond the years Wallace intended *Infinite Jest*'s subsidized time schema—Year of the Whopper, Year of the Depend Adult Undergarment—to represent. Read today, the book's intellectually slapstick vision of corporatism run amok embeds it within the early to mid-1990s as firmly and emblematically as *The Simpsons* and grunge music. It is very much a novel of its time.

How is it, then, that *Infinite Jest* still feels so transcendently, electrically alive? Theory one: as a novel about an "entertainment" weaponized to enslave and destroy all who look upon it, *Infinite Jest* is the first great Internet novel. Yes, William Gibson and Neal Stephenson may have gotten there first with *Neuromancer* and *Snow Crash,* whose Matrix and Metaverse, respectively, more accurately surmised what the Internet would look and feel like. (Wallace, among other things, failed to anticipate the break from cartridge- and disc-based entertainment.) But *Infinite Jest* warned against the insidious virality of popular entertainment long before anyone but the most Delphic philosophers of technology. Sharing videos, binge-watching Netflix, the resultant neuro-pudding at the end of an epic gaming marathon, the perverse seduction of recording and devouring our most ordinary human thoughts on Facebook and Instagram—Wallace somehow knew all this was coming, and it gave him (as the man himself might have put it) the howling fantods.

In interviews, Wallace was explicit that art must have a higher purpose than mere entertainment, leading to his most famous and bellicose thought on the matter: "Fiction's about what it is to be a fucking human being." And here, really, is the enigma of David Foster Wallace's work generally and *Infinite Jest* specifically: an endlessly, compulsively entertaining book that stingily withholds from readers the core pleasures of mainstream novelistic entertainment, among them a graspable central narrative line, identifiable movement through time, and any resolution of its quadrumvirate plotlines. *Infinite Jest,* in other words, can be exceedingly frustrating. To fully understand what Wallace was up to, the book bears being read, and reread, with Talmudic focus and devotion. For many Wallace readers this is asking too much. For many Wallace *fans* this is asking too much. And thus the Wallace factions have formed—the Nonfictionites versus the *Jest*ians versus the Short-Storyists—even though every faction recognizes the centrality of *Infinite Jest* to his body of work. The fact that twenty years have gone by and we *still* do not agree what this novel means, or what exactly it was trying to say, despite saying (seemingly) everything about everything, is yet another perfect analogy for the Internet. Both are too big. Both contain too much. Both welcome you in. Both push you away.

Theory two: *Infinite Jest* is a genuinely groundbreaking novel of language. Not even the masters of the high/low rhetorical register go higher more panoramically or lower more exuberantly than Wallace—not Joyce, not Bellow, not Amis. *Aphonia, erumpent,*

Eliotical, Nuckslaughter, phalluctomy! Made-up words, hot-wired words, words found only in the footnotes of medical dictionaries, words usable only within the context of classical rhetoric, home-chemistry words, mathematician words, philosopher words—Wallace spelunked the *OED* and fearlessly neologized, nouning verbs, verbing nouns, creating less a novel of language than a brand-new lexicographical reality. But nerdlinger word mongering, or "stunt-pilotry" (to use another Wallace phrase), can be an empty practice indeed. You need sentences to display-case the words, and here, too, *Infinite Jest* surpasses almost every novel written in the last century, displaying a consistent and mind-boggling descriptive mastery, as when he describes a sunset as "swollen and perfectly round, and large, radiating knives of light. . . . It hung and trembled slightly like a viscous drop about to fall." (No one is better than Wallace when it comes to skies and weather, which is traceable to his having grown up in central Illinois, a land of flat tornado-haunted vastidity.) As John Jeremiah Sullivan wrote after Wallace's death, "Here's a thing that is hard to imagine: being so inventive a writer that when you die, the language is impoverished." It has been eight years since Wallace left us, and no one is refilling the coffers of the David Foster Wallace Federal Sentence Reserve. No one is writing anything that resembles this: "The second shift's 1600h. siren down at Sundstrand Power & Light is creepily muffled by the no-sound of falling snow." Or this: "But he was a gifted burglar, when he burgled—though the size of a young dinosaur, with a massive and almost perfectly square head he used to amuse his friends when drunk by letting them open and close elevator doors on." We return to Wallace sentences now like medieval monks to scripture, tremblingly aware of their finite preciousness. While I have never been able to get a handle on Wallace's notion of spirituality, I think it is a mistake to view him as anything other than a religious writer. His religion, like many, was a religion of language. Whereas most religions deify only certain words, Wallace exalted all of them.

Theory three: *Infinite Jest* is a peerlessly gripping novel of character. Even very fine novelists struggle with character, because creating characters that are not just prismatic snap-off versions of oneself happens to be supremely difficult. In *How Fiction Works,* the literary critic James Wood, whose respectful but ultimately cool view of Wallace's work is as baffling as Conrad's rejection of Melville and Nabokov's dismissal of Bellow, addresses E. M. Forster's famous distinction between "flat" and "round" characters: "If I try to distinguish between major and minor characters—flat and round characters—and claim that these differ in terms of subtlety, depth, time allowed on the page, I must concede that many so-called flat characters seem more alive to me, and more interesting as human studies, than the round characters they are supposedly subservient to." Anyone reading or rereading *Infinite Jest* will notice an interesting pertinence: throughout the book, Wallace's flat, minor, one-note characters walk as tall as anyone, peacocks of diverse idiosyncrasy. Wallace doesn't simply set a scene and novelize his characters into facile life; rather, he makes an almost metaphysical commitment to see reality through their eyes. A fine example of this occurs early in *Infinite Jest,* during its "Where was the woman who said she'd come" interlude. In it we encounter the paranoid weed addict Ken Erdedy, whose terror of being considered a too-eager drug buyer has engendered an unwelcome situation: he is unsure whether or not he actually managed to make an appointment with a woman able to access two hundred grams of "unusually good" marijuana, which he very much wants to spend the weekend smoking. For eleven pages, Erdedy does nothing but sweat and anticipate this woman's increasingly conjectural arrival with his desired two hundred grams. I suspect no one who has struggled with substance addiction can read this passage without squirming, gasping, or weeping. I know of nothing else in the entirety of literature that so convincingly inhabits a drug-smashed consciousness while remaining a model of empathetic clarity. The literary craftsman's term for what Wallace is doing within the Erdedy interlude is free indirect style, but while reading Wallace you get the feeling that bloodless matters of craftsmanship rather bored him. Instead, he had to somehow psychically become his characters, which is surely why he wrote so often, and so well, in a microscopically close third person. In this very specific sense, Wallace may be the closest thing to a method actor in American literature, which I cannot imagine was without its subtle traumas. And Erdedy is merely one of *Infinite Jest*'s hundreds of differently damaged walk-on characters! Sometimes I wonder: What did it cost Wallace to create him?

Theory four: *Infinite Jest* is unquestionably the novel of its generation. As a member (barely) of the generation Wallace was part of, and as a writer whose closest friends are writers (most of whom are Wallace fans), and as someone who first read *Infinite Jest* at perhaps the perfect age (twenty-two, as a Peace Corps volunteer in Uzbekistan), my testimony on this point may well be riddled with partisanship. So allow me to drop the mask of the introducer to show the homely face of a fan, and much later a friend, of David Wallace.

As I read *Infinite Jest* in the dark early mornings before my Uzbek language class, I could hear my host-mother talking to the chickens in the barn on the other side of my bedroom wall as she flung scatters of feed before them. I could hear the cows stirring, and then their deep, monstrous mooing, along with the compound's approximately ten thousand feral cats moving in the crawl space directly above my bed. What I am trying to say is that it should have been difficult to focus on the doings of Hal Incandenza, Don Gately, Rémy Marathe, and Madame Psychosis.

But it wasn't. I read for hours that way, morning after morning, my mind awhirl. For the first few hundred pages of my initial reading, I will confess that I greatly disliked *Infinite Jest*. Why? Jealousy, frustration, impatience. It's hard to remember exactly why. It wasn't until I was writing letters to my girlfriend, and describing to her my fellow Peace Corps volunteers and host-family members and long walks home through old Soviet collectivized farmland in what I would categorize as yellow-belt Wallaceian prose, that I realized how completely the book had rewired me. Here is one of the great Wallace innovations: the revelatory power of freakishly thorough noticing, of corralling and controlling detail. Most great prose writers make the real world seem realer—it's why we read great prose writers. But Wallace does something weirder, something more astounding: even when you're not reading him, he trains you to study the real world through the lens of his prose. Several writers' names have become adjectivized— Kafkaesque, Orwellian, Dickensian—but these are designators of mood, of situation, of civic decay. The Wallaceian is not a description of something external; it describes something that happens ecstatically within, a state of apprehension (in both senses) and understanding. He didn't name a condition, in other words. He created one.

As I learned—as Wallace's eager imitators learned—as Wallace himself learned—there were limits to the initially limitless-seeming style Wallace helped pioneer in *Infinite Jest*. All great stylists eventually become prisoners of their style and, in a final indignity, find themselves locked up with their acolytes. Wallace avoided this fate. For one, he never finished another novel. For two, he created ever more space between the halves of his career—the friendly, coruscating essayist and the difficult, hermetically inclined fiction writer—so that, eventually, there was little to connect them. Another way of saying this is that the essays got better and funnier—the funniest since Twain—while the fiction got darker and more theoretically severe, even if so much of it was excellent.

The last time I saw David Wallace, in the spring of 2008, he successfully affected artistic contentment, which I now know was the antipode of his true feelings. Nevertheless, I came away from our encounter excited about the work that was to come, which he'd briefly alluded to. He'd given us one novel of generational significance; surely he'd write the novel that helped us define what the next century would feel like. Our great loss is that he didn't. His great gift is that the world remains as Wallaceian as ever—Donald Trump, meet President Johnny Gentle—and now we're all reading his unwritten books in our heads.

David, where be your gibes now? Your gambols, your songs—your flashes of merriment that were wont to set the table on a roar? They're here, where they've always been. Will always be. You have borne us on your back a thousand times. For you, and this joyful, despairing book, we will roar forever amazed, forever sorrowful, forever grateful. I hope against hope you can hear us.

—2016

Different versions of these essays were originally published in the following magazines and journals: "Unflowered Aloes" in *The Boston Review*; "Escanaba's Magic Hour" in *Harper's Magazine*; "Grief and the Outsider" in *The Believer* as "Protesting All Fiction Writers!"; "Writing About Writing About Writing" in *The Believer* as "Sir, Permission to Go AWOL from the Interesting, Sir!"; "Rules of Engagement" in *The New York Times Magazine*; "Euphorias of Perrier" in *The Virginia Quarterly Review*; "Still Rising" in *The Believer*; "The Secret Mainstream" in *Harper's Magazine*; "Kapuscinski's Last Journey" in *The New York Times Book Review* as "On the Road with History's Father"; "No Dying Light" as the introduction to John Gardner's *October Light* (New Directions, 2005); "Symbolic Value" in *The New York Observer* as "Amis in the 21st Century"; "Great and Terrible Truths" in *The New York Times Book Review*; "Cinema Crudité" in *Harper's Magazine*; "A Simple Medium" in *The New Yorker*; "Invisible Girl" in *The New Yorker* as "Voicebox 360"; "The Theory and Practice of Not Giving a Shit" in *Outside* as "The Last Lion"; "Goddesses and Dreams" in *The New Republic* as "You Are Now Entering the Demented Kingdom of William T. Vollmann"; "Everything About Everything" in *The New York Times Book Review* and in slightly different form as the foreword to *Infinite Jest, 20th Anniversary Edition* by David Foster Wallace (Back Bay Books, 2016).

My deep thanks to editors Neil Gordon, Donovan Hohn, Heidi Julavits, Alexander Star, Ted Genoways, Roger D. Hodge, Jennifer Schuessler, Adam Begley, Leo Carey, Abraham Streep, Greg Veis, and Michael Pietsch. Thanks also to my agent, Heather Schroder, and to Dave Eggers, Chris Ying, Michelle Quint, and Adam Krefman at McSweeney's, and Andrew Miller and Maria Goldverg at Vintage. Thank you, finally, to Gabriel Reeve, who provided some crucial last-second help in putting this collection together.